# SOCIOLOGY OF EDUCATION

# Sociology of Education

Dr. S.S. Ralhan
Dr. S.R. Lambat

Commonwealth

**Sociology of Education**



Edition : 2020

ISBN 81-311-0038-3

*Published by* :

**COMMONWEALTH PUBLISHERS**
4831/24, Prahlad Street,
Ansari Road, Darya Ganj,
New Delhi - 110002
Ph. : 23275511, 23257835
e-mail : commonwealthbooks@gmail.com

*Printed at :*
**Roshan Offset Printers**
Delhi

# Preface

The sociology of education is simply the application of sociological tools—that is, concepts like role and status to the study and analysis of school systems. To make this meaningful in terms of one's personal experience is the task of this book.

To run a school, the services of educational administrators, teachers, students and parents are needed.

The sociology of education, therefore, tries to analyse the role of educational administrators, as state or private organisations, the teacher, the students and the parents, probably the maximum application of sociological tools and analysis is in the field of education.

It is hoped the book will provide ample food for educational planners, administrators and the teachers.

***Dr. S.S. Ralhan***
***Dr. S.R. Lambat***

# Contents

# 1

# The Sociology of Education

This chapter will be a humanistic view of the sociology of education. The sociology of education is simply the application of sociological tools—that is, concepts like role and status—to the study and analysis of school systems. To make this meaningful in terms of one's personal experience will be the task of the chapter.

Sociology is both knowledge and a system of finding and organising that knowledge. It is, more than anything else, a large accumulation of empirical studies about persons in institutional life. The sociology of education mainly consists of a number of studies about persons in educational life, how they function, how they define their situation, how they succeed or fail, how they are motivated, etc. Some of these studies will be mentioned as we proceed, but only as they illustrate the relationship between a fact or idea and the routine activities and concerns of the sociologists. An example of this relationship would be the following kind of statement:

> James Colman, in a comprehensive study of the educational opportunities of American students, found that, in many areas, advantages were usually associated with one's race and socioeconomic position. American sociologists are critically interested in the consequences of being black or poor in America, both because they wish to describe the different conditions of American social life, and because they wish to reveal regularities within the American social structure. That is, they wish to know more than the social reality that there are differences, they want to know what difference such differences make.

Usually, sociologists who study the educational system report their findings in terms of rates of difference. The following Table 1.1 is a good example.

This table tells us that there is a relationship between one's socioeconomic status and going to college, regardless of intelligence, or, if we might infer further, of ability. The sociologist in this case has differentiated all the boys according to 'their fathers' occupations (statuses), tested intelligence scores and college aspirations. Since clear patterns appear, we inter that being in different socioeconomic categories makes a difference in the way in which one looks at education. The patterns tell us that there is some utility in making socioeconomic distinctions. They do not tell us, however, how these rates occur, or how they are produced. This requires another kind of analysis, one we can intuit perhaps, but one that is far more difficult to demonstrate, largely because sociology has not developed its tools to tell us why as adequately as it is able to tell us what is happening.

A humanistic sociology of education would be one that considers explanations of how the regularities we discover occur. We want to know, for example, how persons who are black, poor, male, adolescent, etc., are affected by being these things. We want to know more than differential rates of school achievement. We want to know how, for example, it happens that black students don't do as well as white students.

Table 1.1
Going to College

| *IQ Quintile* | *Father's Occupation* | | | | | *All Boys of* |
|---|---|---|---|---|---|---|
| | *(High) 5* | *4* | *3* | *2* | *1* | *Given IQ Level* |
| (High) 5 | 89 | 76 | 55 | 40 | 29 | 52 |
| 4 | 82 | 53 | 29 | 22 | 14 | 30 |
| 3 | 79 | 47 | 22 | 19 | 10 | 24 |
| 2 | 72 | 36 | 20 | 15 | 6 | 17 |
| (Low) 1 | 56 | 28 | 12 | 4 | 9 | 11 |
| All boys of given Occupational level | 80 | 52 | 26 | 19 | 12 | |

J.A. Kahl, Educational and Occupational Aspirations of Common Man, Boys, Harvard Educational Review 23 (summer 1953): 185.

## The Sociologist as a Person

This is a difficult task that I have: to separate the man from his work and then to put them back together again and display him in his humanistic togetherness. While the task is difficult it cannot be avoided for the idea is central to a humanistic conception of sociology. That is, without understanding how the man who does the work is related to the work we cannot understand the way in which humanism fits into sociology.

Sociology is, in itself, only a perspective on the world. It is a perspective that sees society through its own conceptual glasses. This means that persons walking around in the world are viewed as members of some distinct category of persons, performing certain functions, in certain regular ways. The sociologist is a person who has learned to see through those glasses. It is as if one were learning to make out forms that are invisible, and then one day, with the right glasses, one sees a whole new world of shapes and moving forms. In this way the student of sociology learns to see status groups, and racial groups, and bureaucratic patterns where, before, there were only people.

Now, what about the sociologist's old glasses, the ones through which he saw the world before learning how to use the new ones? Or what about the ones he wears when he's not working? Doesn't he sometimes forget to change them when he goes about his work? It depends. It depends upon his belief in the scientific ethos. What this means is that he becomes committed, to a greater or lesser degree, to seeing the world objectively and reporting it that way.

Objectivity, as a professional commitment, requires the sociologist to refrain from allowing his own values to colour what he sees. The whole posture of objectivity is derived from the sociologist's sense of himself as a scientist. As a scientist, he must be not only committed to objectivity, he must also be somewhat aloof from being concerned about the use to which his work will be put once he has finished it.

Now, our concern is whether a humanistic sociology, given this conception of the sociologist, is possible. I don't think so. I believe that, in order to see any humanistic possibilities in sociology, or in the sociological study of the school, we need to reject both the necessity, and the possibility, that the sociologist exist as a true scientist. We have to believe that the man cannot be separated from his values and perspective on the world, and we also have to believe that the scientific study of human beings, individually or in groups, is not really possible. It is not possible because human beings, unlike material objects studied by natural scientists, experience the world, as well as behave in it.

A humanistic sociology begins with this notation, for without understanding the importance of it, we cannot communicate our argument with the scientific approach to the study of persons. I would like to have you consider again the table interrelating IQ, socioeconomic status, and going to college. The two variables used to draw a relationship are IQ and socioeconomic status. Now, does a person experience his IQ and socioeconomic status or can be possess these qualities without knowing of them, or are these qualities something we, as sociologists, have given him in order to study him?

There are no perfect relationships in sociology, and very few strong ones because we can never guarantee that the characteristics we attribute to persons mean anything to him at all. What does it mean to a person to be lower, class for instance? For some, it means frustrations; for others it means being the same as everyone else in the neighbourhood, and for others it is the way it has always been.

Now it is possible to say, as many have, that the meaning of experience to the person is irrelevant to the study of behaviour. Many behavioural scientists will argue that they are simply looking at behavioural patterns and describing regularities from these evidences. What persons experience is not pertinent from this perspective. Although these behaviourists are indeed acting like scientists, without dealing with experience they will never reach scientific precision, since what goes on in a person's head governs the way he acts in a given objective circumstance (*e.g.*, low socioeconomic status).

On the other hand, is it possible to really be objective about the human condition? Most of the sociological research on school deals with the question of inequality, with certain biases operating in the selection of the problem. And what about the meaning of data? Most sociologists are content to let a phenomenon be defined by a symbol of itself, called an indicator. Again, let us examine the indicators on Table 1.1 IQ is a score on a test; "economic status" is father's occupation; and "aspiration" is going to college. Now this is fine, except that, in the extrapolation, we are told that a relationship exists among intelligence, status and aspiration. Do the indicators really mean what they are supposed to mean, independent of any verification as to what they mean to the person who is supplying the researcher with his data? And what about the issue of the data itself? Do the results we get on questionnaires accurately tell us about the person? We really believe that the results on an attitude questionnaire reflect the real attitude of the respondent. He could be lying, he might not know, he might be in the process of changing. It all seems so damn uncertain that you would think that sociologists would declare a moratorium on their labours and consider doing something else, perhaps in another way.

It does appear, short of a moratorium, that many sociologists are willing to admit to their biases and want to attack the structures that they once wished to "analyse". They have set out, empirically and analytically, to uncover the dysfunctions or disjointedness within a society that appears to be running down. In this light, then, a humanistic sociology of education is possible, because a "person" rather than a "scientist" is emerging to do the job.

A sociology of education, in this humanistic respect, must be an applied sociology. The choice of problem and the kind of data we, as sociologists, use must reflect a concern with the human condition. There was once a time, and not very long ago, when the sociologist-scientist shied away from applied research and from work associated with education, since education was, by definition, an applied field. What we are now looking for is the kind of school that is able to overcome the traditional tendency to allow social differences to invidiously effect those who experience those differences. And what we are looking for is a sociology that is able to expose the meaning of those differences to the people who experience them.

## A Conceptual Framework for Understanding Education

Education is a very general concept. It can refer to learning to a system of transmitting the culture, to a quality of an individual reflecting his status as well as his ability, to a formal organisation where students attend classes from 9:00 to 3:00, to a graduate or undergraduate school where teachers are trained, to a means of social mobility. The sociology of education, as an academic discipline or subdiscipline, is, among other things, a way of looking at this phenomenon. It is a way of revealing, describing, and managing it, provides us with a specific framework, which helps us to look at the whole by analysing the components. Sociology, as a general discipline, has evolved a number of working concepts. These concepts can be, conveniently, applied to all aspects of societal life. We can, for example, use the concept of role to aid our analyses of schools as well as political systems, religious organisations and families. What we will attempt to evolve in this section is a sociological description of educational systems, utilising both formal and real-life conceptualisations, as well as experiential qualities of the concepts. Our goal is to make the social structure of schools come alive.

## Social Structure

A social structure is the pattern of relationships and interactions that characterise a specific unit of social life, a system, at one point in time. In order to be a structure, these patterns, by definition, are relatively stable. This stability is maintained by a system of norms, values, and roles, which we will discuss subsequently. In a school, as in other social institutions, we cannot see a social structure. We can only see benches, persons, materials. But the way these are used, the way persons move, the things they do, insofar as we can say these uses and movements are guided, tell us that a social structure exists. If children sit quietly, stiffly, and answer the teacher politely these are patterns. If teachers direct the activities of the class, this is a pattern. If, when a student speaks out of turn, he is punished, this is a pattern. The way in which teachers talk to their principals, the kinds of assignments they give to students, the cost to students of not doing them, are all patterns. The social structure of the school consists of the set of activities utilisation of facilities, and ways that people traditionally use to communicate with each other; in other words, the evidences that tell us we are, without question—even with our eyes closed—in a schoolroom.

We know we are there because of the configuration of individual structures, or components, not because of the existence of any single one. Adults and children, books and papers, even chalk, desks, and blackboards, can be found almost anywhere. But when desks are lined up one behind the other, children seated orderly, an adult standing, books and papers passed around and on the desk, we have a school. If, in the interests of bringing education up-to-date, or to correct some deficiencies in the school's functioning, we change these patterns, we still have a school. Insofar as the new modes become stable through time, we evolve a new social structure. When a college student begins to notice that he does a number of things differently on the campus than he does on the beach, he begins to take account of the social structure. His experience with the social structure can be described more specifically with reference to several concepts which are the foundation blocks of that structure: the norms, values and role.

### Norms

The formal concept of a norm—an ideal pattern of behaviour—suggests that there are certain things that persons are expected or obliged to do. These expectations are usually tied to one's position; that is a student may not be obliged to do some things that a teacher is obliged to do, and *vice versa.* Norms often refer to the limits of acceptable behaviour that apply to everyone regardless of his position in the institution. For example, neither students, teachers, nor administrators are expected to disrobe in the classroom. Often these regulatory norms are formalized as rules, and these rules help persons to know the kind of behaviour approved or disapproved by the school.

Most norms are internalised; that is, they are inside of us. If we behave in a certain way, it is because we expect it of ourselves, not because there is somebody watching. In this way, institutions effectively control the behaviour of its members. In institutions, such as prisons, where most of the members do not believe in its institutional norms, more manifest controls are necessary.

In the classroom, we have both forms of social control: internalised expectations and enforcement. We do not talk back to our teacher; we do not criticise him even if we suspect he is depriving us of an education. We may no longer be aware of our responding to such social controls. If asked, we might attribute our restraint to a specific concern about punishment. Usually, however, we restrain ourselves because we are all participants in the normative system, and to violate some norm requires more psychological exertion than we are often able to handle. The anxiety and nervousness we feel when we consider going against the norm demonstrate its power over us.

Educational systems represent the normative order more than other institutions. In order to socialise students from different backgrounds in common ways, schools have had to stand as examples of the normative system which orders the total society. As Waller described the school many years ago, it operates as an institution which represents the Protestant morality to a degree that most real human beings would not presume to imitate.

## Values

A value is a standard against which things are approved or disapproved relative to each other. We have standards or quality and standards of excellence, standards of beauty and standards of performance. In schools, we have standards of academic performance, ethical standards, standards of popularity and standards of interpersonal relations. These are the standards that most students try to achieve, and in terms of which many are crucified for failing to achieve.

The values that operate to structure school behaviour are those which are reflected in the general culture, based on our American traditions. We value industriousness, success, cleanliness, cooperation, respect for authority and order. We devalue laziness, failure, messiness, physical aggression and lack of restraint.

Students are constantly manoeuvering to attain the values that are important in their lives. Consider what we have all done and continue to do in order to achieve the goals that we have been socialised to desire. We work hard even when we hate what we are doing, we memorise things we will never remember. We compete with each other, feeling badly when we lose and often guilty when we win. When we cannot attain our goal we often pull down others to prevent them from succeeding. This behaviour in the classroom is poignantly represented by the following example from Henry's observation of elementary school students:

> Boris had trouble reducing 12/16 to the lowest terms and could only get 6/8. The teacher asked him quietly if that was as far as he could reduce it. She suggested that he should "think". Much heaving up and down and waving of the hands by the other children, all frantic to correct him. Boris pretty unhappy, probably mentally paralysed. The teacher quiet, patient, ignores the others and concentrates with look and voice on Boris. After a minute or two, she turns to the class and says, "Well, who can tell Boris what the number is?" A forest of hands appears, and the teacher calls Peggy. Peggy says that four may be divided into the numerator and denominator . . . Boris's failure has made it possible for Peggy to succeed; his misery is the occasion for her rejoicing. This is standard condition of the contemporary American elementary school. To a Zuni, Hopi, or Dakota Indian, Peggy's performance would seem cruel beyond belief, for competition, the wringing of success from somebody's failure, is a form of torture foreign to these non-competitive cultures.

Because we value stability, we become uncomfortable when confronted with the possibility of instability in our educational life. When we are permitted a great deal of flexibility in the way we learn, we often become anxious and ask for structure. We want an outline of what we are supposed to know. The one thing in education that we do not seems to value very much is learning. There is very little time to learn when we have to get good grades, which we seem to value much more.

### Roles

Roles are expectations for behaviour for those who occupy a specific position in a social system. Roles are often conceived as actual enactments and linked to the expectation concept by the fact that what people do is ordinarily an indication of what they are expected to do.

Schools, like other formal organisations, are bureaucratically organised. That is, there are a number of positions that are arranged in a hierarchy of status, each carrying more authority than the position below. Being a student is a role, usually at the bottom of the hierarchy. Students want to become nonstudents, just as children want to become adults, in order to gain a degree of freedom they do not have in their present role.

What is a student's role? When we ask about roles, we ask both about what a social type does and what he is expected to do. Persons experience their roles personally, We feel expectations. We feel the pressure of conforming to them and we almost always accede to this pressure. A student asks for information, for grades, for permission to leave the room, for the opportunity to impress the teacher and others. What he does not expect is also descriptive of his role. He does not expect freedom to control his own educational life, nor does he expect to be treated like a responsible human being. He expects to be distrusted and therefore does not object when his exams are monitored or when his teacher asks him to bring a note from his parents explaining his absences.

> Individuals quickly learn the expectations of their specific roles, particularly when such roles are traditional, like son, student, brother, friend, teacher, etc. The pressure of conforming to these expectations is great but one is not required to behave congruent with that conception. When he perceives the expectations and acts accordingly we say that he is "role playing". When he has internalised these expectations such that he is acting in terms of his own set of beliefs about how he should act, we say that he is "role taking".

When the expectations of behaviour for a particular role conflict with a person's self-conception—that is, the way, he feels he is and must be as an individual—then he experiences the kind of role conflict that we call self-estrangement. Most persons, at one time or another, experience this feeling of being called upon to play a part personally uncomfortable to them. Many individuals throughout the country now suspect that this feeling is especially common to the student role. If persons have a sense of how they, as individuals, learn best, and this cannot be accomplished in the traditional student role, then a role strain appears. To reduce this strain, many students either drop out of school if they are old enough, or attempt to declare their independence in any way they can. Much of the current conflict on college campuses is a result of this process.

## Sanctions

Sanctions are forms of controlling the behaviour of members of a social group. They are both general to society at large and specific to institutions or subunits within the society. Having a language and a number of symbols in common, most members of the society quickly recognise a sanction.

In the classroom, students are sensitive to all the forms of reward and punishment. A smile from the teacher, a nod that an answer is correct, a commendation, an election victory, an appointment to a responsible job, a good grade on a test or report card, are all positive educational sanctions, and students work to attain them. They structure their behaviour in terms of them. They work for sanctions rather than knowledge.

A poor grade, a detention, extra homework, being sent to the principal are also sanctions. Most students do their best to avoid them. As we are socialised according to the expectations of specific roles in society, we are also conditioned to be sensitive to the consequences of violating them. In the school, the approval of our teachers and peers are the goals for which we strive. Up to the point where we find that everything we do brings us disapproval, the quest for this approval keeps us controlled or motivated. In this way, a social institution protect its values and norms and maintains the stability of traditional roles.

Sometimes time-honoured sanctions become weak because those persons who are controlled by their wish to receive positive sanctions and avoid negative ones begin to stop caring about certain rewards and punishments. It is at this evolutionary stage of a particular society that change is most possible and most likely. When college students refuse to be threatened by dismissal from school or a court record, then the university has lost its most significant formal means of control. At this point, either manifest enforcement or structural changes must occur. We have witnessed both trends in recent days.

## Status

Status is the evaluation of a role. In American, most positions in the social structure are ranked. They are ranked in terms of the qualities or goals that we value. What we seem to value most is wealth, and persons achieve status to the degree that they secure wealth.

Each institution has its related status values. School status requires the student to attain good grades, access to higher education, and to be popular among his peers. Grades and access to higher education, however, are indirect linked to economic values.

Status in everyday educational life, on the primary and secondary level, is a good report card, the favour of the teacher, having many friends in the classroom, moving up through the grades. On the campus status accrues from being an athlete, a member of a good fraternity or sorority, or a student body officer. There is a status difference between a student and a teacher and between an assistant professor and a full professor.

Status is esteem. We like others to look up to us, to respect and applaud our attainments. To court such esteem often means that we must sacrifice our basic interests, shift away from our best skills. This means, for example, that we may need to abandon our artistic skills and interests in order to attain occupational success. Teachers do not have as much status as engineers, lawyers or doctors. In some cases, this explains why many persons who might have led successful and exciting lives as schoolteachers are leading dull ones as engineers, lawyers and doctors. Status differences also explain why some high school students drop out of school when they are enrolled in other than academic curricula. School systems have never been able to discover a way of improving the status of vocational courses such as industrial arts. School administrators, having the same values as the rest of society, do not esteem the vocations as much as the professions.

There are several ways to achieve status in most social systems. Status is usually a combination of one's success in a number of areas. One's occupation, income, family lineage, education, all contribute to one's combined status. This is also the case with schools. Gordon's study of a high school described three structural patterns, or systems, by which students attained status:

1. the formal system in which status was involved in the process of making grades;
2. the semiformal system which involved students participation in extracurricular activities, through which these students achieved status from being popular; and
3. the informal system which accounted for the status conferred by membership in a particular friendship group, or clique.

In universities, for instance, membership in certain fraternities is more prestigious than in others.

Status is an important concept in sociology; it explains the basic patterns of social mobility, rates of deviance, and the various adaptations to cultural goals. Society is organised around status values and the struggle to attain them. In the classroom, this structure of status values is the most efficient structure by which school control is maintained. When one achieves status in our society, one gains a sense of power and well-being, a feeling that one has successfully met life's challenges and achieved personal victory over others.

## External and Internal Systems

When education takes place in a normal organization, such as a school, it becomes useful to distinguish some of the components of that organisation. Homans distinguished between the external dimension of a social system and the internal dimension. The external system is all the activities which take place that directly justify the system's existence. Regarding the school, we are talking about activities, interactions among students and faculty, and sentiments that evolve in order to move students through the various grades to prepare them for adult life in the society. The use of books, discussions, lectures, instruction; the organisation of curricula, the formal interactions according to role types, the giving and grading of exams; reports to parents, referrals to the counsellor, the note to the vice-principal about the gum-chewing, the suspension for holding hands in the hall, are all example of how the external system operates in the schools.

Personal interactions, communications, and emotional responses among the members constitute the internal dimension of an organisation. When persons revise their activities, rearrange their patterns of interaction, and change their feelings about what they are doing, the internal system is operating and is reacting upon the demands of the external system.

If you have ever observed a teacher lessen the homework assignment because students moan, then you have observed the operations of the internal system. When students reduce their drive according to the informal rule of "don't be a rate buster," the internal system is at work. When universities begin to drastically revise their curricula of their policies towards minority groups, then we see the effect of the internal system operating to change the external system.

Even second graders can perceive the existence of an internal system, although they would not use those words. They know how to convince each other of the mutual necessity of getting the teacher to change an activity or a rule, of the kinds of strategies which will accomplish this. As one child interviewed by the author, responded. "If the teacher keeps on giving us all that work, I'll just stay home, and get my friends to do it too."

## Manifest and Latent Functions

We have, particularly in recent days, heard a good deal about the notion of "working within the system". Most students are not revolutionaries by nature nor by ideology. Everybody seems to willingly admit that there are always problems, and most people are convinced that these can be solved without destroying our traditional institutions. If we agree with the goals and activities established to achieve these goals—the manifest function of institutions—then we find it most reasonable to assume that we can and should work within the system. The problem often is that our perspective of "the system" is incomplete, because we have only locked at its manifest functions. Many institutions fulfil important latent functions and they are supported by society more often on the basis of these latent functions rather than on manifest ones.

The manifest function of universities is to develop the minds of students, to help them think about and solve problems. But when students begin to challenge the basic assumptions of the whole society, the college budget is cut with public support. This happens not because the school failed to fulfil its manifest function—it perhaps accomplished that too well—but because it failed to fulfil an important latent function, which is to produce social conformists who do not threaten the *status quo.*

A latent function is a useful sociological concept. It helps us to describe the structural basis for the existence of many social forms. It can help tell us why some traits exist in society even when there seems to be no useful purpose for them. Many Indian tribes persist in their ritual rain dance. Although the manifest function (to make it rain) is no longer believed by the members, the latent function (to cohere members of a social group) is necessary to the viability of that group. We can ask ourselves about the function of many of our traditions, and by utilising the notion of a latent function, understand a great deal about the social structure. The importance to sociology of analysing latent functions is that it both clarifies seemingly irrational social patterns, like rain dances and wedding rituals, as well as directs our evaluation of the success of an activity away from its "supposed" function to its real function. That is, we don't evaluate rain dances on the grounds of the amount of rainfall produced.

This last value of looking at the latent function of institutions or social patterns is critical to our concern about understanding the system or working within the system. Since moral judgments, and hence social action, seem to arise from the way the public perceives the manifest functions of an institution, analysing latent consequences may reveal beneficial social aspects that had previously not been considered. It is possible, for example, that both the church and state in Catholic countries were able to maintain family stability by permitting prostitution to flourish.

With restrictive divorce codes, the accessibility of other sexual outlets helps to prevent movements that may threaten to change the traditional patterns. Prostitution, in this evaluation, is a spin-off or siphon for every that might otherwise become political to attain similar ends.

In education, some student activities are being judged by the larger society as disrespectful of many traditional values such as law and order, respect for authority, and bureaucratic efficiency. It is possible, however, that such activities are promoting the kinds of change that will make education congruent with the changing culture outside of the school. The more static that schools remain in the face of shifting cultural standards, the more likely that the school will cease to be an important socialising agency. As many students and teachers increasingly consider the school obsolete and irrelevant, university and school administrators will increasingly reassess the function of the school in a quickly changing society.

**The Structure of Competition: Function and Dysfunction**

Students are required to complete with one another for a variety of educational rewards. They compete in terms of standards of achievement established by the school in line with traditional performance expectations. The manifest function of competition is motivation. Persons are motivated to achieve their goals in terms of these standards. The latent function of competition operates to control the behaviour of students by keeping them rigorously committed to the goals they seek. It maintains their conformity, since deviance diminishes the qualities they need to compete for the rewards of the school. We have come to believe that worth is determined by the number of people competing for something. It makes A's and B's worth something by the sheer act of forcing people to compare for them. In the final analysis, competition clouds our vision of worth in learning. We come to believe that what is worth something is whatever you get by competing for it, rather than what you want to achieve.

A dysfunction is a consequence of seeking certain manifest or latent goals which adversely affect some members of society.

There are several dysfunctional consequences of competition. Let us consider these in the context of our educational system. First of all, we need to find out who is adversely affected. Although probably everyone is, the most serious affected by the dysfunction of competition are the school dropouts, the "losers," who enter the adult world vocational training or the possibility access to higher education.

There are two other groups in the competition, however, the "survivors" and the "winners". The survivors are those who barely make it through high school. They usually have the credentials to enter a junior college, but seldom a four-year school. While they are the junior college, they are "cooled out," a term used by Clark to designate the process of sidetracking or modifying aspirations so that a students seeks a career as a medical technician rather than a doctor. What is the human dilemma for this person? What does it mean to him to have his aspirations raised only to have them sent crashing as he realises that his real status in society is only a second-rate position? For this person, it is sometimes easier to fail in the system and then develop his own structure for facing life rather than be coopted to seek high status and then be relegated to a inferior position.

The "winner" can be described in terms of his academic achievement, his popularity among his peers, and his easy transition from high school to college. But what has his victory cost him? Let's first look at female winners.

The educated woman in America has competed with males academically for at least sixteen years. In the process, she has been encouraged to think of herself as intelligent, knowledgeable, cultured. As a housewife, she lives in a world of people one to three feet tall, shifting her dialogue from. "That's an interesting point to consider," to "That's a good baby". The millions of tranquilisers consumed in suburbia by the trapped housewife speak of the strain such women experience from the difference between their expectations and their rewards. If success through competition is an internalised social habit, what happens to the fulfilment drive when women become mothers and housewives? It may seep into the marriage, and we note that divorces are common today, or it may require rechannelling, whereby these women pay psychiatrist billions of dollars yearly to help them accept their new roles.

The "successful" man in America drinks three martinis before he is able to take a bite of food. He has ulcers, is overweight, has chronic anxieties fights with his wife and children, goes into depressions, and sometimes commits suicide when his career flounders or goes sour. He is the organisation man, the dysfunctioning product of American competitiveness, who, like a prizefighter, keeps swinging long after he has lost the fight.

What we have done in judging the function or dysfunction of competition can be usefully repeated in judging the functions of differentiation within the classroom, extracurricular activities, bureaucratic organisation, achievement an intelligence tests, and so on. Most educational structures exist because they serve some function, and an astute educator should be capable of analysing the manifest and latent consequences of these functions and assess how well they operate.

## THE SCHOOL AND OTHER SOCIAL UNITS

The sociology of education is a field concerned with the interaction of the school with other institutions, such as the family and church, and other social units, such as adolescent peer groups. We can discuss briefly the kinds of interactions which are studied and written about in the literature.

### Education and the Economic System

Here we are interested in the way a person's income, his education level, his social status within the community, and his occupation relate to the kind of education his children receive. One of the early important studies in the field was conducted by A.B. Hollingshead, in which he demonstrated that a student's educational behaviour was related to his parents' social position in a small midwestern community. He did this by developing measures of economic standing, some of which were based on reputation and others upon objective indicators, such as occupation and income. According to these measures, he then divided the community into five social classes. The next step was to look at the academic performance of the students from each class level. He found, as he expected, that students from the upper classes enrolled more frequently in college preparation course, developed cliques only within their own class, had higher professional aspirations, dropped out of school less frequently, and received better evaluations from school personnel.

In a small community where everyone attends the same school, a study of economic advantage such as this one can reveal dramatic differences. Today, most schools are homogenously grouped as to the economic standing of pupils' families. Nonetheless, most of the studies of a child's economic position show a distinct relationship to his educational attainment or aspirations. As one's social position increases, so do one's successes.

**Race**

When we speak of race as an American sociological category, we ordinarily mean to differentiate between white majority and non-white minority groups. The most prominent minority group in the literature of sociology is the Negro. In education, the dominant focus has been upon the black man's position in the opportunity structure. It is well-known that he, like Mexican-Americans and Puerto Ricans, is under represented, in proportion to his numbers, in institutions or higher learning. His graduation rates from high school are lower than for Caucasians. His position within the school is inferior; that is, that schools, through many channels and activities, favour Caucasians.

Educational sociologists are concerned about the discrepancy in educational opportunities. They, like the Kerner Commission on Civil Disorders, are interested in the structure of racism, how these inequalities occur, and how they are produced. Several ideas are relevant to this kind of analysis:

*1. Differential Socialisation*—This simply means that the social habits learned in the homes of Negro students are not conducive to educational success. The aspiration level of black students, in terms of making it through the school system and on to higher education, is low. A black person's commitment to delayed gratification is not quite the same as that of a Caucasian. His language is often less than "perfect" English. He has not internalised the value of passivity in social interaction. He approaches others physically, often with aggression.

2. *Middle Class Standards*—This notion is similar to the first, applying here to the school rather than to the student. The middle standards of the school are universally and often rigidly applied. They are established according to the achievement performances of students who have accepted and internalised the ethic of hard work and educational success. Standards for moral behaviour and standards for academic achievement are equally important in the evaluation of the student. This means that persons who are industrious, respectful of authority, clean, physically unaggressive well-groomed, and use standard language form, are rewarded with educational prizes such as grades and honours.

3. *Unequal Distribution of Human and Material Resources*—Anyone who has visited a typical ghetto school recognises that the environment is different from that of a typical suburban school. The rooms and buildings are older and usually in need of repair; the audio-visual equipment is either non-existent or badly used; the teachers are more hostile; the work that students perform is either routine or repressive. Kozol and Cole have vividly described the educational conditions in such schools. Although these are individual and not really sociological observations, the data from the Coleman report and elsewhere substantiate the picture.

4. *Segregation vs. Compensatory Education*—Here we are faced with the assessment of a real ongoing problem. Social and educational reformers are trying to break down the structure of racism. We know that improving the facilities and instruction for lower-class black students helps, but this does not meet the demand for integration. "Separate but equal" is a myth. Evidence suggests that black children in integrated schools improve faster than their peers in the all-black schools.

5. *Home Rule*—The decentralisation of educational authority and control is a popular theme in the socio-educational literature. Black leaders believe that segregated schools have

value only if black personnel make the major decisions in these schools. This issue has created strange bedfellows. In California and elsewhere, both political conservatives and black radicals are interested in decentralising schools, although, we suspect, for very different reasons. While the black leaders hope to provide a better education and stronger and more positive black identity in community schools, conservatives appear to like the idea of self-help and self-determination. At the same time, private enterprise is viewed as a possible form of school management. This means, in one sense, a profit and loss business for Negro entrepreneurs in the ghetto who contribute services of the community-owned school.

## The Family

Literature that relates family life to education usually focuses on the economic theme. The socialisation, be child-rearing, activities of families have usually been studies in relation to social class differences. Other kinds of topics in this area would be:

1. the working mother and her effect on the educational success of the child,
2. children of large and small families,
3. broken homes,
4. family geographic mobility.

The interaction of family and schools has not been viewed in any particularly new or productive way. That poor people's children become poor people, and that children of migrant farmers experience educational barriers are obvious conclusions. Often, however, these data help make a case for policy decisions, if politicians are interested in bringing about some changes. A more challenging and currently relevant consideration is one which would analyse the way in which family beliefs and patterns can help explain deviant phenomena such as college dropouts, drug-taking among school-children, and political radicalism on the campus. The question of whether or not adolescent and college-age "deviants" are going through a rebellious stage, or have found a genuine ideological commitment, a unclear. How can we explain the fact that students whose parents have lived a life of middle-class conformity are rebelling? What notions will help explain the disaffection of middle-class children from the educational aspirations of their parents? The struggle of disenfranchised whites and blacks to change the system may only be possible with the support of persons within the system—students who are educationally successful and who want to change that system.

### The Peer Group

Along with the family, the peer group represents, particularly for adolescents, a significant influence. Ofen, when expectations of family and peer group class, the child conforms to the peer group. Sometimes the same confrontation occurs between the adolescent peer group and the school.

The youth group constitutes a distinct entity, what Coleman has called an "adolescent society". He has shown how the character of adolescents and their value system has influenced the organisation of the schools they attend. If they like football, the school will have an athletic emphasis. If they are eager to study and get into college, the school will take on an academic posture.

Students who work together for common purposes have been shown to influence not only the way each other thinks but also the degree of commitment and involvement that each will assume. The society of "young radicals" who have been making an impact upon the college scene are stimulated less by their successes than by their association with other in a common purpose. Much of the research and writing emphasis of the near future will be upon such students. They exist on the college campus and in the high schools. They also exist in ghetto elementary schools and they are starting to organise very young. Their impact upon the system of education is an interesting and important question.

## THE SCHOOL AS A SOCIAL SYSTEM

Many sociologists have attempted to view the school as a microcosm of the larger society, as an organisation with functions, roles and bureaucratic relationships. We have talked about this somewhat in the first part of this chapter. C. Wayne Gordon, whom we discussed earlier, has usefully broken the school down into three systems and attempted to explain how students achieve overall status through their participation in each system. This analysis allow us to observe a graphic relationship among all three positions. Persons in similar status positions are shown to choose each other as friends, and tendency for good students to be popular students is revealed.

From another perspective, we see the way the system allocates persons to the occupational world. Parsons analyses the selection and evaluation of persons based upon achievement and the way students develop capacities and commitments to function adult roles. Students are categorised according to their cognitive and ethical performance; that is they are judged by the school grades and their "respect" for the teacher. Once these categories are established, students are allocated along channels of success or failure commensurate with these definitions.

Students are ordinarily defined early in their school career by their performance and personal style, from which their status can be predicted. This status label is one that they usually carry, on one that carries them, through their entire academic career. One of the consequences of this definition is that students almost never become free to act in opposition to it.

For example, when a student who has been defined as a high achiever fails a test, we normalise this unpredictable happening by saying that he had a bad day. If a student who has been defined as a low cognitive achiever does well, we say he cheated. If a high moral achiever violates a rule, we look for the source of his being upset. If a low moral achiever spends a week conforming to all the rules, we suspect ulterior motives.

## SCHOOLS AND SOCIAL CHANGE

The school has always mirrored, if not exaggerated, trends and patterns in the larger society. When our society shifted to a more scientific mode, after the Russians sent the first satellite aloft, schools mobilised their science facilities and shifted their emphasis accordingly. The history of the relationship between social changes and educational changes is a parallel history. In order to understand the interaction between schools and society, we can trace certain historical shifts in our cultural patterns.

## Urbanization

In rural society, interaction was personalised. This means that we identified he mailman and shopkeeper by name rather than by uniform. Students in school were linked to their families in several ways. Teachers would deal with children in terms of the skills that were needed in the home, or discipline children commensurate with the status of their families. Urban society demanded another set of school-home relationships, since the family no longer serviced all the needs of members. Living in the city required a different set of behaviours for family members, and families required a different set of services from the schools. Since occupational succession (sons following in the footsteps of the father) was no longer the pattern, children had to be educated to find their own oceupations in industrial society. As the function of the schools changed, so did the patterns of interaction. Since community schools were homogenous, and since most students were enrolled for vocational training, students needed to be differentiated. This was also necessary for the management of large groups. To facilitate these new requirements, the schools had to develop ways of grouping, advising, and training students that were different from the past. In the same manner that urban persons would define others, usually in terms of occupational labels, schools evolved their own form of labelling. Students became labelled in terms of achievement, moral behaviour, and later, in terms of vocational choice and curriculum. College preparatory students, for instance, were expected to be high academic achievers and vocational-course students were expected to achieve less. That may be why we get less.

## Social Mobility

By 1945, at the close of World War II, the United States was becoming an affluent society. The efforts of labour unions, combined with the general prosperity produced by a war economy, raised the mass of society upwards on the socio-economic ladder. But status within the prestige structure could not be based on income alone. A large segments of the society looked towards education to preserve and increase their status.

The children of the working class were sent off to college to ensure a better and easier life than that enjoyed by their parents. Education seemed the major path to social and economic success. Public schools came to be viewed more as selecting agencies than training ones. The competition for the rewards of the educational system, linked closely to occupational opportunities, began early. You who are reading this book are familiar with the process, and can understand how competition for grades, honours, popularity, and college entrance replaces much of what we think of, in the pure sense, as learning.

Mass social mobility led to other conditions which seriously affected the educational quality of the school. Those who were not included in the rate for success became clearly discernible as members of educationally disenfranchised minority groups. The economic success of some and the failure of others led to ecological migration in a pattern we have called *de facto* segregation. These success patterns began to evolve into a process of increasing specialisation, requiring greater amounts of formal education. All persons caught in the whirl of intensified striving for social rewards were in some way mutilated, separated from their fellow humans. Segregation and specialisation have this common potential: social and personal alienation.

The prosperity of the 1950s and 1960s led to redistribution of humans into ecological arrangements called slums and suburbs. The organisation of the schools has become patterned in terms of different educational goals, for those who have and those who have not. Discrepancies of personnel and facilities become obvious to any observer. Teachers in the suburbs are better trained, better experienced, better paid, better supported by specialists and facilities, than their counterparts in the slums. But one changing pattern has become apparent and that is in the way the poor have discovered their political and social influence. A political manoeuver, a parents' strike, or a riot, can influence school administrators to become responsive to the needs of ghetto communities, and can influence government agencies to set up programmes to encourage equality of opportunities. Between the forces of conscience and politics, the poor are beginning to have a chance for the same kind of education offered to the middle classes. Those of us who have been through the system and succeeded might respond that there doesn't appear to be any good reason for them to want it, but this too may be another effect of affluence. When persons are struggling to climb a mountain it seems selfish and patronising of those at the top to yell down, "Don't bother, it's a gravel pit up here." The point is not that we are witnessing a cycle of succession-rejection, but that frustrated peoples are separated by opposite motivations. The poor want "up" and "in"; the middle-class dissenters or dropouts want "down" and "out". This is why a coalition of black and students, for example, is unlikely.

## Institutional Interaction

Society is made up of a number of institutions with a separate, yet interdependent, institutional life; that is, what happens in the home is affected by economic, political, religious and educational patterns. Changes in one sector affect changes in others. The shift from a farming to an industrial economy, for instance, brought about decreased fertility rates, since children were no longer needed as workers. As the pattern of children succeeding to their fathers' occupations became outmoded, schools began to expand their educational function. As the role of women in the family changed, schools had to accommodate a whole new set of feminine aspirations.

The school today has, despite the complaints of many, evolved into an educational structure for the common man, requiring that any child old enough to attend must go to school. Child labour in the factory has become obsolete with developments in child labour laws, and with the increased application of democratic ethic. A democratic nation requires an enlightened electorate, and with universal suffrage, all citizens need to be educated. Unfortunately, the only aspect of fulfilling this requirement has been compulsory attendance.

In recent days we have observed a growing concern on the part of many administrators and students that politics has become part of university life. In Washington D.C., as well as in many state capitals, legislators are introducing bills to control the behaviour of students. Many politicians are capitalising upon the fears of many conservative citizens that college students are a threat to the kind of life, that their generation has created and in which they hold a comfortable and vested interest.

Another social unit, although not an institution in the sociological sense of the word, has seriously influenced educational life; the peer group. As a force controlling values and behaviour the strength of loyalties between age mates has never been greater than it is today. We can speculate on the reasons for this. The increased solidarity of the peer group appears to be linked to the phenomenon of decreased family dependency. The family, like the formal organisation, has become a group of specialists, each member being involved in activities not shared with anyone else. What we have come to call the generation gap is a product of this evolution. Lacking any set of common values, young people turn to each other for support in these values. Rapidly-changing social experiences have made it difficult for members of one generation to teach their children what to expect of the world they are facing on a daily basis. The peer group has had to assume this socialisation responsibility. Male-female relationships, for example, seem to change dramatically every ten or so years, and an adolescent taking his cues from his parents is apt to find himself socially incompetent.

The interaction of formal educational structures with the peer society has developed a pattern which sometimes creates dramatic confrontations. On a routine basis, the school has for some time, been responsive to student interests. In high schools and colleges, a whole network of student interest activities (sometimes called extracurricular) has been established. Often teachers will use educational materials that will reflect the interests of certain student groups, such as the car, sports, surfing and dress and music fads. Rules of deportment have changed in many places as a result of student values. Some schools and school districts have made what they consider to be concessions to student values towards dress and personal grooming. The length of skirts and hair informal dress, hair tinting, and similar issues have provided school administrators with an ongoing experience of confrontation with the adolescent society. In more recent days, on both high school and college campuses, the issues are more significant. Essentially, students appear to want to be treated as whole human beings with a sense of responsibility and some legitimate claim to participating in decisions which affect their lives. Special interest groups, such as organised minority students, have pressed their claim beyond the standard university structures into the larger community, asking that the school feel some responsibility for the life in the ghetto. This can be done, they argue, in several ways, the most important being improving the educational opportunities of members of the non-white communities through more permissive admission standards and through financial support for qualified as well as special students.

Social life today is highly interdependent, as we have seen. For those who do not wish to experience social change, either by ignoring the whole social scene in hopes that it will to away, or by resisting it politically, the future appears very threatening. The future for those who are just beginning to sense that they can play a part in making it, appears very exciting. Classrooms and campuses are currently charged with this kind of excitement, and even though the forces of repression, trying to dam up human striving and potential, may have their day, it is too late. Too many on the campus have experienced a taste of educational freedom, of experiencing power and some control over their educational life. This will never be relinquished.

## The Scientific Revolution

Social change has come about, in part as a response to scientific developments. Science, in our society, has always been linked to technological efficiency which in turn is linked to industrial profits Americans, since the turn of the century and for some years before, have grown up with the understanding that many people were engaged in the task of finding better ways of doing almost everything. We believe that, through science, we can eventually achieve every task. Today's generation does not find it surprising that we have landed men on the moon. Change is inherent in the process of discovering "better" ways—change in our daily routines, our entertainment and our world of work. We, as individual, are always keeping up with and adapting to changes produced by scientific innovation. Furthermore, we are confident that in the hands of scientific technology we are well cared for. We undergo strange medical treatments of which we are ignorant, cross continents in machines that we don't understand, comply with computerised estimates of our bills and bank balances, and subject our best China and furniture to mechanical cleaning processes. We trust science. We must, because our lives are based upon it.

This attitude towards science has carried over into the school. Citizens come to expect that their children will be taught with the most modern techniques and facilities available. Parents from one community will protest vigorously the fact that another community has employed teaching machines while theirs has not. We do not appear to care much about the irrelevance of what we are taught; we are only annoyed if we are not taught in new ways. It is not science itself which has worked for or against a better education. In some important ways, it is our attitude about it. Politicians, for example, can allocate billions of dollars for space exploration and the public does not object since, one fine morning on colour TV, we can all watch the blast-off and landing. But if allocations for education become too high, politicians will fight each other regularly. The products of this money are hidden, the results are not obvious, cannot be viewed on the TV. Most citizens, like most educators, cannot differentiate between a good educational product and a bad one. The student in his black robe receiving a piece of white paper looks the same whether he has received a good education or a bad one. For this reason, educational changes do not occur as rapidly as changes in other segments of our lives.

Technological changes, however, have forced the patterns of educational life to undergo some revision. New technology has created new jobs and made others obsolete. Specialised training had to accompany the development of new specialties and specialists in education had to emerge to teach and guide students towards those new specialties.

The most profound effect of the scientific ethos upon education, however, came not from the development of new machines, but from the discovery of more "scientific" theories about how people learn. We took from psychiatry and psychology many ideas about learning and motivation, and in a relatively short period of time, began to base our classroom organisation and related activities upon it. Students were grouped in certain ways, tested frequently for intelligence, interest, aptitude, and personality, counselled for personality problems, and managed interpersonally as if he (the child) might fall apart at any moment. In many classrooms, the shift was from complete non-concern about the emotional component of the learner to an oversensitivity by which the child's personal strengths were in doubt and his mind was ignored.

Technology has, in some ways, been utilised as an educational tool. The teaching machine, based upon a set of ideas about how rewards can be programmed into the learning activity such that learning occurs, is gaining wider acceptance. Perhaps other, more sophisticated technology will follow in the years to come, until one day we can all just take a pill and have immediate knowledge of the laws of physics. We continue to rely upon science to patch up the holes that we discover in the educational process, and to provide us with new discoveries, new inventions, new techniques. The amazing thing about educators, and those citizens who are concerned about solving the problems of education with some brilliant new discovery, is that they are unable to associate the problems that our society is currently experiencing with this attitude in the first place. Where has all our social and personal alienation, disruption, and disorganisation come from if not explicitly from those forces which have made us a specialised, technological and impersonal society?

### Social Movements

Some of the most dramatic changes in educational structures have come about as a result of large groups of persons banding together to demand change of our major social institutions. When black people began to challenge their treatment by whites on a mass basis, dramatically signaled by the bus boycotts in Birmingham, Alabama, the civil rights movement took on a dynamic posture. The Supreme Court decision to desegregate the schools in 1954 followed, and the demand of black people and many supporting whites made it necessary for educators, as well as politicians, to begin to think about policy. Integration and comensatory educational programme, such as Headstart, began and large sums of government money for bringing dropouts back into the school and for training teachers for the ghetto were allocated.

Minorities of Latin American descent, in the Northeast and Southwest, have taken their cue from the black movement, and are demanding a better American experience. The schools appears to bear the brunt of challenge since these groups, like other American, recognise the function of education as a social equaliser. The civil rights movement itself has passed the stage of calling for integration, since this seems to be the most superficial aspect of what non-whites view as American racism. Racism, as a concept, involves more than individual prejudice and discrimination. It involves are notion of a total institutional structure organised to provide rewards differently, depending on one's race. The call for decentralisation of the schools, for community control, is the next stage of confrontation with the educational establishment. This kind of arrangement would put not only teacher selection and recruitment in the hands of citizens of the community, but would also call for a radical restructuring of the school curriculum in which white middle-class values and ideas would not be the central values and idea stressed in the classroom.

Minority students have made some of their most vigorous protests on the campuses of American colleges and universities. They have called for an increase in the number of minority students, ethnic studies programmes, better integration of faculties, and the support of non-white students financially and through a system of tutorials.

The face of the civil rights movement has grown angry and hard in the last few years, and the demands are becoming more difficult to satisfy all the time, since educators look futilely for some specific change that they can provide to assuage the anger. "What can we do for you?" they ask. They, for the most part, have not learned that the white educator must understand the structure of racism in all its manifestations and put an end to it wherever he finds it. It is his system, he has made it in his image, and he alone knows how it works. He must provide leadership in restructuring the school, for eradicating those patterns which dehumanise the relationship between persons and perpetuate invidious consequences of being non-white in America or in American schools.

### The Humanistic Movement

The most serious threat to the core structure of American society as we know it is a movement as yet unnamed and in whose success lies a new conception of the value and function of education. It cuts across ages, sexes, races, statuses, religions and nationalities. It involves all those who wish to see a society in which isolation, deprivation, and anxiety is not the price of everyday living. The force was born out of our present stage of depersonalised institutional living. It is nourished by our industrial progress, our meaningless affluence our job conditions where men are only roles, and our schools, where students are regarded as products.

The symptoms of this kind of living can be discovered in persons running everywhere seeking for affiliation. They seek organisations which will take them in and care for them, like Alcoholics Anonymous, Synanon, and a host of religious cults. They seek therapy by the droves, sensitivity training, group dynamics. They seek happiness in drugs, drinking, or sexual orgies. Or they seek relief of the condition itself and for themselves by affiliating with others who want to bring about change. They become agents.

Many in this latter category are college students. In them the spirit of protest is most vital. Students are demanding educational reform, in the direction of a more humanistic education where there is freedom for the individual to explore the limits of his own potential.

The college has not been unresponsive to this mood. There is more flexibility in curriculum choice, more innovative experimental courses, experimentations with new forms of evaluation of student performance. It is becoming more difficult to dismiss faculty members of whom the students approve, and students are gaining access to many important committees involved in curriculum planning, policies related to student life, and the recruitment of faculty.

The spirit is being felt in the public schools also. High school students are pressing their own demands and winning the right to be more themselves. In the elementary grades, many teachers are experimenting with new ways to involve students in their own experience. There is pressure emanating from a growing force for more personalised living, to make schools-human places, to return students to their life as children, to allow them to believe that it is worthwhile, perhaps even special, to be a child and to be an ongoing performer seeking institutional rewards.

Society is at a juncture where the forces of technological efficiency and institutional regularity are in a life-and-death struggle with those persons who are victimised and who know it. Education and educators can play a passive role, as they have always done, and accommodate to traditional social expectations and lead us further down the path towards total depersonalisation, or they can serve as an active agency of social change. They can do this by making the school the kind of therapeutic environment that is required for persons to grow as individuals in productive affiliation with others, and to be total human beings.

# 2

# The School in Society

## Nature of Social Institutions

Social Institutions, their origins, their development, their variabilities, their possible perfection, have been of interest to people everywhere and in all times.

Some have believed that they were spontaneously created by their gods and then "revealed" to men. Others have given the credit to a master or group of masters who were inspired.

When people subscribe to such beliefs, they are prone to consider institutions inviolate and to retain them as such no matter what social changes may occur and cause lags between the institutions' credo and actual living conditions.

The current sociological agreement today suggests that institutions are the outcomes of man's attempt to meet his needs. This assumes that they change from time to time and take different forms and outlets from one group to another. Since origins are lost in antiquity, attention is settled on what is the nature of social institutions, their variations, their interrelationships and their tendency to change.

The term social institution is used in many ways by the layman. Whatever has come to be relatively permanent and established with some favour is often called an institution. So-called "characters" of a community are often spoken of in this fashion. The building or buildings which serve as the centre of assemblage or the dispensing of functions are often so identified. Churches, synagogues, mosques may be synonymous for many people with religion. The capitol or the mayor's office may be equivalent to government, and the school house, the college, or the university may connote education.

Again the institutions may be identified with the people, the agents who interpret and enact the institution. In religion this may be thought of as the priest, the minister, the rabbi; in government as the dictator, the president, or chairman; and in education as the teacher, the principal, or the professor.

Sociological definition of social institution is a more specific one. One of all the definitions proposed by various writers, several characteristics are held in common to distinguish them from other social phenomena. Each has a structure or elements which compose it and are organised and integrated to a degree where certain functions can be performed. These characteristics include:

First, social institutions rest upon and develop from basic human needs, desires and interests.

Second, each is a configuration of material objects, of their symbolification, attendant beliefs, rituals, and consequent behaviour patterns which we term folkways and mores.

Third, there is a degree of permanence and universality in structure which is dependent upon the complexity and specialised nature of the society.

Fourth, these institutions have functions whereby the structure is utilised in performance. In simpler cultures these functions are often sharply differentiated and materially exclusive. Today the opposite is more often the case. It is not too difficult to gain agreement as to central tendencies, but where functions begin and end is often a matter of disagreements. The school ably illustrates this impasse.

All will doubtless agree that one school function is instruction in the basic skills of communication, such as reading, writing and arithmetic. Shall communication be understood to include the art and science of living successfully and fully in groups through relaxed, socialised classroom activities which vary from art expression through sex education to music instruction, is for many a moot, or more exactly, a highly debatable issue.

All agree that the function of education is the transmission of the social heritage, but whether it is to be done *per se* or by and with critical analysis with change imminent, will split most drawing room conversation pieces into two politely warring camps.

Not only do social institution structures and functions vary, but they may vary in the same culture at different times in terms of value status.

Religion is accorded an all important role in some societies. In others it occupies a competitive or unpopular role. Within our own society we can readily trace its changed status from the means of personal life and group social control to a purely elective position in a now secular society.

A fifth characteristic of institutional structure and function, as implied above, is change. As one wag has put it, "About the only thing one can be sure of these days is change."

Sociological literature and that of social anthropology is amply supplied with attempts at scientific study and analysis of changes in social institutions. The Middletown studies and community studies in general illustrate this trend.

Somewhat different but equally penetrating analyses of the school as a social institution include Newton Edwards and Herman Richey, *The Role of the School in the American Social Order;* Robert J. Havinghurst, *Who Shall Be Educated?;* Benjamin Fine, *Are Our Children Cheated?*

If there are any general findings which both these general and specific studies of social institutions have in common, it is that in spite of inertia and conservatism changes occur in social structures and their processes of function.

Likewise these changes are not traceable to any one factor or set of factors. Rather it is to be observed that an invention or discovery in one area of life, like the proverbial pebble in the pool, starts reverberations in all other areas, for relationships are reciprocal.

Just as needs, wishes and interests call forth social structures to satisfy them so will new inventions and discoveries disturb the approached equilibrium and set in motion, if not new needs, newer definitions of them.

If the structure has become so solidified that it will not consider such growth and development, the results may be varied. Stalemate may ensue and/or revolt by smaller or larger segments of those who feel thwarted.

It is important to add that with institutions, as with personality development of the individual, neither the hereditary, the geographical, or the social-cultural factors can be considered as all important. Each influence helps to set the stage as it were, but alone it does not determine.

It is apparent that certain institutions, such as the economic, are more closely related to environmental factors than, say, religion and family are, but these latter are by no means independent of geography. It is also probably true that the simpler societies are closer in their institutional framework to geographical influences than are more complex societies. Man by improvements in his cultural equipment, learns to become less dependent upon his immediate environment, and is even able to alter radically his geographical surroundings by the application of science and technology . . . cultural factors and process play their part too . . . Every element, material and non-material, that goes into the making of an institution had to be invented somewhere, sometime, and by someone. They have been transmitted from generation to generation for countless centuries, either by imitation or inculcation. They have also been diffused, being carried from their point of origin to the far corners of the earth . . . To understand any of our institutions, therefore, we need to bear in mind the hereditary, the geographic and cultural factors that determine its form, that affect its function, and that operate in causing it to change. It is also important that we assess properly the influence of these various factors for they are not all of equal importance, and their signifcance is not uniform at all times or in all situations.

## A BRIEF HISTORY OF THE SCHOOL AS A SOCIAL INSTITUTION

### A "Relatively" New Institution

Schools appear to have been one of the later formal social institutions to emerge. In the simpler, smaller, preliterate societies education and socialisation were practically synonymous. The family and the intimate and face-to-face, primary group life of the village transmitted the heritage to its children.

Much of this was done by word of mouth where traditions, customs, and the roles and statuses they prescribed for community members were concerned.

As great a portion of the culture was transmitted by the actual performance of duties and activities in company with family or other community members. Thus, a child learned about hunting and fishing by the actual experience of so doing. Here was perhaps the first really progressive schooling where children learned by doing, hearing and seeing.

In addition, preliterate people recognised the modern fact that changes in physical growth and development entail social growth and development changes.

To emphasise these signs of maturity, to prepare and cause the youth to anticipate these advances, to be certain that cultural facts would be passed on in an approved way and that the new generation would faithfully play the roles assigned, so-called "rites of passage," or initiation ceremonies, were carefully planned and carried out. Tests of physical prowess endurance as well as of mental attributes were rigorously performed.

In such societies no child could be unsure of his roles and statuses. Nor would he be in conflict over what attitudes to assume, what vocation to choose, what religion to embrace, or what political theory to support. Likewise under this educational system be had no doubts as to when he was adult, when child.

His initiation ceremonies were in effect his graduation exercises and established him securely in his society. This is in sharp contrast to present day ones which often serve, as one student remarked, only to set young people adrift. Mead puts it very well when she says:

> So a girl's father may be a Presbyterian, an imperialist, a vegetarian, a tee-totaler, with a strong literary preference for Edmund Burke, a believer in the open shop and a high tariff, who believes that woman's place is in the home, that young girls should wear corsets, not roll their stockings, not smoke, nor go riding with young men in the evening. But her mother's father may be a Low Episcopalian, a

believer in high living, a strong advocate of States' Rights and the Monroe Doctrine, who reads Rabelais, likes to go to musical shows and horse races. Her aunt is an agnostic, an ardent advocate of women's rights, an internationalist who rests all her hopes on Esperanto, is devoted to Bernard Shaw, and spends her spare time in campaigns of antivivisection. Her elder brother, whom she admires exceedingly, has spent two years at Oxford. He is an Anglo-Catholic, an enthusiast concerning all things mediaeval, writes mystical poetry, reads Chesterton, and means to devote his life to seeking for the lost secret of mediaeval stained glass. Her mother's younger brother is an engineer, a strict materialist, who never recovered from reading Haeckel in his youth; he scorns art, believes that science will save the world, scoffs at everything that was said and thought before the nineteenth century, and ruins his health by experiments in the scientific elimination of sleep. Her mother is of a quietistic frame of mind, very much interested in Indian philosophy, a pacifist, a strict non-participator in life, who in spite of her daughter's devotion to her will not make any move to enlist her enthusiasms. And this may be within the girl's own household. Add to it the groups represented, defended, advocated by her friends, her teachers, and the books which she reads by accident, and the list of possible enthusiasms, of suggested allegiances, incompatible with one another, becomes appalling.

As communities became larger and more closely knit with other communities, as inventions occurred and were diffused, the cultural content gradually became both great enough and specialised enough so that general family and community members could neither know nor be skilled enough in all its aspects to transmit it.

Consequently, as Murdock points out, even advanced primitive peoples began a new and specialised social institution known as the school.

In other words, wherever the existing social institutions can no longer perform all the functions needed, when the culture has become too large, complex, and specialised to be passed on by lay people, a new institution tends to arise. Its structure and its processes reflect those of other institutions within its culture, and its aims are derived likewise from tribal or societal experience. So it was, and is, with the school.

## Aims of Education

The aims of preliterate educational practices appear to have been centered upon inducing conformity to group structure and process by securely fitting the individual into the scheme.

Formal agencies of education have also followed this aim in a number of societies. In addition, they have expected the educational system to train for strong physical bodies and alertness in mental ways for the good of the states' military aims. The education system of Sparta is a commonly cited example of this. So important was the aim that the state took the child from the home at seven years of age for intensive physical culture training as well as that of military science.

Some educational systems have deliberately separated the sheep from the goats in a determined effort to train leaders not only in the military sense but also as leaders in political, economic and social life.

Salvation has often been the objective of formal education.

> Among the early civilisation the Jews were somewhat slow in establishing schools, but in the fifth century B.C. the synagogue began to be a center of instruction, and schools were eventually established. The emphasis was upon religion, the Holy Scriptures forming the core of the curriculum. The early history of Christianity offers examples of formal education devoted to religious aims. The rapid spread of Christianity throughout the Roman world following the conversion of the Emperor Constantine in A.D. 312 presented a multitude of problems to the church. The pagan philosophers had to be refuted, converts had to be instructed, Christianity had to be propagated, doctrines had to be expressed in convincing and intelligible language. To these ends the Church developed a variety of schools—catechumenal (for new members), catechetical (for training priests), cathedral (for training bishops) for the purpose of elucidating, propagating and defending its doctrines.

Throughout history as in more current times, there have been those who sought other utilitarian aims such as most of those mentioned above.

At certain times and in certain places the aim of the school has been to provide a liberal education—that is, to free the individual from the domination of the group; to help him to be informed, articulate, sensitive to life's values, and able to think and act as a responsible being; and to train the mind to be disciplined, curious, sensitive, rational and skeptical.

Other aims have included such as the belief that all education should be functional in a vocational way. A child should be pointed always toward the niche in society he will fill, should learn to be satisfied with the same and be "A good citizen," whether it is the life of case and "conspicuous consumption" or that of the vast army which makes the world's goods and performs services.

## THE SCHOOL IN AMERICAN LIFE: HISTORY OF SCHOOL ROLES AND FUNCTIONS

### Colonial Schools

The American colonies must be viewed not as just settlements along the shore edge of a continent but as integral parts of an expanding European civilisation.

> They were in fact Europe's western frontier, and they were bound in a thousand ways by the traditions and customs of the Old World, by its ideology and by its religious, social, economic and political institutions. The history of colonial life, therefore, is in no small degree the history of transplanting European culture in American soil. But that is by no means the whole story. The colonists did not hesitate as they struggled to subdue a raw continent to modify inherited ideas, values, and institutions to meet their needs.
>
> One of the inheritances from England was an educational system which reflected the class system. In the early colonies as in the countries from which the settlers were derived, secondary and higher education—Latin grammar schools and colleges—served primarily the needs of a small directive class. Schools concerned with the teaching of reading and writing in English—where they existed at all—were primarily terminal schools for the masses. They were designed to teach the children of the common people to read, to grasp the principles of some religious sect, and so socialise youth in terms of the existing principles of social organisation.

When one attempts to trace the development of the early system of education in the New England colonies, he meets with conflicting views. Cubberly regards Massachusett's attempt to establish universal literacy by its Acts of 1642 and 1647 as "not only new educational ideas in the English speaking world, but that they also represent the very foundation stones upon which our American public school systems have been constructed".

The Beards disagree violently

> These laws, which seem to have been honoured in the breach as well as in the observance, have been greeted by a modern education as making for the first time in the English language "a legally valid assertion of the right of the state to require of local communities that they establish and maintain schools of general learning." The unwary are liable to be misled by this contention. Unquestionably the first of these acts was conceived partly in the spirit of the English poor law; while the second flowed from a great desire to impose on all children the creed of the Puritan sect. The fact that the education was ordered by "the state" was of no special significance, for the state and church were one in Massachusetts at the time; indeed if the Mathers were to be believed, the church was superior to the state.

Whichever viewpoint may be correct we can be sure that

> the men who founded New England, who led Pilgrim and Puritan across the seas to establish Bible commonwealths in the wilderness, had worked out, in their own minds at least, a definite social design . . . The social order designed by the leaders was a closely knit church-state. As the leaders of New England read their history, sacred and profane, God had never looked with favour on the rule of the many either in church or commonwealth. Consequently, they proposed the establishment and maintenance of a social order in which the popular will have only limited expression.
>
> It is clear that the town schools of colonial New England were designed to meet the needs of a Puritan social order. It is clear, too, that the pattern of these schools was so rigid that it did not yield to the pressures of an emerging capitalistic society.
>
> In the Middle Colonies, no less than in New England and in the South, the transplanted Europeans strove determinedly to maintain the old and familiar culture in new surroundings.
>
> Educational development in each of the colonies established between New England and Maryland was retarded by the disorganising influences of clashing cultures. In no other section were the people so sharply divided in social origin or in social

outlook. In no other section did the Protestant theory of the personal relationship between God and man find such varied expression as in the divided and constantly dividing religious affiliations of the inhabitants. In no other section was the population so heterogeneous with respect to nationality. All mother Europe contributed to the constituency of the population, and the only non-English peoples to found colonies within the limits of the original thirteen established them in this middle region.

In the area of private and higher education, considerable progress was made. Over the Middle Colonies, as elsewhere in America, the Renaissance and the Reformation cast long shadows; for many years the classical and religious traditions held education firmly in their grip. As a result, education was, in large measure, divorced from the realities of American life except as it served religious ends or the purposes of a small aristocratic class. Slowly, however, the influence of classicism and ecclesiasticism weakened, and education began to play a more dynamic role in the social and economic life of the people. The private schools and the colleges were the avenues which led away from old inherited European traditions, and nowhere were these institutions more liberal than in the Middle Colonies.

The Southern Colonies presented still another picture.

If any region in the New World was to bear the name "New England," it should have been the area stretching from the Chesapeake Bay southward rather than the northeastern corner of what is now the United States.

Migrants to the South had embraced a much less thoroughgoing Protestantism than those who had taken refuge in New England. By and large, they had no quarrel with the Anglican Church, and few of them were impelled across the sea by the desire for religious freedom. But on the whole, the Anglican clergy in the South were not an impressive lot. Their influence on political development was relatively slight; they tended to follow rather than to shape social policy.

The educational ideals and practices of the Southern colonists were only slightly changed by the transit to America. No phase of Southern life reflected more truly its English origin than did education. A militant middle class was demanding education, but this demand reflected the growing importance of this class rather than the development of any marked democratic or liberal tendencies. Members of this expanding and power-seeking group looked upon education as a means of enhancing prestige and assuring worldly success, but there were as yet few to argue that children generally should be provided with more training than required to fit them to participate, at levels proper to their social stations, in the political, economic and religious life of the day.

## Nineteenth-century Developments

The period from the Revolution to the Civil War was characterised by the formulation and gradual acceptance of the principles of democratic liberalism; by the development of a more democratic social structure; by the rise of the common man to a position of importance, politically and otherwise; by a bitter struggle to control the national state on the part of Southern planter interests and the rising capitalistic East; and by the growth of the feeling of national unity. As new forces transformed American life, it became apparent that the educational arrangements designed to meet the needs of colonial society were no longer satisfactory. A few far-sighted leaders saw at an early date that a system of education publicly supported and controlled and free and open to all was required to meet the needs of the emerging democratic state. This point of view, however, found slow acceptance in practice.

Education in the West was slow to develop on a large scale, but from the beginning its purpose and its ideals were more genuinely democratic than was the case in either the South or the East. In the West there was greater emphasis on the preparation of youth to perform their civic duties in a democratic republic, and education was designed more than elsewhere to prevent the rise of social classes, to make social mobility a reality, and to release the moral and intellectual capacities of the individual.

While science and invention, translated into technology, were modifying the foundations of American life, another change, quiet and unheralded but of revolutionary importance, was taking place. As each decade registered a further decline in the birth rate, it became apparent,that a demographic revolution was under way. The slowing down of the rate of population growth; the changing age structure of the population; regional, rural-urban, and class differentials in fertility; and internal migration—all these were creating problems of the first magnitude. Scarcely any aspect of public or social policy was left unaffected by population change.

The educational development that have occurred in the United States during the past three quarters of a century can scarcely be understood unless viewed against this broad background of economic and social change. More important still, educational statesmanship today requires an understanding of the forces that have transformed and are still transforming our traditional pattern of institutional arrangements.

These social changes have had a profound effect upon the development of American educational institutions. They were responsible, in part, for the expansion of the educational enterprise to include within its services most children and youth as well as a large part of the adult population, for the enrichment of the curriculum, for the almost endless attempts to order the instructional programme so as to give it system and co-ordination, for the development of new types of structural organisation, for the changing relations of government to education, and for the improvement of the quality of instruction through the scientific study of education and the more effective education of teachers.

The expansion of the educational enterprise was accompanied by ceaseless effort to construct and reconstruct a curriculum to meet the needs of American life as they changed and as they came to be more adequately understood. Fortunately, in the United States no central government has been in a position to control educational policy. Each community has been more or less free to formulate its own educational values and to implement them in such ways as it deemed best. This experimentation, however, has been carried forward within the framework of certain common ideals and has had as its common goal the discovery of a curriculum content—a body of experience—best suited to the changing conditions of American life. Conflict of values and confusion of purpose there have been, but much of this conflict and confusion must be regarded as the product of different ways of arriving experimentally at a common goal.

Structure and function in human institutions are always closely related. Such has been the case with respect to school, college and university in the United States. As the purpose of education has moved in the direction of a cultural democracy and as attempts have been made to frame programmes to meet the changing and varied needs of the people, the structural organisation of education has been repeatedly modified in the hope that each unit in the system would perform its own peculiar function more adequately and that a closer articulation and co-ordination of the total programme would be achieved.

## The School as a Modern Social Institution

Even so brief an historical examination of the school in relation to American society in different period points out the action, reaction and interaction constantly going on between the school and society.

The role and position of the state as a power instrument, the particular stage of development of the economic, religious, and political factors, the concepts of the individual's worth and how he is located in the society's status levels have all been interrelated in their effects upon the structure and processes of the American school.

The school, in turn, has exerted its influence. Sometimes it has retained structures and processes long after they have outlived their usefulness, thus creating imbalances and lags. Sometimes it has coasted along content with the "present," the *status quo*, even "intent" upon its sheer perpetuation. Sometimes it has conceived of its role as an active agent in cultural change in one direction or another. Often schools and school people have simply muddled through. Today they issue is no less sharply drawn. Schools make their choices in a changing world along several avenues. Two widely different ones serve a summary purpose.

> One purpose of education is to draw out the elements of our common, human nature. These elements are the same in any time or place. The notion of educating a man to live in a particular environment as, therefore, foreign to a true conception of education.
>
> Education implies teaching. Teaching implies knowledge. Knowledge is truth. Truth is everywhere the same. Hence, education should be everywhere the same.

And on the other side :

> The school should endeavour to preserve and continually reinterpret and recreate the democratic way of life which has made public education possible. The school has as its basic purpose the creating of a living and learning situation which will provide for the

maximum development of the individual and the group in a democratic setting. Recent aims have included the recognition of the human being as a constantly developing organism whose optimal development is desired regardless of his intelligence, social or economic level. Herein the role of the school is thought of as that of the developing and utilising of the method intelligence in solving problems of human concern.

Such a school attempts, in the words of Alberty:

1. To provide an education environment directed toward the optimal development of all American youth regardless of intelligence, level, or social or economic status.

2. To provide for each student the richest possible experience in democratic living within the school and to help the student to intellectualise such experience in terms of democratic values. This calls for active participation in group living and continuous practice in the recreation of values.

3. To provide for each student the conditions for optimal physical and mental health defined in terms of adequate functioning in democratic living.

4. To help each student to develop and utilise the method of in telligence in solving problems of human concern.

5. To help each student to achieve a dynamic understanding of our democratic culture through the intelligent examination of the conflicting values and practices of the immediate and wider community.

## The School as a Current Object of Attack and Criticism

In an era of rapid and uneven social change cherished institutions of a democratic society are always subject to attack, and the current scene is no exception. In popular magazines, in pamphlets, in screaming, brightly coloured propaganda sheets, in newspapers as well as in some more scholarly publications, one runs head on into attacks on our public schools. In fact, if the reader is at all impressionable, he might readily think that the entire countryside is irate at the schools and clamoring for their complete revision. The thoughtful student, however, is more apt to wish that someone would bring the evidence together, would analyse it in the light of research methods, and in terms of "who," "when," "where," and "by whom sponsored".

The results of such a scholarly attempt may now be read in a monograph entitled "Let's Look at the Attacks on the Schools".

Dr. Alberty and a number of his advanced graduate students undertook this study in order to discover both what the literature would reveal and what a study of their own would contribute. A survey of the literature revealed that there were, in the main, ten basic criticisms levelled at schools as follows:

1. Schools are not effectively teaching children the fundamental skills.
2. Schools are not developing obedience, respect for authority, a sense of responsibility, or a sense of the importance of hard work.
3. Schools fail to stimulate competition among students and to reveal to parents the comparative standing of their children.
4. Schools are trying to educate many young people who cannot profit sufficiently from such education.
5. Schools have not been effective in interpreting their programmes to the public.
6. Schools fail to develop a wholehearted allegiance to the American way of life.
7. Schools are taking over the functions and responsibilities of the home and other institutions.
8. Schools are not teaching boys and girls to make a living.
9. Schools are not keeping pace with social change.
10. Schools personnel are not competent to deal with complex problems the modern school faces.

The accompanying data on both sides of these issues points to several conclusions. First, one or another, and in some isolated cases all, of the criticisms may apply to a given school system at one time or another. Also the attacks on the schools as a whole are never substantiated by reputable research findings.

In respect to the first criticism, studies in many communities, both large and small, show that pupils in the newer curricula master reading skills as well or better than comparable pupils in conventional schools.

Since a variety of reading tests were employed in the studies, the consistent trends of evidence seem well established. Also achievement on a variety of arithmetic tests in various communities provides evidence that pupils in the newer curricula are attaining standards equal or superior to comparable pupils in conventional schools at both the elementary and secondary levels. In general, the newer curricula produce pupils who surpass pupils of the conventional curriculum in language skills and usage. In spelling achievements there is no difference. In secondary schools studies of English are also favourable to the newer curricula.

One very important further point made by the authors in their survey of the basic skills should be given much consideration. They find that not only are the so-called basic skills not neglected but the newer curricula are emphasising the broadening or the number of basic skills to include, such as initiative, social responsibility, ability to work cooperatively with others, and a concept that leadership resides in all and therefore the person must assume responsibility for his actions, to mention but a few.

Incidentally, the discovery of these curricular aims and outcomes is in itself able answer to criticisms two and three. When you know what grades on a grade card, with attendant cut-throat competition, can do to a child's honesty, his happiness, and his general outlook on life, the reader is apt to conclude that evidence has to be interpreted in the light of education aims. If one assumes the values assigned to traditional schools of "hard work at an assigned task" whether it has meaning or not to the student, then it is probable that students are not so engaged in modern schools. But if one takes the viewpoint that "learning is most effective when the task is accepted by the learner as being worthwhile and when its accomplishment is accompanied by a feeling of genuine achievement," then modern schools are doing an excellent job.

The criticism that schools are trying to educate many who cannot profit therefrom seems aimed mainly at secondary education for even these critics agree on the need for a literate population. The criticism appears to say "that the schools should be geared to the needs of the few, the intellectual elite" rather than to the needs of all American youth as democratic ideals would hold.

It is undoubtedly true that so long as curricula remain pointed toward college entrance requirements while the larger percentage of graduates finish their formal schooling at this level, schools are not giving the kind of secondary education which provide for needs and hence optimal development, nor are they preparing youth to make a living by such tactics. But the answer is not less education but "redirected education toward meeting the needs of all youth."

On the issue of the failure of schools adequately to interpret the American way of life, the workshop group points out that merely saluting the flag and reciting the Preamble to the Constitution does not insure appreciation unless effort is made to interpret and relate the principles learned to daily living.

> The modern high school student knows the dangers of totalitarian government and has had practice in recognising and evaluating propaganda for what it is. He is not likely to become a victim of this and other vicious schemes that are utilised by totalitarian governments. Loyalty to the American way of life goes deeper than a pledge of allegiance, beautiful words, and flag waving. One must experience democratic practices and living (in schools) if these values are to be protected, retained and extended.

Analysis of the literature on this criticism suggests that much of it is springing from "front" organisations and/or from such individuals as Allen A. Zoll.

The studies suggest that many schools have been remiss in the interpretation of their aims, programmes, and the like to their constituents. There is evidence also to show, however, that school people are increasingly aware of and interested in this area. In fact, some have gone so far as to say that an enlightened citizenry is one of the best means both of avoiding and of fighting these attacks on the schools. However people may feel, if they do not have the facts they cannot adequately support their schools and school people. And in the lapse of time often necessary to become armed with these facts, the attacking forces enlist many will-meaning but naïve citizens.

The criticisms concerning the taking over of home functions and the failure to keep pace with social change are closely interrelated. The increasing urbanisation, development of technology, speed up of communication and transportation, and general increase in complexity and specialisation of the culture tend to lead us from primary to secondary ways of living. It is a commonly accepted sociological datum that when this occurs, institutional structures as well as processes of functioning will be affected. Some functions will no longer be feasible for one institution but will be so for another. Very often what seems a lost function is but a difference of performance in the function. For example,

> "Doesn't it make you mad to have a teacher send home word that your boy should have glasses or that he doesn't get along well with the kids and the school suggests he be allowed to be seen by their social worker?", raved the discontented parent.
>
> "It would not bother me in that way at all," responded the second parent at the meeting. "In this complicated business of living these days I should be eternally grateful that people who could look at him objectively and with superior training, took such an interest and had such concern for my child. I should know that they want for him what I want for him, adjustment and happiness. No, they aren't taking away our functions, they are re-enforcing them and evidently better than we if our children have reached them in the state you describe."

On the issue of the quality of teacher personnel, the study indicates that although the teaching profession is not up to the standards that many think desirable, there is evidence of improvement as higher salary scales are achieved, as better facilities and equipment become available, as requirements in training advance, and as staff relations improve. It is worth noting that in a nation-wide survey of student reaction to teachers the students, representing all types of schools, liked three out of four of their teachers and considered them helpful, interesting, stimulating, democratic and intelligent. Their dislike for the fourth teacher was related mostly to temperament and personality. Only one tenth of the reasons for dislike included "too old fashioned, too old to be teaching, or doesn't know the subject."

And finally, what do laymen say when surveyed by such as the Elmo Roper study for *Life magazine*? Roper's data showed that a majority (67 per cent) believes that children today are being taught more worthwhile things than children were twenty years ago. Almost all parents think the school should play as important a role in the socialisation of children as the home. A rather large number (67 per cent) feel that teachers are more competent than they were in 1930. This is not to say that the respondents did not find weaknesses in the schools. They did and do. This is healthy and necessary if criticisms are made in relation to specific as well as general situations and are of a constructive nature. For the very nature of social living demands constant examination, re-examination, sometimes deletion, often extension as communities perform what well-adjusted, growing personalities must also continually perform—life reconstruction.

## REFERENCES

Berry, Brewton, Part VI, Social Institutions, in Seba Eldridge and Associates, *Fundamentals of Sociology* (New York, Crowell, 1950), p. 492.

Mead, Margaret, *From the South Seas* (New York, Morrow, 1939), pp. 202-203.

Murdock, G.P., *Our Primitive Contemporaries* (New York, Macmillan, 1934), pp. 384–435.

E.P. Cubberly, *Public Education in the United States* (Boston, Houghton, 1934), p. 17.

Charles A., and Mary Beard, *The Rise of American Civilization*, Vol. I (New York, Macmillan, 1927), pp. 179-180.

Hutchins, Robert, *The Higher Learning in America* (New Haven, Yale University Press, 1936), pp. 66-67.

Harold Alberty, *Reorganizing the High School Curriculum* (New York, Macmillan, 1947), pp. 52-54. Used by permission.

Harold Alberty and others, "Let's Look at the Attacks on the Schools," (Columbus, College of Education, The Ohio State University, 1951).

Harding, Lowry W., "How Well Are Schools Now Teaching the Basic Skills?" *Progressive Education*, Vol. 29, No. 1 (October 1951), pp. 7–15.

# 3

# The School as a Social World–Specialised Aspects

## Ascendancy Relationships—Suggestions as to Newer Concepts and a Way of Studying Them

### The Concept "Leadership"

As was mentioned in the discussion on the formation of child groups, lines of association begin appearing almost simultaneously with interaction. These association lines are not merely in terms of choice as to composition of the group members but also in terms of what group position will each person hold.

As someone has said, if two people were placed in absolute isolation, one of the two would shortly assert dominance over the other. It would be done in terms of competition it is true, but also in terms of cooperation, or, more aptly, cooperative-competition. For basic to the very idea of competition as a social process is the idea that it is impersonal, continuous, and in the main carried on according to rules, understood and/or expressed. Such a process has then, as a major part of its concept, cooperation.

Within this frame of reference, people play different roles from time to time largely dependent upon the social situation, its components, needs, facilities, its definition of leader, behaviour, etc.

In other words, some people, some children are more dominant in social relationship, some are less so, and some are now dominant and now more submissive. We tend to attach the name "leader" to the more dominant, ascendant person and "follower" or "led" to the more submissive roles played.

What, then, has been, and is, the concept of leadership? What people assume these roles? What are their characteristics? What are their ways of instituting their leadership?

Leadership has been variously defined as "the influencing of opinion," as "the directing of activities of a group," as "acts which make a difference in group effectiveness," and as "actions by people which influence people in shared direction."

Earlier studies of leadership centered on qualities and characteristics. These have ranged from descriptions of essentials to detailed studies of size, weight, scholastic ability, manner of dress, beauty, etc., as traits of leadership.

Pigors suggests that the essentials of leadership are (1) a common cause, (2) a leader, (3) followers, (4) and the current situation.

Terman found leaders as rated by their associates to be either first or last in health, dress, social status, scholastic work, boldness of manner, and speech fluency. As Terman suggests, they stood at one extreme or another in these personal-social characteristics.

Hunter and Jordan in their extensive study of college students found significant differences between leaders and nonleaders in terms of age, weight, and the like. Leaders as compared with nonleaders were significantly younger, were lighter in weight (possibly because of being younger), had parents who were college trained, had parents belonging to the professional classes, had law or journalism as vocational preferences, were superior in tests of intelligence and of vocabulary, and were higher in scholarship.

Lists of leadership qualities are well illustrated by such lists as those by Bernard and Allport.

Bernard's list consists of the following:

1. Striking physical personality.
2. Size.
3. Good looks.
4. Appearance of strength of body.
5. Appearance of strength of character.

6. Ready speech.
7. Oratorical gift of emotional appeal.
8. Readiness in repartee.
9. Sympathy.
10. Sense of justice.
11. Humanitarianism.
12. Honesty.
13. Good faith.
14. Insight.
15. Courage.
16. Persistence.
17. Good natural ability.
18. Originality.
19. Initiative.
20. Good intellectual training.
21. Soundness of judgment.
22. Mental flexibility.
23. Forethought.
24. Intellectual vision.
25. Moral vision.
26. Positive idealism.
27. Cheerful, even temper.
28. Poise.
29. Self-confidence.
30. Organising and executive ability.
31. Knowledge of human nature and society.

Allport lists the following:

1. Trait of ascendance.
2. Physical power.
3. High motility.
4. Tonus.
5. Erect, aggressive carriage.
6. Tenacity.
7. Face-to-face mode of address.
8. Reinforcement of energy.
9. Restraint.
10. Inscrutability.
11. Expansiveness in field of action.

12. High intelligence.
13. Understanding.
14. Keenly susceptible to social stimulation.
15. Tact.
16. Zeal.
17. Social participation.
18. Character.
19. Drive.

As Britt once suggested, "it is questionable whether such generalised lists can aid anyone in achieving a position leadership, for there seems to be a definite specificity in qualifications for leadership. The traits that suit a leader for one purpose do not necessarily suit him for leadership in all activities. To say that a leader is one who has size and good looks may apply in the world of a candidate for political office, but does not necessarily apply to a leader in the world of science . . . Leadership in any one activity requires a certain amount of skill in that activity as well as evidence of other skills. A person cannot lead in all spheres; he must at times be a follower. In other words, if you wish to analyse the social psychology of leadership so that the materials may be useful to you personally, you should choose some particular situation and then, by observational or experimental methods, make a careful study of leadership in that particular kind of situation."

### A Plan for the Analysis of Leadership

In line with this suggestion, we present a paradigm for the analysis of leadership. In the words of Seeman and Morris this pattern stresses the fact that the group and individual variables commonly examined in leadership studies may be viewed in five ways—as results, concomitants, determiners, or conditioners of the leader's behaviour and as criteria for evaluation.

Such an approach to the understanding of status within school groups would be of inestimable value to the teacher and/or counsellor with reference to abilities and potentialities. Though the material quoted below is being utilised largely in research of adult groups, its framework is readily adaptable to any age level.

This newer and challenging approach to the study of leadership is being developed in the Ohio State Leadership

Studies under the direction of Carroll L. Shartle, *et al.*, Seeman and Morris describe this interdisciplinary approach as follows:

1. ***Who it the leader***—It should not be assumed that the nature of the group under investigation will entirely determine how the leader is to be designated. This is also a function of the theory and definition of leadership involved. It is possible, by one definition, to designate as "leader" the individual in high office who has been chosen for study; while, by another definition, we cannot call him "leader" until he has demonstrably made a difference in the group, i.e., has exercised influence. The problem of designating the leader is of crucial concern in the study of leadership, especially in view of the fact that the office holder as leader is a common stereotype in our culture.

2. ***What is defined as leader behaviour***—The individual designated as leader behaves in accordance with the demands of many roles in addition to that of leader. Clearly some of his behaviour is to the considered as leader behaviour, and some is not. It seems essential, as methodologies of observation are worked out, to establish theoretically the limits of the phenomena to be observed.

3. ***How is leader behaviour to be described and analysed***—The focus, for the most part, has been on either leader *evaluation* or on the *traits* of leaders, while the leader's behaviour has been largely ignored.

   The staff of the Ohio State Leadership Studies has made the description of leader behaviour one of its chief responsibilities. Instruments designed to observe and analyse the behaviour of leaders are being developed. We have found it useful to think in terms of *what* and *how* of leader behaviour: on what organizational functions does the leader spend his time and how does he perform these functions? Is he dominant? separated from the group?

   Who shall describe the leader's behaviour? The description may be made by the leader himself, by his subordinates, by his peers, by his superiors, or by the investigator, either as a participant observer or otherwise. The methods currently being used are listed in the chart: all may be applied to obtain descriptions of leader behaviour from the entire range of personnel listed above. One of the instruments currently being analysed (3K) contains one hundred and fifty items describing leader behaviour in terms of nine categories (3C), calling for responses by the leader himself, his subordinates, and others. This instrument can also be used to explore leadership ideologies (What should an ideal leader do?).

A Paradigm for the Study of Leadership

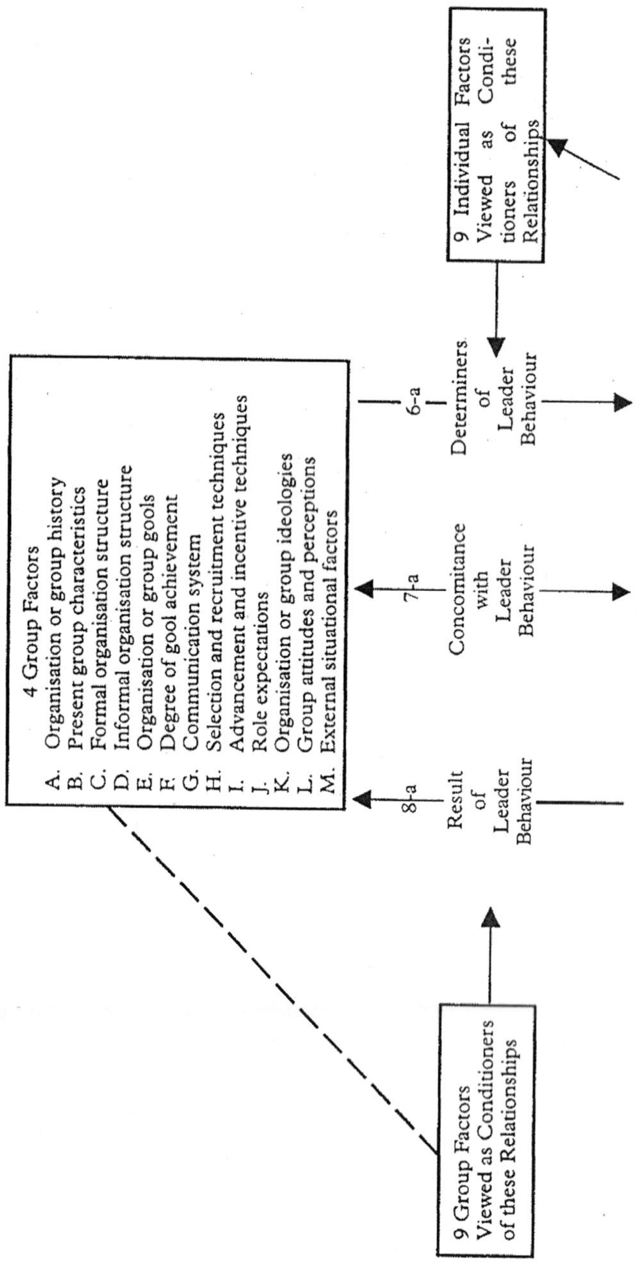

**1. Definition of the Leader**

A. Individual in a given office; in a standardised position of high influence potential.
B. Individual who exercises positive influence acts upon others.
C. Individual who exercises more, or more important, positive influence acts than any other member in the group.
D. Individual named by the group as leader.
E. Individual who exercises most influence in goal-setting and goal-achievement.

**3. Leader Behavior Description and Analysis**

*Content*

What does the leader do?
A. Time spent in various kinds of activities (planning, evaluation, supervision, etc.)
B. Time spent with various people (sociometric patterns).

How does the leader do it?
C. Frequency of various categories of behaviour dominance, integration, etc.
D. Responsibility, authority, and delegation patterns.
E. Prediction of behaviour in given situations.
F. Influence patterns in group situations.

*Method*

By whom is the description mode?
G. Self-description.
H. Group member description.
I. Observer description.

By what method
J. Interview.
K. Behaviour checklist
L. Time distribution analysis.
M. Sociometrics.
N. Direct observation, participant, non-participant
O. Rating scales
P. Situation tests.

**2 Definition of Leader Behaviour**

A. Behaviour involved in the execution of a given position.
B. All the behaviour of the individual selected as leader.
C. Any positive influence act.
D. Behaviour of any individual that makes a difference in the behaviour or characteristics of the group.
E. Behaviour of an individual when he is directing the activities of a group.

8-b Results | 7-b Concomitance | 6-b Determiners

**10a Group-centered Evaluation**
(Group factors viewed as criteria)

A. Goal achievement of group.
B. Group satisfaction and morale.
C. Group efficiency production per time and cost unit.
D. Group survival: member turnover; success in competition with other groups.
E. Achievement and maintenance of democratic values : utilisation of members in decision-making.

**5 Individual Factors**

A Biographical information.
B Psychological characteristics.
C. Physical characteristics.
D. Ideologies.
E. Perceptions and attitudes.
F. Position in organisation or group.
G. Length of time in position.
H. Salary and other rewards.
I. Method of achieving position.
J. External situational factors.

**10-b Individual-centered Evaluation**
(Individual factors viewed as criteria)

A. Personal success of leader advancement salary level, office, honours.
B. Choice of leader by group members.
C. Effectiveness or other merit ratings by group members or others.
D. Self-rating by leader job satisfaction.
E. Degree of conformance to expected role behaviour.
F. Degree of role change made by leader.

*Source:* R.T. Morris and M. Seeman, "The Problem of Leadership: An Interdisciplinary Approach," American Journal of Sociology, Vol. LVI, No. 2.

4-5. ***What group and individual factors are significant for leader behaviour***—The category "group factors" refers to the characteristics of the group in which the individual designated as leader exercised the function of leader. These factors are distinguished from "individual factors" in that the latter refer to the characteristics of the individual designated as leader. The variables listed in these two sections of the chart are suggestive rather than exhaustive. Four major types of variable have been focused upon for present study:

(a) *A job analysis and organisational structure approach,* in which the central effort is upon describing what leaders actually do (3A and 3B); and on how this is related to organizational structure, *e.g.*, informal work patterns (4D), or echelon level (4C).

(b) *A communications and leader effectiveness approach,* in which are examined, first, the relation of leader effectiveness to specific leader differences, *e.g.*, the ability to estimate group opinion (5E) and, second, the relation among multiple criteria for effectiveness, *e.g.*, high group morale (10-aD) and ratings by subordinates (10-bC).

(c) *A status factor approach,* in which the emphasis is upon leadership as a status phenomenon with major attention given to exploring the relation of the leader's and followers' behaviour to status factors at work in the organisation or community, *e.g.*, the relation of leader behaviour to commitments about or perceptions of status differences in society (4C and 5E).

(d) *A group dimension approach,* which seeks to explore situational differences in leader behaviour, *e.g.*, differences in leader operation associated with differences in group size, homogeneity, togetherness, etc. (4B).

6. ***Why does the leader behave as he does***—We are interested here in discovering the group or individual factors which determine differences in leader behaviour (6-a, 6-b). As such factors are found, we will be in a better position to test our findings by controlled experimentation in the selection, training, and evaluation of leaders.

7. ***What phenomena are concomitant with gives kinds of leader behaviour***—Though the ultimate effort is to isolate the crucial determining variables, all the studies listed in sections 4-5 above are primarily, at the present time, studies not of causal but of concomitant relations. To illustrate, Seeman and Morris found, in a study of the relation of general-status attitudes to leadership

ideology, that teachers who were committed to maintaining larger status differences in a wide variety of social, political, and economic situations were those who wanted most direction, and clear "leader" rather than "member" behaviour, from their "ideal superintendents". This suggests a concomitance between the status ideology of superintendents themselves and their behaviour as described by subordinates. Seeking out such concomitances is a vital preparatory step toward the establishment of causal patterns.

8. *What are the results of leader behaviour*—The primary concern in describing results of the leader's behaviour is with what we have called the "group factors". There are also, however, questions which center on the individual factors as results: Does dominance by the leader (3C) lead to given patterns of advancement for him in an organisation (5H).

9. *What factors serve as conditions*—Here the individual and group factors are viewed as conditioners of relationships between given leader behaviour and other factors. Hemphill found that the reported behaviour of "superior" leaders differed significantly in terms of the size of the group in which they functioned. The differences were in the direction of greater tolerance for leader-centered direction in larger groups. These findings suggest that the size of the group is one important factor conditioning the relationship between leader behaviour and his evaluation by subordinates. Similarly, the relation suggested in section 8 above between supervision pattern and the communication system in the group may hold only in groups of a given size or in groups having a given type of formal organisation.

10. *How are the results of leader behaviour evaluated*—Two kinds of criteria can be used: those which evaluate leadership in terms of the results for the group and those which focus simply upon the individual who is the leader.

    Criteria for effectiveness may vary systematically with the individual making the evaluation: different people want different things of leadership; or with the situation: what is effective leadership in peace may not be effective leadership in war.

## Democratic Leadership

We are all convinced of the superiority of democratic groups but we frequently are not so aware or convinced of the fact that this superiority is directly related to:

> . . .appropriate leadership in these groups. And democratic leadership requires attitudes, understandings, and skills which are more, not less profound and complex than those required by the autocratic leader. These attitudes, understandings, and skills can be learned, but they will not be learned without educational thought and effort.
>
> Too often and too long we have thought and said that leaders are "born, not made" and fully as mythical have assumed that the social situation will automatically provide its own leader. It is high time that proponents of democratic grouping and procedures recognised and accepted the responsibility for training of democratic leadership. The first requisite for this viewpoint is a clear recognition of what is to be developed. What are some leadership functions?
>
> 1. It is important that we see "leadership" in terms of functions to be performed in helping groups to grow and operate productively not in terms of qualities inherent in persons. [This means that] one set of leadership functions, then, has to do with services required within the group in helping it to grow to greater maturity.
>
>    *(a)* A group must set common goals and purposes. This is done by working through differences among its members. Leadership must help clarify differences, bring in relevant information which will help resolve issues that divide.
>
>    *(b)* A group must keep balance between long-range and short-range goals. Leadership must aid here by seeing that one type of goal is not forgotten in planning for another.
>
>    *(c)* Groups must be helped to keep plans "realistic," to practice plans before trying them fully, and to test them in practice.
>
> Finally, groups, having planned and acted, must evaluate what they have done. They need help in getting evaluation data, in interpreting it, and in amending cherished plans if evaluation requires it.
>
> 2. A second set of leadership functions, therefore, has to do with services required by any group in keeping its processes of planning, acting, and evaluating productive and geared to the changing environment in which it lives and acts.
>
> In the mature group leadership is not resident in any one person but is delegated in terms of different group members, their particular interests and aptitudes. Some functions may even be reserved for the group as a whole.

## Principles of Leadership Training

1. Leadership can be learned by children only as they practice the skills of productive group work in a variety of group settings.

   This implies extensive experience in student-led groups. But experience in group work in not enough to insure that the skills and understandings are well-recognized or well-learned.

2. Self-evaluation by the group of its own ways of working and group planning to improve the groups procedures are necessary to insure that leadership functions are adequately understood and practiced by all children.

   A good starting point for this evaluation is a time when group discussion and action is confused, frustrating, at a stand still.

   "The group which discovers out of its own group experience that there is a relation between the language its member use in making a suggestion and the kind of hearing the suggestion receives, that summaries of where we've been and where we seem to be going help keep a group on the beam, that minority or unpopular opinions often contribute much to a groups thinking, and the right of these opinions to be heard needs to be safeguarded is learning to identify, support and practice the functions of democratic leadership."

   One other, often, neglected area of leadership training needs emphasis.

3. New patterns of relationships are frequently resisted by children and adults because they are perceived as threats to self-confidence. Trying out new patterns requires a free and permissive atmosphere in which this ego threat is reduced to a minimum.

   This says that "the right to make mistakes" must be a part of group understanding; that consequent criticism is directed in terms of *group maturity* at the *leader* or *member* role not at the person himself.

   Role playing may be of great help in such connections, criticisms may be readily accepted under such circumstances because it is the *role* not the *person* which is being evaluated, but the insight and security and skill in new ways of working are just as real and keen.

## "Fringe" Relationships of the School

Many teacher experience papers bear out Waller's contention that the school social world "contains some hangers-on, some marginal members who from one point of view are members of the school as a social body and from another are complete outsiders, some persons without any fixed legal status in the group but often with a good deal of influence."

The janitor or custodian appears to fill such a role especially in smaller communities. Out of 520 personal experience papers written by returned teachers in educational sociology classes, only 25 did not mention the janitor as a personage to be reckoned with as a "person of power".

This is perhaps all the more significant when it is recalled that 162 papers were written by teachers from communities of 150,000 population to 300,000. The 25 who did not so mention the custodian were from communities of 300,000 or more.

The consensus of opinion seemed to be that if the janitor were on your side, he could do you much good not merely with supervisors and administrators but also with community members. If he did not like you and "the way you kept your room," his opportunity to bear tales was unequaled.

People who work in lunchrooms, cornor-store "hand-outs," and the like likewise often influence student thinking and consequent attitude toward teacher activities out of all proportion to their social position.

It has been suggested that this may be due to the fact that these adults represent themselves as harmless and manipulable mother and father substitutes. In so doing they encourage youngsters to establish and carry on a rapport with the older generation at the some time that they are able to "get even" with it by gossip, criticism, and so forth.

School "cops" also fit this fringe roll. Often they are beloved characters for whom alumni ask more often than they do for teachers or administrators.

The influence of alumni is very real, and frequently very potent, as both student participants and observers point out. Their interest is likely to focalise on athletics. At the college and university level they are often carefully courted through alumni associations, class reunions, chain letters and journals. The object of this attention is not difficult to find. Both contributions to funds, scholarships, and even enrolment are derived from alumni. At the high school level some attempt is made also to maintain the interest of alumni, but, in the main, success is only with the most recent, those who live close about and the very old alumni, who find it a nostalgic release.

One interesting analysis of alumni is presented below:

> Indeed, there seems to be an inherent necessity that the better sort of alumni, the more intelligent and the more successful, should always elude the tentacles of the alumni secretary. There are exceptions, of course, but the rule seems to hold. When a man goes back to his alma mater for a reunion, whether that alma mater be a prep school or one of the most advanced professional schools, he does it for a taste of the joys that were his when he was a youngster in school. But if he has attained a satisfactory adjustment of his life on the adult level, he will not be likely to hanker for a revival of adolescent associations. Thus, it is the unadjusted and the failures in life who are in general most enthusiastic about keeping up their school connections; if they have adjusted themselves to adult life, their interests and desires will have moved on irrevocably from their school-day memories. Indeed, it may be argued that a man who after five years still persists in telling stories of his college achievements has failed in life. He may not have failed to secure position, or professional advancement, or wealth, but if his emotions and his intellect have not become involved in situations of life far more interesting than those old situations of schools, he has failed in life.
>
> While we are attempting to generalise about alumni, we should state that there seems to be a considerable difference between those alumni who merely hold to the values of school life because that was the most interesting time of their lives and those alumni who break away, are inducted into a rapidly expanding world of adult interests, and afterwards encounter their alma mater in their expanding social world. From this latter group are gathered those excellent individuals who, though weighed down by a thousand and one other interests, persist in serving their alma mater as a means to a wider social service. From this latter class are recruited those lay advisers and administrators without whom it would be very difficult to conduct the work of any school.

Though there may be differences of opinion concerning the inclusion of the school board as a school fringe, the fact remains that it is *in* and *of* the community and *in*, if not *of*, the school social world. Theoretically, it sets and stands for policies and hires a school staff to carry out these policies. Actually in many smaller communities, the school board, composed largely of lay members with little or no specialist training, demands a final voice in matters which require considerable training and which in the opinion of informed people would seem to be matters for staff handling.

It is an easily documented fact that school-board members are chosen with little or no regard for training or experience in educational pursuits. As shown by studies of community conduct codes for teachers, school-board members are apt to translate their role as a highly conservative one. It would be interesting to know what causes a mildly liberal community member to swing sharply conservative once he assumes the role of board member.

## SELECTED INTERPERSONAL RELATIONSHIPS WITHIN THE SCHOOL SOCIAL WORLD

### Staff Relationships

The importance of "staff relationship atmospheres" are exceeded in importance, if at all, only by teacher-pupil relationship atmospheres. Obviously, the two are closely related, for few people are able to follow consistently and happily one social atmosphere in one area of interpersonal living and a very different one in other areas.

In earlier days, and in some isolated places still, where single salary scales are not the rule, rivalry and discontent were, and are, often rampant between elementary and high school teachers. This was especially true if both were housed in one building, as in small communities.

Likewise, under the older concept of supervision relationships between classroom teachers and supervisory and administrative people were too often of dubious, if not downright, antagonism and hatred.

These social structures and processes were obviously derivatives from the efficiency complexes which business and industry developed during the era of rapid growth and expansion. It is often said that the army line and staff organisation amplified by business and industrial giants has been taken over *in toto* as the school also became too large, too expanded to be handled by the people as a whole. The pattern of movement from simple, community-wide direction to committees (boards of education) to school superintendents is the usual pattern in the shift from primary to secondary modes of living.

A structural parallel between army and school organisation is readily drawn. In the army the line officers are in authority from general to Brigadier General-to Colonels, to Majors to Captains to Lieutenants to Sergeants and finally to corporals. The staff officers are specialised experts who can handle technical matters. They are without authority and cannot issue orders though they may have any of the above rankings. Generals issue orders but usually not without consultation with the staff officers.

With some differences, many schools are organised in similar fashion. The executive officer is the superintendent, but he delegates responsibilities to assistant superintendents, principals, vice-principals and department heads. In the school the staff officers are the psychiatrists, the guidance people, the psychiatric social worker, the librarians, the testing experts, and the like. Their job is an advisory one to the people in the above ranks.

But what is the current scene? What are the attitudes of both teachers and administrators toward "actual and preferred practices?"

A recent doctoral dissertation reveals interesting and challenging factual material on the subject.

After considerable research, Williams devised an inquiry which tested whether school policy formation and implementation was democratic, *laissez-faire,* or authoritarian, as well as testing the degree or level of development at which the group was working. Authoritarian categories included such characteristics as:

1. The administration decides on policies and announces them to the staff.
2. Individuals who have seniority use their experience and prestige to away policy formation.
3. The teacher is so much in the background that he contributes little to policy formation.

4. In order than routine matters the administration carries out instructions from the superintendent's office.
5. Irrelevant considerations or fears dctermine policies used.
6. Factions oppose each other on matters of basic policy.
7. Precedents and traditions determine policies.
8. The administration uses veto power on matters of policy.

*Laissez-faire* categories included such characteristics as the following:

1. Mistakes are made without assuming responsibility for actions or conduct.
2. Each teacher handles situations as he sees fit.
3. The administrator handles situations in terms of expediency.
4. Cliques, stool pigeons, suspicions, favours, and "back bitings" influence policy formations.
5. Pressure groups flout or reverse policies by agitating or by influencing public opinion.

Democratic characteristics were as follows

1. Teachers' expressed preferences are considered as to work that is assigned them.
2. Teachers are given liberties and responsibilities consistent with their individual abilities, interests and dispositions.
3. The administration secures staff consideration of the problems, issues, and values which need to be considered in policy making.
4. Cooperative concern for the common good is the basis of policies.
5. Teachers are given opportunity to question or suggest policies.
6. The administrator works with his teachers. Suggestions take the place of commands.
7. Teachers are permitted and expected to share in the forming of school policies.
8. Committees are established to formulate policies which will be presented to the entire staff.
9. Staff meetings are planned ahead of time on a cooperative basis.

10. Members of the faculty help formulate the issues to be discussed in staff meetings.
11. Matters are discussed pro and con, put to a vote, and the majority decision becomes policy.

In country secondary schools administrators felt by slightly higher scores (95) than teacher (89) that democracy prevailed in their systems activities. In the county elementary schools there was so small a difference in administrators (97) and teachers opinions (98) as to be negligible. Secondary school administrators and teachers were farther apart in their opinions.

In exempted villages the elementary teachers gave the school a score of only 92 whereas administrators gave a 99 score. Secondary teachers and administrators presented scores of 92 and 99 respectively, also showing greatest consistency in opinion.

In city systems elementary teachers and administrators were again close together as were secondary people with a score of 91 for teacher and 90 for administrators.

Further breakdowns of the over-all findings allow for several conclusions from the Williams study.

1. Policy formation (and by implication) policy implementation is increasingly coming to be regarded as the joint responsibility of teachers and administrators.
2. The enthusiasm of teachers for participation in policy formation rises or falls according to the degree to which they are permitted to take part in the process.
3. There is an inverse relationship between staff participation and administrative administration. As staff participation increases, administrative participation decreases.
4. Both teachers and administrators feel that free discussion of needed policies is of paramount importance.
5. Most administrators and teachers feel that majority vote is very democratic and very satisfactory.
6. Very few schools strive for consensus in arriving at desired policies.
7. Committees form a major role for study of problems and in the presentation of recommended solutions for them.
8. Actual practice falls far below beliefs and desires of both teachers and administrators.

9. Teachers and administrators in about equal numbers believe in cooperative procedures, although administrators are slightly more enthusiastic then are teachers.
10. Administrators as a whole are slightly more anxious to move toward democratic procedures than are teachers.
11. There is a very close relationship between the goals sought by teachers.
12. Both desire an increase in teacher participation.
13. There is little difference between attitudes of the two groups on policy formation.
14. Often administrators do not realise their use of dictatorial methods, or teachers do not realise their actions as participants in administration.
15. After policies are set up, it is often felt that teachers should help administer them more than they do.
16. The democratic staff process provides almost unanimously experiences that are effective, satisfying, while undemocratic procedures provide experiences which are unsatisfactory and ineffective.
17. Staff agenda need to be prepared and presented to teachers well in advance of staff meeting.
18. When changes in policy are desired, democratic procedures are more frequently used than undemocratic or doubtful procedures.
19. In-service training is provided through democratic staff participation.
20. There should be a continual evaluation of policies which have been formed.
21. There is need for a basic set of values to guide formation of school policies.
22. No one person has enough ability and information to supervise and administrate a school at its highest efficiency.
23. Staff members are more effective when they feel that they are an accepted part of the school organisation and not just pawns of a supreme administration.
24. Only 29 per cent of the schools that were studied have definite written policies.

25. Where there is not cooperative procedure in administration of school policies, the teachers alone administer the policies twice as often as do the administrators.
26. There is practically no variation in the degree of democracy thought to be present in the exempted village, the county and the city schools.
27. Exempted schools are more democratic than small community schools in their staff policy-making procedures, while city schools are least democratic.
28. Administrators feel schools to be more democratic than do teachers.
29. There is a definite preference for democratic organisation rather than authoritarian or *laissez-faire*.
30. Often the administrator or a board member stifles the desire of a staff to participate in policy by having earlier reversed or disregarded staff decisions.
31. Veto power on the part of the administration is used sparingly.
32. It is believed that in large staffs committees should first study and analyse the problems, then present tentative findings to the entire staff for further study.
33. The most democratic policies now in use are those which concern school trips, guidance, assembly programmes, and textbook selections. The least are those which concern corporal punishment, school accidents, religious instruction, and school budgets.

**Teacher Social Roles**

Heretofore we have spoken of teacher living in terms of interpersonal contacts with children as related to effects of teacher personality and social climate upon children.

It is now necessary to consider the backgrounds of classroom teachers. Who are they? Where are they on the social-cultural status scheme? What is expected of them as persons in the school's community life?

Though the social position of the teacher varies somewhat in terms of regions of the United States, size of communities, and the personal-social characteristics of the individual, teachers are derived largely from middle-class backgrounds. Some studies suggest their orientation to be largely lower-middle and upper-lower with main emphasis upon lower-middle and middle-middle. This is said to be especially true of the Middle West and the Far West.

In studies of social backgrounds of teachers, parent occupations are largely farmers and businessmen, usually small business owners.

In one study of women students in teachers' colleges Methodist and Baptist religious denominations accounted for more than half of these would be teachers. These denominations more than any other in this country are middle class.

Elsbree and others have considered these backgrounds as dangerously limiting factors. "Coming as they do mostly from lower-middle class, they bear all the marks of the relatively unfavoured social and economic group. To fill in these cultural gaps in the experiences of teachers is a task of considerable magnitude".

With such backgrounds in evidence, it is safe to say that teaching has been "chosen" by many people because it served as a possible social elevator for those who elected to be teachers. Though there may have been historically disagreement as to its rating as a profession, it has until very recently been the profession requiring least formal training.

With such background teachers tend to present, perpetuate, and enforce middle-class mores, attitudes and skills. This very often results in penalisation of lower-class children. One who is on his or her way up, unless he thoroughly understands such sociological factors and backgrounds, will see only as "bad" and "nasty," the child who uses the language and techniques of his lower-class level within the schoolroom and on the playground.

The expectations and anticipations established for middle-class youngsters may well be not only impossible but undesirable and frustrating to him.

Since few upper-class children appear in public schools, they escape this impact in the main. It is true that their teachers in private schools are also largely middle class, but there teacher role and function is restricted to teachings which have upper-class value.

> It has been said that like other professions—teaching is regulated by at least two basic kinds of controls—by laws imposed from the outside and by codes of ethics developed within the teaching group. More than in other professions, there is a third, and perhaps even more rigorous type of control in teaching. This consists of the attitudes, values, expectancies, and norms of the public—the type of control which defines the kind of person a teacher should be and thus determines to some extent the characteristics of those who enter the profession. These factors likewise play a part in deciding who shall continue in the profession and are therefore instrumental in forming are "teacher" as an occupational type. Although the teacher type has never been expirically delineated, some of its elements have been analysed by a few students.

This study has attempted to answer this question by securing replies to the inquiry: "Should the following types of persons be employed to teach in the public schools of your community?"

> In Table 3.1 employability quotients have been arrayed from highest positive to lowest negative response, using school board member totals as a base. Inspection reveals a number of generalised findings. For instance, female applicants who are married are definitely disapproved of by school-board members (—32.1), only mildly reacted against by lay persons (—12.0), definitely approved by students training to be teachers (12.4). More likely than not, the student vote in the last instance is probably based upon anticipated competition with married women for teaching positions.
>
> A non-local resident is favoured more by school-board members than by community lay representatives, a rating position not duplicated on any other item in the entire list.
>
> In the words of one Southern student. "The only place Negroes would be employed to teach would be in coloured schools, and I naturally assumed this was the meaning of the question."
>
> Attention may be called to one final comparison of scores. Apparently school-board members would employ a person in bad health in preference to a known Communist, though the difference in score is so small as to lack significance.
>
> In many instances the reactions of school-board members are so

different from the young people among whom they may be expected to find teachers for their schools as to be a matter of grave concern. Evidence also indicates that the longer students are in college the more liberal they tend to become, a fact, which we have singled out for sociological interpretation.

Table 3.1
**Employability Quotients of Potential Applicants for Teaching Positions in the Public Schools of the Nation**

| | *As Rated by* | | | |
|---|---|---|---|---|
| *Potential applicant for teaching position* | *356 School-board members* | *2,095 Lay persons* | *9,122 Pub. Sch. teachers* | *3,054 Education Stud'ts.* |
| 1. A known Protestant | 76.5 | 84.9 | 93.5 | 93.5 |
| 2. Native-born, foreign name | 56.3 | 73.2 | 88.5 | 89.9 |
| 3. Non-local resident | 48.3 | 46.0 | 78.4 | 89.1 |
| 4. City-reared person | 45.8 | 66.6 | 85.4 | 90.8 |
| 5. Out-of-state applicant | 15.4 | 27.5 | 69.4 | 64.9 |
| 6. A known Catholic | —21.3 | 9.5 | 53.1 | 68.0 |
| 7. A known pacifist | —22.8 | 5.3 | 29.7 | 40.4 |
| 8. A married woman | —32.1 | —12.0 | 36.5 | 12.4 |
| 9. A known Jew | —41.3 | 2.3 | 44.8 | 41.5 |
| 10. A known militarist | —62.0 | —50.1 | —42.1 | —25.0 |
| 11. A light Negro | —82.1 | —54.2 | —54.2 | —33.6 |
| 12. A dark Negro | —85.7 | —66.0 | —63.4 | —49.4 |
| 13. A known radical | —88.0 | —72.5 | —63.6 | —48.2 |
| 14. Person in bad health | —93.3 | —87.9 | —54.7 | —89.6 |
| 15. A known Communist | —94.1 | —83.2 | —77.5 | —57.9 |

Light Negroes and dark Negroes are significantly differentiated in only one instance—the response of the community group—a finding contrary to common-sense expectations and probably due to the tendency to think of Negro teacher applicants as seeking positions, not in "the schools of your community," as stated in the instructions, but in Negro schools.

*Source:* Florence Greenhoe, *Community Contacts and Participation of Teachers* (Washington, American Council on Public Affairs, 1941), p. 32.

Various writers have called attention to the several types of mores and to their coercive power. One set of moral codes is the "organisational mores," the approved ways and sanctions on which our social system rests, *i.e.*, competitive labour, representative democracy, compulsory education, race prejudice and nationalism. A second set comprises the humanitarian mores, the urges for social betterment, public welfare, and charitable activities. A third set of mores is the scientific, defined as "the assumption of order in nature, a faith in man's power to predict and control natural processes, and a courage to make known the findings and implications of research."

The mores have obvious effects upon each of the four rating types discussed in this study. Lay persons, especially those of the so-called middle class, are the carries and transmitters of the mores par excellence. School-board members are enforcers of the mores in respect to school and community relations, and if our findings are generally valid, these same board members are overly conservative in the attitudes. That is, they cling more closely to traditional beliefs and practice than do community lay representatives. Presumably, this arises from two major sets of circumstances. School-board members are usually fairly well advanced in years, and advanced age has a position correlation with a desire to preserve the *status quo*. Secondly, school-board members are in general a property-owning group, and wealth makes for conservatism.

Students are born into the organizational mores of their communities. As indicated earlier, the vast majority of students who are training to become teachers are from the villages and small towns of the nation. They absorb their original mores as a matter of course, and they come to college as representatives of the moral system which has influenced their formative years. At college, and especially in education and arts courses, they come in contact with liberalism and its emphasis on democracy, humanitarianism and social idealism. They develop the relatively liberal views which account for the scores and rank order position in the presnt survey. What happens when these students seek employment as teachers, or when, having secured a first position, they are again caught up in small-town community life, is told, in part, by the study on conduct codes for teachers.

With perhaps a few unimportant exceptions, conduct codes for teachers have been objects of scientific study only during the present decade. Prior to 1930, the literature shows no quantitative investigations and the case studies to be found are mostly in the form of autobiographical records such as *The*

*Hoosier Schoolmaster*. The first fairly systematic study is the work by Howard K. Beale. A careful study of Beale's volume reveals that community controls apply in nine major respects:

1. They frequently indicate where teachers must not live, for example, with certain families, in an apartment, or outside the local community.
2. They prescribe appropriate dress for teachers, including facial make-up hair coiffure, and style of dress.
3. They define many of the teacher's leisure-time pursuits, such as dancing, card playing, smoking and drinking.
4. They regulate associations between teachers and members of the opposite sex who may be students, town persons or teachers.
5. They bring pressure to bear on teachers to participate in such approved community activities as teaching a Sunday school class and contributing to worthy causes; and they seek to enjoin teachers from participating in disapproved activities and movements, such as the Teachers Union, an affiliate of the American Federation of Labour.
6. They prescribe extracurricular activities in which the community takes a strong interest, such as competitive athletic contests, school celebrations, musicals, etc.
7. They seek to regulate the time teachers spend in the school community by reacting against week-end trips or limiting the number of such trips.
8. They forbid running for political office by teachers, and they indicate disapproval of participation in politics, especially in issues affecting the school.
9. They clearly indicate that teachers are expected to attend institutes or summer schools; at times they enforce this view through promotions or adjustments in salary schedule.

The same community attitudes, frequently found in materials published by other investigators, are also evident in the cases cited in the present study. Apparently codes vary by localities, are stronger in small communities than in large cities, are more rigid for women than for men, and are everywhere undergoing liberalisation as a consequence of urbanisation.

Reaction of four rating groups to teacher behaviour represented in Table 3.2. These data find basic interpretation in terms of a sociology of social control.

> In sociological theory social control is usually distinguished from physical control. By the latter is meant the manipulation of another person by sheer physical force, such as carrying a child off the street and out of the pathway of automobiles. Social control, on the contrary, accomplishes the same end by and through the "cooperation" of the person involved; that is, the person responds to some such stimulation as a command, threat or explanation and takes himself off the street. Used in this sense, social control is of two fundamental types: formal and informal. By formal control we mean the kind of stimuli and pressures which are exerted by laws and official rules having the sanction of the punishing power vested in the state or in any of its governing bodies. Informal control connotes the non-legal forms of manipulation—praise, blame, rewards, suggestions, etc. While teachers are subjected to both formal and informal control, the present study has been limited to the latter type.
>
> From time to time one is impressed with the manner in which college students training to become teachers think of themselves as "free souls". They live in an atmosphere of semi-anonymity and limited personal responsibility. They come and go and govern their conduct by the liberal and tolerant standards of the "college crowd". Conditioned to this way of life, they are unprepared for the situation which will confront them as teachers. For one thing, they become "public personages" in the small community. Moreover, they become heirs to the community controls worked out long ago and passed along as part of the towns heritage. By one means or another, they are made familiar with community expectations and this control process continues as long as they are teachers. Our purposes have been to examine, in more detail than has been done, the various areas in which community controls operate and to canvass the adjustment patterns which the teachers themselves report. The most obvious implication of a practical nature is the teacher's conception of self as developed in reference to conduct taboos. If teachers feel that their freedom as citizens is unduly limited, they grow restless and unhappy and cannot, therefore, do their best work.

## Summary

The school is like an organism. Every aspect is interdependent with every other. Anything which affects one aspect has

**Table 3.2**
**Net Approval and Disapproval Reactions of Representative Groups to Teacher Behaviour**

| *Teacher Behaviour* | *As Rated by* | | | | | |
|---|---|---|---|---|---|---|
| | *356 School-board Members* | | *9,122 Teachers* | | *1,363 Students* | |
| | *Male** | *Female* | *Male* | *Female* | *Male* | *Female* |
| 1. Owning an automobile | 61.3 | 60.0 | 64.4 | 59.6 | 81.0 | 79.3 |
| 2. Dating a town person | 31.7 | 28.9 | 49.7 | 46.5 | 65.8 | 64.2 |
| 3. Dating another teacher | 19.6 | 19.5 | 35.2 | 40.5 | 67.3 | 66.7 |
| 4. Leaving area over week-ends** | 0.8 | 0.9 | 9.9 | 5.5 | 5.8 | —6.7 |
| 5. Pay for coaching, speaking, etc. | —2.8 | —3.1 | 30.4 | 29.0 | 23.3 | 21.8 |
| 6. Single teachers living in apartment | —6.2 | —11.2 | 24.6 | 24.5 | 36.4 | 29.7 |
| 7. Buying clothes, etc., outside area | —8.5 | 19.4 | —4.3 | —4.0 | —1.6 | —1.5 |
| 8. Smoking in private | —9.8 | —46.2 | 11.5 | 11.2 | 35.0 | 1.4 |
| 9. Not attending church | —9.9 | —69.0 | —54.8 | —54.5 | —61.6 | —62.2 |
| 10. Playing cards for money | —18.2 | —56.6 | 69.2 | 70.0 | —72.3 | —77.6 |
| 11. Joining Teachers Union | —22.5 | —23.1 | 9.1 | 8.5 | 22.2 | 22.4 |
| 12. Dancing at public dances | —23.9 | —26.4 | 5.7 | 4.2 | 25.7 | 19.0 |
| 13. Playing pool or billiards | —25.0 | —38.2 | —8.0 | —17.8 | —3.6 | —47.2 |
| 14. Living outside community | —27.2 | —29.7 | —11.7 | —10.8 | —37.4 | —39.1 |
| 15. Teaching controversial issues*** | —34.9 | —36.7 | —1.2 | —1.4 | 34.2 | 32.9 |
| 16. Smoking in public | —48.1 | —80.7 | —25.2 | —61.0 | —16.1 | —66.7 |
| 17. Playing cards for fun | —48.1 | 16.9 | 54.3 | 54.5 | 66.8 | 76.1 |
| 18. Making a political speech | —55.7 | —55.9 | —34.9 | —40.5 | —53.7 | —60.3 |
| 19. Running for political office | —56.1 | —56.4 | —33.4 | —34.2 | —58.4 | —57.7 |
| 20. Drinking alcoholic liquors | —80.1 | —81.3 | —71.8 | —73.2 | —76.5 | —76.7 |
| 21. Dating a student | —86.0 | —65.7 | —84.4 | —86.4 | —68.8 | —76.7 |
| 22. Use of rouge, etc., by a women | | 0.4 | | 45.5 | | 65.3 |
| 23. Women teaching after marriage**** | | —43.2 | | 4.7 | | —25.5 |

*. Male (teacher) female (teacher). ** Item reads in questionnaire "leaving community often over week-ends." *** Item reads "teaching controversial social issues in the classroom." **** Item reads "A woman who continues to teach after marriage."

*Source:* F. Greehoe, *Community Contacts and Participation of Teachers* (Washington, American Council on Public Affairs, 1941), p. 51.

repercussions on all other aspects. It is in truth the microcosm of the macrocosm. Within its patterns of living operate all the social structures and processes of the microcosm which are reproduced or reflected in terms of the young.

Ostensibly schools are set up and conducted for the youth of the land. In reality, this conception is far from attainment in many schools. As one visits, listens, and observes, one too frequently comes away with the impression that schools are often run so that teachers may have jobs.

Those who would work in the complex interrelated, interdependent social world of the school need to give attention to a study of its basic structures and processes. This needs to be done not merely in terms of what is but also in terms of what research shows are possibilities for constant appraisal, reappraisal and replanning in the light of the larger social world, its tempo of change, needs, and general backgrounds.

Of equal importance is the study and understanding of the interpersonal relationships within school life, such as teacher-pupil, teacher-teacher, teacher-community and "fringe."

The specialised culture of the young is very real and very satisfying for those who live within it. And this specialised culture is perhaps the agency most effective in binding personalities together to form a school.

The following chapter will attempt an analysis of that culture which rises as a product of the school's social world.

## REFERENCES

Pigors, P.J.W., *Leadership or Domination* (Boston, Houghton, 1935), p.16.

Terman, L.M., "A Preliminary Study in the Psychology and Pedagogy of Leadership," *Pedagogical Seminary and Journal of Genetic Psychology* (1904), pp. 413–451.

Hunter, E.C. and A.N. Jordan, "An Analysis of Qualities Associated with Leadership Among College Students," *Journal of Education Psychology,* Vol. 30 (1930), pp. 497–509.

Bernard, L.L., *Introduction to Social Psychology* (New York, Holt, 1936), Chap. 34.

Allport, F.H., *Social Psychology* (Boston, Houghton, 1924), pp. 419–424.

Stewart H. Britt, *Social Psychology of Modern Life* (New York, Farrar and Rinehart, 1941).

Seeman Melvin and Richard T. Morris, "The Problem of Leadership; An Interdisciplinary Approach," *American Journal of Sociology*, Vol. LVI, No. 2 (September 1950), pp. 152–155.

Stogdill Ralph M., and Carroll L. Shartle "Methods for Determining Patterns of Leadership Behaviour in Relation to Organisation Structure and Objectives," *Journal of Applied Psychologyy*, XXXII (1948), pp. 286-291; and Shartle, "Leadership and Executive Performance," *Personnel*, XXV (1949), pp. 370–380.

Hemphill, John K., "Group Factors in Leadership. I : Relations Between the Size of the Group and the Behaviour of Superior Leaders," *Journal of Social Psychology*, Vol. 32 (December 1950), pp. 11–22.

Benne, Kenneth D. "Leaders Are Made Not Born," *Childhood Education*, Vol. 24 (January 1948), pp. 203–208.

Waller, W.W., *Sociology of Teaching* (New York, Wiley, 1932), p. 80.

Kilpatrick and others, *The Educational Frontier* (New York, Appleton-Century, 1933), p. 221ff.

Elsbree, Willard S., *The American Teacher* (New York, American Book, 1939), p. 555.

Greenhoe, Florence, *Community Contacts and Participation of 9,122 Teachers Selected as a National Sample* (Washington, American Council on Public Affaiss, p. 28.

Beale, Howard K., *Are American Teachers Free?* (New York, Scribners, 1936).

# 4

# The School's Culture

## THE SCHOOL'S SEPARATE CULTURE

Teachers have always known that it was not necessary for the students of strange customs to cross the seas to find material. Folklore and myth, tradition, taboo, magic rites, ceremonials of all sorts, collective representations, participation mystique, all abound in the front yard of every school, and occasionally they creep upstairs and incorporated into the more formal portions of school life.

There are, in the school, complex rituals of personal relationships, a set of folkways, mores, and irrational sanctions, a moral code based upon them. There are games, which are sublimated wars, teams, and an elaborate set of ceremonies concerning them. There are traditions, and traditionalists waging their world-old battle against innovators. There are laws, and there is the problem of enforcing them. There is *Sittlichkeit.* There are specialised societies with a rigid structure and a limited membership. There are no reproductive groups, but there are customs regulating the relations of the sexes. All these things make up a world that is different from the world of adults.

The school is a locus for cultural diffusion, that the school transmits the culture from one generation to another as well as skills, attitudes, and prejudices; yet these social products are seldom passed on intact. For the child does not experience these things as do the adults who are attempting to transmit the norms and customs of behaviour.

In terms of his physical, physiological, mental-emotional, and social-cultural maturity quotient, he sees them differently than adults. Very early in life he experiences the world in terms of very small, simple wholes which are extended, as has been said, by a series of "Aha moments". The results of these insightful moments build his selfhood.

This seems to say that the norms and patterns of childhood arise in part at least from "imperfectly experienced adult situations".

> The culture pattern followed out by children may be a survival, for when culture changes, it often happens that what was formerly a serious activity for adults is continued in the play of children. Indian fighting, sword play, Hallowe'en festivities, fairy tales, and the use of the bow and arrow have lost their worth in the adult world, but they have retained a certain value in the mental world of childhood. Sometimes economic activities survive and are continued in play because they have great intrinsic interest and have disappeared from the adult world only because they were unable to hold their own in competition with more efficient and prosaic means of getting a living. This has been true of hunting and fishing. There is in the development process a gradual evolution in the complexity of social situations and of the adjustment which the person makes to them; the fact that these social situations sometimes reproduce the actual situations of an earlier state of society has led some common-sense observers to believe in the theory of recapitulation.

This separate culture of the young is easiest seen and studied in peer grouping and within the school. The unsupervised playground probably approaches "pure child culture" most closely. The cultural forms within the school pattern are the next best objects of study.

This suggests that such differences in perception and conceptualisation may well lead to conflict between the adults who are attempting to induct the child into society and the child who sees otherwise.

As pointed out by Kingsley Davis, this is true at all age levels, but often painfully so at adolescence. It is often suggested that awareness of this potential conflict has caused those who were able to project themselves back into the child's world with intensity and understanding to "attempt to make the transition easier by presenting to children a finely graded and continuously evolving culture, organised into ever more complex configurations."

Recent curricula and teaching methods are evidence that educators understand this important principle and are attempting to bridge these gaps by meaningful activity programmes within the academic field.

But this recognition is not so new at that. The history of the growth and development of "extracurricular activities" is the story of teacher recognition of the factor. The difference is largely in the point of focus.

Educators of other times and of other schools of thought today are trying consciously, or unconsciously, to keep academic things intact and meet the needs through a whole galaxy of "school activities". In the main these are "teacher-initiated" and "teacher-managed," at least in the beginning. Should the young attempt to take them over and mold them to suit themselves to free them from stifling, adult domination, the ensuing conflict negates much of the intended ameliorating influence. Youth is charged with insubordination, impudence, lack of appreciation, and "wanting to run everything".

Waller spoke tellingly when he wrote, "So completely is the individual immersed in his own age and social level that he often has difficulty in realising that any other kind of culture exists".

One can only conclude that adults who experience violent and continued conflict with children and youth are so bound by their adult views that they forget the thoughts and feelings of their younger years.

The resiliency of childhood allows it to set up a buffer subculture of its own. As emphasised earlier, this has two main centers of orientation: child peer groups, especially those unsupervised (at least ostensibly) by adults and the school. In the former children are free to set up their activities largely in terms of their own desires and devices. The culture of the school, however, "is a curious melange of the work of young artisans making culture for themselves and old artisans making culture for the young; it is also mingled with such bits of the greater culture as children have been able to appropriate."

This culture may be studied from many vantage points. For our purposes, we have selected traditions, ceremonies and activities.

## Traditions, Ceremonies and Activities

The traditions of the school appear to derive from several sources. As evidenced in conduct codes for teachers, there is a body of tradition which comes from the school's community, a purely outside tradition, but a powerful one. These traditions are concerned with the community's expectations of the role to be filled by the school in the socialisation of its children. Suffice it to say that the very existence and insistence upon schools themselves is a western tradition.

The "outside" tradition defines also at least for nonschool adult community members, the status positions of teachers and students.

Teachers shall be older than students or at least able to appear older and in command of the situation at all times.

> The old shall teach the young, and not that the young shall ever teach the old, which would be at least equally justifiable in a world that changes so rapidly that an education twenty years old is out of date.

Teachers and students are expected to maintain a discernible social distance and the penalty for failure to do so is for the teacher, at least, a loss of status and prestige in both the student world and the adult world.

Teachers are also expected to treat all students with equal attention, respect and opportunities. Favouritism is the cardinal sin.

What is sometimes termed intermingled tradition is that derived partly from outside and partly from inside the school.

> In so far as this tradition of teachers is derived from outside a particular school, it is drawn by teachers from the general culture and from association with members of the teaching profession everywhere. In so far as it is a purely local product, it is produced by the teachers in the institution and is passed on from one teacher to

> another. We may mention some cardinal point of the teacher tradition as it is usually encountered, making due allowance for local variations. There is a teacher morality, and this morality regulates minutely the teacher's relations with his students and with other teachers; it affects his relations with other teachers, especially where the standing of those teachers with students might be affected. There is a character ideal of the teacher; nearly every group which lives long in one stereotyped relation with other groups produces its character ideal, and this ideal for teachers is clearly observable. Teachers have likewise a certain traditional attitude toward each other. The most obvious manifestation of the traditional attitude is the ceremoniousness of teachers toward each other and toward the administration of the school. It seems clear that this is the ceremoniousness of a fighting group which does not care to endanger its prestige with underlings by allowing any informality to arise within itself. Another interesting observation that has often been made about particular groups of teachers is that they discriminate markedly between veterans and new men. This distinction is in the folkways. Occasionally there is a more or less definite ceremony of initiation, more rarely, actual hazing.

Traditions within the school have been originated by both teachers and students. In some instances teachers originate traditions because they were a part of their own background or because they seem to give cultural respectability to the institution. Or they act as means of gaining popularity with students and/or as means of controlling students' behaviour.

Traditions set up and carried out by students vary in structure and process between schools, but have certain basic characteristics which can be mentioned.

Student-teacher relationships come within this area. In the earlier grades children "like" the teacher, and there is customarily no disgrace in behaving toward her as a veritable mother surrogate. If the teacher is a man, he is openly declared a father surrogate. By some more errotically precocious girls and boys he may unashamedly be spoken of as a later love object.

In later elementary and high school, however, one likes the teacher but not too well, at least openly, unless, of course, it is a permissive atmosphere with democratic implementation.

Student to student loyalty is a strong tradition. Many youngsters suffer undeserved punishment rather than "squeal" on their bodies. While giving information concerning others may be taboo, just as strong feeling exists if in a democratic framework wrongdoers "admit" mistakes and one does not. For example:

> Never again can we trust Joey. We all admitted we played with the dry ice when we weren't supposed to, but Joey. He lied on his cub-scout honour, and Mother, he raised his hand to God. No more Joey for us boys.

Green hats for freshmen, school letters for upper classmen, jeans, sweaters, T-shirts, low-heeled shoes and bobbysox, sweaters and skirts with pearl necklaces, plus many, many more clothes choices are part of the tradition of dress. And woe betide the child who dresses other than in the designated tradition of dress.

Language, or as someone has said *slanguage,* is also traditional not only within the school but also within maturation levels. Once a pleasing object or experience was "hot stuff," "tricky," "sweet," and more recently "near," nifty," "mellow." As Whyte suggests for *Street Corner Society,* so too the school child is surrounded by a language which to the uninitiated is often unintelligible.

Some high schools and many colleges and universities carry rigidly enforced traditions of where different grade levels may walk, sir, to whom they may speak, and certain services which one class level must perform for another. These traditions involve a sanction of mores proportions. For the school pupil, they are *right, necessary* and *true.*

Every school population has ceremonies for implementing traditions. Sometimes they consist of simple informal things, such as slaps on the shoulder, verbal signs of passing from novitiate to member, or just payment of dues.

Again the ceremonies may be formal, replete with symbolism, such as initiation ceremonies, mock trials, hell weeks, and the like. Shudder the novice may, but refuse to perform, however outlandishly, he will not, as some tragedies from fraternity initiations will illustrate.

Whether the activity is athletics, clubs, or secret societies, the traditions take on stability and immortality as they are carried out through the rituals and ceremonies of the school's activities. Because of the limiting factor of space two examples of school culture as shown in structure and processes will illustrate the point.

## Fraternities as a School Cultural Phenomenon

> A student probably joins a sorority or fraternity, not because he feels identity with that group, not so much because he thinks he is like that group, but because he wants to be like it. Such a group holds prestige value for him. He has heard fraternity mentioned in such ways that it holds "glamour" for him. There is the matter of secrecy, the desire to participate in activities that are not for the mob. The fraternity holds prestige values because it has been so closely identified with college life. Fraternities have drawn within their membership individuals who, themselves, have high status and prestige value. They hold such status and value because they have excelled in areas which are of concern to youth, such as athletics. Alumni become famous writers, actors, governors, businessmen. The prestige which these individuals carry is shed upon the group to which they belong—to the whole state, or university, but, in particular, to the intimate in-group, the fraternity. The individual's own ego expands in the reflected glory of the campus hero. To belong to such and such a fraternity makes X a marked man; to him is attached the prestige of the group.

The term "fraternity" itself carries prestige value, largely because of its association with the values of school life. Added prestige is given by the use of Greek letters. The Greeks were a classic people, great in art, literature, athletics, war, politics, philosophy, etc.

The fraternity has what may be called polarity. It is a fixed thing on the high school or college campus. It has a name, a history, a ritual. To the lonely boy or girl coming to the campus, it beckons because of its offer of security, the provision of an intimate we-circle of closely interacting personalities. In it the individual may sink himself, and feel that he is anchored, that he belongs.

Fraternities more or less control many of the activities of the university, which are most meaningful to the student. This control may extend to such things as athletics, the school publications, extra-curricular activities, social functions. Organised power and strength have their own prestige values.

A fraternity is also a unity of interacting personalities. This is to say that it is more than a solid entity, totally given to singleness of purpose. We have said that individuals seek membership in a fraternity not because they *are* like that group but because they *want to be* like it. Within limits the fraternity draws its members from a variety of social sources, those members having different backgrounds. The fraternity has its own culture—its characteristic traditions, values, attitudes. It has a history. There may well be a fraternity type of personality. The incoming new member does not represent this type of personality. Without knowing exactly what it is doing, the fraternity immediately sets about shaping each individual into the fraternity-type personality. A process of socialisation goes on which is analogous to the same process in the family. By individual counselling, through "round table" discussion, by bull session, by precept and example the neophyte is shaped into the fraternity personality. He is rewarded by approval or other techniques; he is punished by ridicule, by "lecture," and even by the paddle. He learns what sort of girls he may date—those whom he may date for college affairs and dates—and those whom he may sexually exploit. He learns the proper attitude toward the professor, the apple polisher, the independent, other fraternities. He learns what clothes and jewellery are taboo.

Ordinarily, it is not difficult to mold the personality into proper form. The individual seeks the approval of his group and its constituent members. He reacts easily to suggestion, imitates consciously and automatically mannerisms, dress effects, etc. He stands always ready to defend the group against outsiders, against certain allegations directed at his fraternity or fraternities in general. He comes to hold all the symbolisms of fraternity in high value—the pin, the "boy gives girl pin" complex, the hand clasp, the ritual, the whistle, the sentiment that we must stick together and pull together. The inner workings of campus politics come to be entrancing to him, and he defends them for all he is worth.

But in still another sense the fraternity is a group of interacting personalities. If there are group purposes, group values, group techniques, there are also individual purposes and values. There are statuses within the fraternity. Some of them will be official statuses usually achieved in some manner. There are certainly ascribed statuses that are assigned to the freshman pledge. Status may derive from the holding of office, or from some other factor: wealth, athletic ability, scholastic ability, wit, and the like. The members hold attitudes toward each other as well as toward the group as an entity. Fraternities sometimes pluck a "lemon"—a member who outwardly conforms to fraternity standards, but whose personality pattern does not fit in with those of a number of the group. There may also be groups or cliques within the larger group.

Between the members there will be behaviour derived from varying attitudes toward one another. There will be rivalry, competition, sometimes open conflict.

There are then those attitudes of institutionalism which govern the behaviour of the member in all outside relationships. These attitudes and their attendant behaviour patterns, make him a fraternity man—both in the eyes of outsiders and of the in-members. There will also be types or patterns of behaviour within the group which are governed by the institutional attitudes, such as those with respect to the conduct of fraternity business and fraternity order, the performance of certain social functions, the support of a brother because he is a brother, the glowing response to the achievements of a fraternity brother (the pride felt in the fact that Governor Blah is an alumnus member).

On the other hand are those attitudes which motivate individualistic behaviour. These are manifested in the interplay between personalities, in the seeking of status within the group, the playing of roles of various kinds.

Much the same structure and similar processes are to be observed in the school club with several exceptions. Few clubs have the lure of secrecy, with all its symbols, rituals, and the like.

Some may have longevity, but fewer will have the cultural prestige hangover of the Greek letter society.

Likewise the control exerted over the individual member is not likely to be so potent as in the sorority-fraternity exclusiveness construct. It may well be in fact a well as in theory that the social-cultural interpretation of the term Club as over against the more controversial terms sorority and/or fraternity, sets the stage for its "halo" among non-members as well as members.

## Athletics as a School Cultural Phenomenon

As has often been pointed out by analysts of school activities, "their catch-on," their appeal is directly related to the spontaneity of their base. In other words, do the activities have behaviour patterns which have such intrinsic interest for students that they will gladly brook faculty connections?

The sorority-fraternity appeal as discussed previously is one of intrinsic interest sans, in large measure, faculty intervention. Many have hazarded the guess that the escape from adult domination is one of the secret society's greatest appeals to adolescents, and at the same time one of its greatest potential dangers.

We should now like to pay attention to one area of school activities which seems most successful in providing the spontaneous base just mentioned to the extent that adult connections are accepted by students. An important factor in this is the "set form," as Waller called it, which individuals can observe on the basic assumption that the "group welfare and prestige" are at stake. And from this observance can and must come "merit and distinction" in the eyes of both the whole school and outside adults as well.

For the athlete who plays the game, the forms to be observed such as training rules, long, arduous practices, even the often tedious trips not to mention the grueling minutes of the game are well recompensed by the shouts of his name as he scores, by the we-group spirit and enthusiasm of his classmates, by the respect and admiration of the townspeople, and finally by the letters, sweaters, banquets, and press releases which show him to be the maker and carrier of glory for his old alma mater.

But what of the substitute, the "fall guy" for the first stringer? At least he has identification with the glamour, the honour, and in defeat, the sorrow, and commisseration of the defeated but unbowed contenders. The spectator also can and must feel a similar identification if there is to be "support" for the team.

Here too, form and merit enter into the planning. Cheering sections are carefully organised, drilled, even uniformed sometimes. Booster clubs assume considerable prestige as not merely those who provide "things," follow the team, and generally display loyalty, but also as keepers of the school's good sportsmanship reputation.

Whichever game is considered is surrounded by form, and this form is handed on from one school generation of players and spectators to another with very few variations. Uniforms, plays, yells, rituals such as rallies, after-the-game dances become traditional and are part and parcel of the form and merit concepts.

A student paper illustrates this individual and groupal identification which occurs and under what circumstances.

> I always loved athletic competition, and on the sand-lot I could manage rather well. But I could never make the team in high school. I trained twice as conscientiously as most of the first team (who always boasted they never trained at all), I worked at practice until I was weak from exhaustion, and I was sure I "internalised perfection of response" for several special roles, but somehow the coaches always thought that I was willing and "a great help to morale," but I wasn't quite in form, they said. So I played the bench throughout high school. But I was never bitter. We played football at night under the lights, and nothing could be more thrilling. The colours, the yells, the feeling of something bigger and more important than you personally, did something to all of us. When Waller says a game is a sublimated fight, I think he's right. The cheerleaders work people into a frenzy with their Fight, Fight, Fight yells, the crowd echoes in a roar, the coach tells you to go in and "fight 'em to a standstill," and when we were losing, we sang, "We'll go down fighting."
>
> While this is fine for the spirit of the team and the school, it can also be a detriment. Rivalries between small towns as between big universities can become so intense that to lose that game may mean

> a coach's job. As a result he often keeps star players playing when to do so endangers their future health.
>
> This game as a fight business is further shown by the ways of controlling the situation. There are elaborate sets of rules for every game and penalties for infractions plus a referee and in most situations now, more than one referee. It's hardly safe to be *The* referee on a tight basketball game floor or on a football field.
>
> Yes, I think athletics is the most developed, detailed, formalised, and most loved and participated in school cultural pattern. Bands, school papers, language clubs, and class plays are fine and surely worthwhile, and I was on the staff or had parts in all of them while I was in school, but I would have given up every one of them if I could have carried that ball over the goal line just once each football season!

## School Culture in Terms of Processes of Social Interactions

As one studies the over-all social-cultural process of social interaction, he finds that it breaks down into several subprocesses.

All of these subprocesses operate within the social and cultural world of the school. Some writers are interested mainly in analysing from the viewpoint of conflict as the basic process. Social educational analysis is more concerned with what Park and Burgess earlier designated as cultural process or the interpretation of persons and groups, with the goal of sharing experience and history.

In the words of Park and Burgess, "Assimilation is the process of interpenetration and fusion in which persons and groups acquire the memories, sentiments, and attitudes of other persons and groups, and by sharing their experience and history, are incorporated with them in a common cultural life. In so far as assimilation denotes, this sharing of tradition, this intimate participation in common experiences, assimilation, is central in the historical and cultural processes."

Accommodation, on the other hand, is a living arrangement which has been worked out through compromise, systems of dominance and submission, and the like. "Accommodation has been described as a process of adjustment, that is, an organisation of social relations and attitudes to prevent or to reduce conflict, to control competition, and to maintain a basis of security in the social order for persons and groups of divergent interest and types to carry on together their varied life activities. Accommodation in the sense of the composition of conflict is invariably the goal of the political process."

It will help us to grasp the meaning of the school as a social-cultural institution if we try to place it with regard to these processes. To be strictly accurate, we must think of these processes as going on within the school as well as without it, of the school as a microcosm that mirrors the macrocosm.

When the political process is still in the stage of overt conflict, various conflict groups attempt to use the schools for passing on their truth to the unbiased younger generation. Sectarian schools are for the most part established for this purpose, but it is perhaps only of the worst of these that Ross's aphorism that they are means of conducting children into society through a tunnel holds true. Economic groups are able to influence profoundly the policies of established schools, and on occasion to establish chairs and schools for the promulgation of their doctrines. In a leading eastern college is a chair that was endowed for teaching the fallacies of socialism. One of the greatest of the business schools was established, at least in part, as a means of crushing out various heresies concerning the protective tariff.

The list of those who have sought to use the tax-supported schools as channels for their doctrines is almost as long as the list of those who have axes to grind. Prohibitionists, professional reformers, political parties, public utilities, sectarians, moralists, advocates of the open shop, labour unions, socialists, antivivisectionists, jingoes, chauvinists, and patrioteers—all have sought to control the curriculum, the composition of the teaching staff, and the method of instruction.

Opposing groups work out various compromises by virtue of which the schools can be made accpetable to all parties. Thus, the school is shot through with accommodations, some of which have grown so old that their original purpose has been forgotten.

In that assimilation of group to group which Park and Burgess think of as characterising the cultural process, the schools play a most important part. That is particularly true of the schools of a nation which, like ours, is seeking to amalgamate into one whole the representatives of many diverse cultures. The main burden of Americanisation falls upon the public schools, and there is every likelihood that it will continue to do so. The schools Americanise by immersing the young in the culture and tradition of the country, by inducing them to participate as much as possible in the activities of the American arena. The things that the children of the foreign born learn at school, and on the streets before and after school, are often in conflict with the tradition which their parents are trying to transmit to them. Children usually learn to speak English better than their parents, and they more rapidly acquire a superficial familiarity with American life, so that frequently they feel superior to the parents and are most unwilling to take advice from them. Since the home plays a large part in the formation of law-abiding attitudes, and since the view of American life which these children get is at best incomplete and distorted, Americanisation through the schools usually entails a certain amount of disorganisation for the second generation of immigrants. Adult education of immigrants has also been organised on a wide scale. Though less immediately effective, it is yet a very powerful means of leading the immigrant to the participation in American culture from which Americanisation results.

The common experiences of a group of people living together under any circumstances which give a semblance of unity operate to give the group that sense of a common past which is the mark of assimilation. Time is of the essence of the cultural process. There is, however, in the cultural process a many-sided interchange of attitudes and definitions of situations, of techniques and knowledge concerning the elements of culture. It is this process of transmission and interchange which we shall have particularly in mind when we speak of the cultural process from this point on. The school serves as a medium in which this interchange takes place.

The ordinary school does not serve as a centre of inventions, although there are many institutions of higher learning which, through the support of experimentation and research, are taking over this function. The ordinary school does not share in this, but serves rather as a very important subcentre in the process of cultural diffusion.

Particularly on the mental side of culture it is the task of the schools to mediate new things to the local community. Sociologists have found that many of the unadjustments in modern society are traceable to what is known as cultural lag, to the fact that non-material, or adaptive culture, does not change so rapidly as material culture. Thus, our systems of law, religion, and morals are authentic antiques, but our automobiles and radios and talking pictures are modern. Much of the maladjustment of society is due to this failure of the machinery of social control to change with a rapidity equality that of mechanical culture.

The existence of cultural lag is ascribable to a number of factors. There is a low rate of invention in non-material culture. And it is also true that new ideas spread slowly and meet with much oppostion be cause many of them are against the mores. The schools could do much to accelerate the diffusion of non-material culture, but they have not usually cared to assume this function.

We come now to the second phase of the cultural process, which consists of the transmission of attitudes, techniques, and knowledge to the younger persons of the community. This process is incidental to the succession of generations and is necessitated by the fact that all men are born equally ignorant. Much of the work of forming the young is done by other institutions, and certainly the family is more significant in child life than the school, but the importance of the school in the cultural process seems to be increasing; its formal position has always been central in the process, and there are indications that the actual significance of the school in child life is not destined to diminish.

The amount of schooling which children undergo foreshadows, and some would say determines, their future earning capacity and the level of society on which they will find their life. A crude selection, then, goes on in the schools, a social selection of those destined to fulfil certain predetermined social functions.

Partly it is the schools themselves which select. The native intelligence of children sets certain absolute limits to their achievements. No amount of schooling can make the moron perform satisfactorily above his fated level. The schools, by their curriculum which must be mastered before the student can pass on, sift and resift their human materials, selecting on the basis of intelligence chiefly, but allowing considerable weight to other qualities such as a pleasing manner, emotional stability, and diligence.

The schools must sort all the human material that comes to them, but they do not subject all children to the same kind of sorting process. Other things being equal, the schools tend to bring children at least up to an intellectual level which will enable them to function in the same economic and social stratum as their parents. But the children of the poor tend to drop out early, and very frequently for reasons quite other than incapacity to learn; they drop out because their labour is needed at home, because they are ashamed to attend school in shabby clothes, because there is no tradition in their group of going beyond the literacy stage in education. Equally important with economic factors are the social assets of a family, its standing in the community, its level of cultural participation, its traditions and ambitions—these factors likewise limit social mobility.

The functions of the school as an agency of the cultural process and as a channel of vertical mobility are sometimes blended; indeed, these two functions in their individual reference are often indistinguishable. Education brings one into touch with the main stream of culture. The aspiring student embraces this wider cultural participation in the hope that it will make of him something somehow different. Yet this being different is indissolubly connected with having a different place in society. A university confronts a gifted freshman as a vast array of cultural riches; he may appropriate these and realise himself in learning to use them. The cultural process, which must start a new with every generation, automatically assigns men to their proper posts. The manner and extent to which they assimilate the cultural heritage determine the niche they will fit into in the social structure.

One of the important things that the school does is to separate individuals into classes corresponding roughly to certain occupational and social strata. When the matter is pragmatically considered, that conclusion seems inescapable. One is tempted to inquire whether this view of education corresponds with that social philosophy which is known as democratic theory and which is regarded as the fundamental orientation point for discussion of social policy in our society.

We turn now to a consideration of child-school-community relationships and how they may, and in many instances have been, beamed toward the assimilative end result of social interaction.

## REFERENCES

Waller, W.W., Sociology of Teaching (New York, Willy, 1932), p. 103.

Davis, Kingsley, "The Sociology of Parent-Youth Conflict," *American Sociological Review* (August 1940), pp. 523–535.

Park R.E., and E.W. Burgess, *Introduction to Science of Sociology* (Chicago, University of Chicago Press, 1924), pp. 735–736.

# 5

# The Community Approach to Education

We have assumed in this treatise that the rearing of children is the most important job of this or any other generation. But this does not mean merely bringing them to physical maturity unharmed. For a child to be well adjusted it is necessary to help him at every maturity level to live easily and comfortably with other normal persons to attain behaviour patterns and attitudes that do not differ too greatly from the standards of right and wrong, and to be personally happy and socially useful. Such a person lives up to a high level of his potentialities, and continues his process of social growth and development in the direction of social, emotional, intellectual and moral maturity.

In other words, mental health and maturity are as important, many would argue more so, than mere physical health. Obviously the two are so interrelated as to be inseparable.

Today the need for such child rearing is accentuated a thousandfold by the level of development of the society and culture in which children must live and grow. The statistical evidences of the need are not of the nature to inspire complacency.

Beyond the evidences of personality conflict and maladjustment evidenced in such areas as divorce, mental disease increases, and the like, lie equally disturbing data concerning the mental hygiene aspects of children themselves.

One reputable research into the mental health quotients of children and adults in a country will illustrate. It must be borne in mind that the study is of a rural and semi-rural area where folklore has it that we may expect adjustment and happiness in greater degree than an urban milieu is expected to afford.

The following paragraphs summarise some of the major findings with respect to the prevalence of mental hygiene problems:

(a) *What did the draft reveal?*

Based on the record of one of the two local draft boards which, between them, covered the country, it was estimated that at least 10 per cent of the men of military age (18–37) had personality disorders serious enough to disqualify them for effective military service. This included those rejected with some personality disorder as the leading cause for disqualification. This group alone made up 6.3 per cent of all the men examined and 23.6 per cent of all those rejected.

It should be remembered that the Army psychiatrist at the induction station based his judgment very largely on the man's civilian record of adjustment. Most of these men, therefore, were more or less seriously maladjusted in civilian life.

It may be assumed that many of those who were rejected for obvious and disqualifying physical defects at the local board were also notably lacking in mental health, though they had no psychiatric examination. Many others were rejected for a variety of physical difficulties which in all probability were bodily manifestations of personality disorders. Finally, a considerable number of men whose emotional difficulties were not detected by psychiatric examiners, or not considered serious enough to bar them from services, had to be discharged later because of "nervous breakdown".

In addition to rejections for personality disorders, 1 man in each 100 of those examined had to be rejected because of mental and educational deficiency. One in each 200 was epileptic and was disqualified for that reason.

(b) *What did the study of school children show?*

A rough screening, with tests and ratings, of all third and sixth-grade children provided a basis for an evaluation of their mental health. It was found that:

(1) At least 18 per cent of all third graders in all schools in the county were poorly adjusted and in need of some kind of mental

health aids. An even higher proportion of the sixth-grade children showed evidences of poor mental health. In that grade it was estimated that about 21 per cent were poorly adjusted children.

On the basis of these percentages it was estimated that more than 1,200 poorly adjusted children are to be found in the first eight grades of the Miami County Public Schools.

What General Conclusions were reached as a result of the study?

About *one in every five* elementary school children in Miami County presents evidences of poor mental health of some degree of seriousness. Large numbers of these children are evidently maladjusted to a very serious degree and are in grave need of specialised guidance services to meet their mental health needs. Many are less seriously maladjusted and may somehow "get by" without specialised help, although they, too, could profit if it were available.

Mental health problems were much more prevalent among boys than among girls.

Such problems were especially acute among children who were retarded in their school progress and whose advanced age made them misfits in their class.

(c) *What was shown by the study of juvenile delinquency?*

From 1940 through 1945, a six-year period, 1,168 delinquency cases were brought before the County Juvenile Court for official or unofficial action. Juvenile delinquency cases brought to court reached a peak in 1943 when 260 cases were subjected to court action. That was nearly 4 per cent of all children of juvenile court age. These figures do not reveal the total prevalence of delinquency, since the larger number of offences involving children are dealt with by schools, by parents, by law enforcement officers and by other authorities.

Juvenile delinquency is considered a mental hygiene problem since many children are offenders because of personality distortions or undergo distortion as a consequence of the treatment their behaviour provokes. Misconduct in children is often a way of reacting to inner conflicts and frustrations. These, in turn, may reflect external pressures and deprivations which leave basic emotional and social needs unmet. Delinquent behaviour is often a substitute gratification for real but unmet needs of the child.

This study confirms the conclusion of many other studies which show that personality disorders occur as often among farm people as they do among non-farm residents, and perhaps more often. Estimates of maladjustment among elementary school children in Miami County showed two interesting things in this regard:

(a) At both the third and sixth-grade levels the incidence of maladjustment, as estimated on the basis of rests and ratings, was less among farm children than among those from non-farm homes.

(b) But the advantage enjoyed by the farm children was much less among sixth graders than among those in the third grade.

The draft board records showed that the rejection rate generally was higher for farm men than for non-farm men. It was also found that the incidence of personality disorders was greater among farm workers than among other registrants. This study points to the conclusion that, from the point of view of mental health, farm residence is probably an advantage for younger children, but that the advantage is lost with increasing age. Among men of military age, those in other occupations have the advantage over those concerned with farming. This may be due in part at least to migration of disproportionately large numbers of better adjusted youths away from farms and from farm occupations.

If it is true that basically unhappy, frustrated, children tend to become adults with similar risks, and if it is also true as it seems to be, that happy well-adjusted children, free from severe tension and strain, tend to become happy well-adjusted, efficient adults, the importance of both home, school and community cooperation in child rearing becomes readily apparent. With this viewpoint few would disagree though some few people and groups will still maintain that "raising kids is their own business," and "they don't need any help from crack-brained educators and outsiders." Equally eloquent was the teacher-student who replied:

> And believe me their children show the results. Such youngsters are often the social isolates and rejects in the school world.

Heretofore, we have suggested a point of view toward childhood and have pointed out how it may be implemented in child life associations, such as family, peer groups, and classroom situations. This kind of discussion has been parallel with that of pointing out the "what is" aspects of relationships. We need now to consider the interaction of all these influences—the integration of school and community always with reference to the growing, developing organism, the child.

## Traditional—Progressive-Community Approaches

Schools have always played both a receptive and a directive role in social change. Sometimes it has been done rather blindly, sometimes with clarity of insight and purpose. It is doubtless true, however, that whatever the case in high places, the classroom teacher has too often merely gone along.

Today and for the future it must be otherwise. Each teacher who comes into contact with youth needs to be aware of his philosophy of education and living, needs to be familiar with its implications not only from the standpoint of curriculum building and methods of instruction, but also from the standpoint of impact upon child growth and development.

It is the bias here that the community approach is a natural and logical outgrowth of other approaches which may have suited their ears of evolvement. This is to say that in the light of the social trends mentioned above, it appears to offer the most satisfying and fruitful means of inducting the child into adulthood in a changing world. This says also that there may be other modes, perhaps already originating, which will replace this approach as changes continue to occur.

May we then consider the three approaches mentioned in terms of their (1) conceptions of the child and his role in school and community, (2) conceptions of the teacher and his role in the classroom, and (3) conceptions of the school and its role within the school community.

By implication, many of these concepts have been explained earlier. The purpose in coming to them again is to sharpen and review and to point a way and course of action.

The traditional school conceives of the child as a miniature adult. This means in effect that he may be expected to be and do much as adults with the exception of feats of skill. Bolted down desks, protracted periods of sitting quietly at these desks, selection of subject-matter and activities all are evidence of this concept of childhood. In short, as you see the child so will you arrange his school plant setting, his learning outcome expectations and ways of proceeding to accomplish them.

"The child is a vacuum," quoth one education professor in his pompous fashion. "Yours is a great responsibility. You must so fill that vacuum with worthwhile facts and ideas that he will have them ready to hand when the occasion arises."

Or listen to one who phrased it a bit differently. "The child is a slate on which the teacher writes. Guard well that you write only the great from our heritage." A lá the Great Books, one is tempted to suspect.

Or again, "The child is a sponge. He increases in stature as he absorbs."

Such statements point readily to a further concept of the child. He is considered the carrier, the transmitter of the culture *per se*, and its potential enacter. The teacher's function then is so to cull the heritage and so meticulously to arrange and indoctrinate it as to cause the *status quo* to be perpetuated.

Such a school is a place of learning to be sure but not necessarily of education. Bode's remark is classic when he wrote: "At the turn of the century there were those who began to see the child otherwise and as important to do something about it."

As is often the case, when the break with tradition set a new social movement in motion, the swing for a while was toward the opposite extreme. So-called progressive educators regarded the child in no way similar to a miniature adult but considered him a being in his own right. In the effort to shake off the excess baggage which had been characteristic of traditional education, there was tendency to swing to the opposite pole and assume the meeting of pupil interests, likes and immediate needs as the basic factors in his education. The role of the teacher was now that of friend and guide, rather than that of disciplinarian as in the cultural transmission oriented school.

As might be expected, some teachers became merely glorified fellow student-travellers in *laissez-faire* situations which were mistakenly set up in the name of democratic education.

There were from the first in the movement, however, those who did not confuse the woods and the trees, who recognised that child-centered did not mean child-licensed; who were aware of the sociological fact that the "musts" of the culture were ever present as well as student likes, interests and needs. These people were also well aware that the job of education was not an either/or stampede but a challenge and opportunity to consider the needs and interests of *both* adult society and young society and to provide induction for the young into adult society not blindly as mere culture carriers, but as dynamic, thinking societal members. These educators were interested in so educating that the young would be able, critically, to appraise personal and societal needs and interests, to enact them where they stood the tests of time, change, and the current social scene, and to be unafraid to revise them when lags became apparent.

Unlike the alarmists' predictions, such education (sometimes referred to as progressive education with a small "p") has not turned out incompetents in the three R's or revolutionists who wish merely to tear apart or continually to emasculate the culture with no constructive attitudes of mind. Nor has it built cynics, agnostics, and atheists as predicted.

Instead, the studies point to people who have performed creditably in college and on the job, who have been rated as superior in such personal-social traits as initiative, social responsibility, and concern for the rights and privileges of others and who are able and willing to take a stand and whatever consequences may result.

Among those more far sighted there gradually developed the cognisance that the child-centered approach needed broadening. There arose an emphasis upon what was called the "community school". Here the attempt was to consider the "whole child," not merely as an individual but also in relation to community social order and processes of social interaction.

In a number of instances this relating process became so concerned with the local community as to become bogged down in its problems and concerns with little or no integration with the larger whole.

Sometimes the concept of education became lost along the way, and schools tended to become largely service institutions. This is not to imply that the interactional position of the school and community should not allow for service projects. It does say that when the activity has reached the place where it is no longer a learning experience for children, it should be replaced by something which does posses learning potentialities for the child group.

An example of the above will serve to illustrate. A visitor watched the boys in the shop programme "fixing" Model T Ford trucks, of which there were quite a number in this relatively isolated community.

"How long have you been repairing Ford trucks?" the visitor asked.

"All year," replied the principal proudly.

"How long will you continue to repair them?"

"As long as they need it," was the reply.

Even a cursory observer could see that the students involved had passed both the period of maximum learning and interest. Several were obviously bored and resentful of "working for nothing".

The *Community Approach* to education has a chance to miss many of these pitfalls of the more restricted so-called community school. In a community approach the school is conceived of as *one* agency which must interest, plan, and carry out plans in connection with *all other* agencies within the community. Where need exists, schools and school people will be quick to pick up the ball and start the thinking and acting. Once that function has been discharged, however, they will be ready and willing to release the authority and the activity itself, if need be, to others who may carry it on as well or better. In fact, community social education implies the educating of children, youth, and adults to the level where they do just that—assume the continuance of an activity, leaving the school and school people free to foster real education for others and in other needed areas of which there is never a dearth in a continually changing social world.

This is not a new or novel theory. Many so-called "community schools" have followed this policy, and for a long time. If the literature is read carefully, however, it is possible to point out many instances where the *school* was the containment of the idea and insisted upon maintaining such a position rather than assuming the role of a community participant.

## Criteria of a Community School Approach

In order to test whether or not a school has community approach, it is necessary to build a set of criteria. A particular school might reach the goal in all or most of these. Another school might reach but one or two, but it would still realise some of the potentialities of a community approach to education. From the literature and observation in a number of community-oriented schools, the following criteria have been evolved:

1. A community school is a cooperative enterprise, involving shared undertaking. There is opportunity for democracy to function through participation in planning, decision-making, executing and evaluating. Opportunity is given to all to help set goals and make choices, and guidance is given to all to help assure the carrying through with the choices made. Further, a community school cooperates with other agencies in promoting services for all the age groups in the area.
2. A community school is available and friendly, easy to get to, and into. Not only does it serve as the centre of a natural area geographically, but must serve as the centre of a group of people sharing a common interest.
3. A community school has people in it, all ages, all times. The facilities of a school plant are in use other than the school hours. The auditorium, gymnasium, school grounds serve many people of all ages and at all times.
4. A community school lays stress on human interrelations and makes a human needs approach to learning. It is still responsible for transmitting any of the cultural heritage that youth needs but evaluates the success of the learning in terms of changes in the individual an in the environment. "It is a dynamic social agency pointed specifically toward the enrichment of life for the men, women and children living in the geographical area influenced by the school in question."
5. A community school uses the resources of the community as the content of education. The school still takes the responsibility for the traditional subject-matter but through the use of community resources, both

human and material, translates and interprets that subject-matter that it may be vital to the individual as he lives in his community. From first hand experiences an insight into the social and economic assets and limitations of the community is gained, from which more desirable social attitudes develop in terms of sensitivity to needs and knowledge of ways to take action.

6. A community school relates local life and values to the world community. The participation in near by experiences are interpreted to show their interrelation with the larger area. The beginning will be with the need at hand, it must go beyond the immediate community.
7. A community school finds a way to do things, other than talk. Beyond the vision of desirable changes and attitudes that should be gained must be purposeful planning to achieve them. The degree of success will depend on the proportion of people who share in the idea, its implementation and its continuance.

In the following accounts compiled from the literature and from direct observation, the attention is directed to the initial activities of schools in the community approach direction. Some of the programmes have been in existence for a number of years and are well known throughout the country. Others are quite recent and several have not been described in writing before.

**Round Valley**

Round Valley is a village of 1,000 population with about one-fourth of them being Indians. The school principal and faculty felt that the citizens were poorly informed regarding the school system and what it was trying to do for the children. It was proposed that a community council which would study school procedures and policies might be a successful way of interpreting what was then current and of obtaining community suggestion for next steps in the work of the school.

The principal called a meeting for the purpose of forming a council, requesting each of the 16 civic organisations to send a representative. A chairman and secretary were elected, after which the principal became an ordinary participant.

The council during the first year began with a study of school matters, such as report cards and the need for establishing a kindergarten. Recreation for school youth and adults soon became the focus of attention. Still within the first year, night classes were organised. Between the night classes and the adult phase of the recreation programme, there were more adults using the school plant at night than there were children using it in the day.

The plans for the immediate future included work on medical service. The town had no doctor or dentist, and periodic dental service was already being arranged through the school. The council also was beginning to study some problems of race relationships.

Round Valley meets at least six of the criteria listed of a community school. It should be noted that the first steps were made when a small group of people took action upon an immediate problem. The people were not aware, at that time, that they were launching a community school. Rather, one problem after another was taken up; more and more people were involved; success with small plans led to longer range planning. Now, anyone can look back and see that a community school approach has developed gradually. As important, the school and school people have played the role of participants on equal bases with other organisations within the community.

### Panama City

Parker Grove School, located just outside of Panama City, enrolls approximately 300 pupils in grades 1 to 8. The school is situated near the centre of a fairly distinct community. The homes are small and rather scattered, with space for gardens and pastures. Filling station-grocery stores serve the immediate needs of the people, but the main shopping centre is in Panama City, about 8 miles distant. There are no libraries or forms of organised recreation.

In the spring of 1945 the faculty of the school discussed the advantages that would accrue to the pupils if the school library were kept open during the summer, one afternoon each week. The suggestion was then discussed with the P.T.A. The plan finally worked out for that summer included three parts: (a) the use of the library, (b) the establishment of a crafts room, (c) a pre-school roundup of first-grade pupils. Teachers and P.T.A. mothers both contributed time and effort.

The work met with so much success and such an enthusiastic response from the pupils that the second summer all three phases of the work were expanded. Members of the community other than parents were drawn in to help with the crafts work. More and more adults began to take advantage of the library and crafts opportunities.

An interesting fact in regard to the second summer was that all of the teachers were going to be away at summer school. After the middle of June the parents carried on the work by themselves.

## The Sloan Project in Applied Economics

The Sloan Project in Applied Economics has as its ultimate goal the improvement of living through the school programme. In its experimental aspects, the Project is attempting to find out through long-range observation and experiment how specifically children are influenced in their daily living by what they study in school regarding three basic areas—food, shelter and clothing. The many schools cooperating with the Sloan Project almost invariably develop into community schools, since the ultimate aims of the community school and the Project are almost identical.

In most schools the work starts with something that can be done within the classroom or building itself—the beautification of the building or grounds, improvement of ventilation, care of the clothing the pupils are wearing, providing of a hot dish to supplement packed lunches of the school which has no lunch programme. Schoolwide projects are often undertaken involving committee work. No matter what the point of departure is, work soon extends into the community and enlists more and more community organisations and lay people, often, at first, in search for information and help. The help of County Agents and Home Demonstration Agents is frequently used almost from the start.

In many instances the work of the schools in food, clothing, or housing has led to the formation of a school community health council which involves all the agencies having a contribution to make to the health of people, regardless of age level. In a number of cases the Health Councils have broadened their scope to include recreation and their other matters.

### Geneva

Geneva is a three-teacher school in an agricultural region. Most of the children are transported to the neat brick school house. Adult members of most of the families work on the celery farms in the area.

The principal and his wife, who is the primary teacher, lived in the area and taught in the school for a number of years. They came to know the families well, to see the needs of children, and to realise that the school could do more toward improving the quality of living for these children than it had in the past. Because the need for a more varied diet was apparent, the principal and middle-grade teacher planned a school vegetable garden with the pupils. While the garden work was going on, a lunch programme was inaugurated. The school did not wait for lunchroom equipment but began with what cups and spoons could be brought from home. A cow was secured later, and the pupils learned how to care for the animal and the milk.

In subsequent years the children also undertook garden and household project at home and reported progress at school. The teachers made several visits a year to the homes to help with the projects and visit with parents. Parents, meanwhile, were coming to the school to assist with sewing and with canning for the lunchroom.

Later years saw a widening of a variety of undertakings. The children's lives were barren of any music experiences, and so a small school orchestra was gradually developed.

### Parker District School

In 1923 fourteen small elementary schools forming a semicircle around Greenville, South Carolina, were consolidated into one district. A major reason for the reorganisation of the districts was the hope that a high school could be established that would appeal to the youth of the area. Previous to 1918 there had been no high school at all. In 1924 the high school enrolled 55 pupils and was housed in three rooms.

In an effort to find out what a really appealing programme would be like, the entire faculty engaged in intensive curriculum study with the purpose of revision. Specialists in curriculum revision were brought in then to lead the faculty study groups at intervals during the year. A summer camp was held for further faculty study. Some teachers travelled to other states to visit schools that had already embarked on curriculum revision. Effort after effort was made to increase teacher vision. One observer reported that it was hoped to fit the school to the needs of the child by fitting the teacher to the needs of the child.

Centres of interest and units of work were the first year modifications resulting from the study of child needs. This study of needs led the faculty to the point of view that "American schools exist only to help improve the quality of the people's living and to help each person achieve the happiest and most useful life of which he is capable." The school is to work in and with the community for this improvement of the quality of living.

The subsequent activities are reflected in the growth of the school and its facilities. In 1942, it accommodates 1,400 pupils and is composed of 12 building units, which show its variety of service to the community; a three-storey classroom building; an annex for the library; a cafeteria; conference rooms; a vocational building including arts and crafts shop; a gymnasium; an athletic field arranged for variety of sports, day and night; a maternity shelter where mothers can receive prenatal, delivery, and postnatal care; a museum; gardens; a warehouse with a wood working department; an annex for a music room and recreational hall; and a year around camp. Adults have access to these facilities an share in planning next steps.

### The San Diego, California, Community School Camp

About seven years ago the idea for a public, year-round camp in San Diego County came from a group of nature-loving citizens. In it they saw possibilities for healthful development. Parent-teacher groups, county and city superintendents of schools, a member of the County Board of Supervisors, plus some individuals, sponsored the idea. From this group a five-member board was formed which negotiated for the land and buildings.

The programme started the first year with boys and girls from the sixth grades. Land has since been secured for a second camp which will be part of the high school curriculum. In this second camp, the high school youth will devote half of the time to a work experience, the other half to study and recreation.

The community has become very much aware of the programme and its benefits, and consequently proud of its part in the enterprise.

The two aims of the project have been: (1) to make democracy real and understandable to boys and girls through experiences in out-of-doors living, and (2) to give every child of appropriate ages a camp experience.

In the summer the camp has been available to other groups such as 4 H Clubs, Boys' Clubs, and church groups.

### Curriculum Planning on a Community Basis

A curriculum-planning workshop was the means by which the small village of Joshua, Texas, moved toward community thinking. Curriculum planning was the concern of a group of homemaking teachers in service. The year before Joshua had discontinued its programme of homemaking but had retained the teacher. This teacher was a member of the workshop. She presented the situation as a real problem which gave an opportunity for the workshop members to share in thinking about ways of solving it.

The teacher had the support of the superintendent, and with him appointed an advisory council of people who were interested in better family living. This group had representatives from the high school student body, teachers, administration, school, board and parents. The members of the workshop met for discussion, did much reading, and had meetings at Joshua once a week. At the first meeting the superintendent described the school and the economic and social factors affecting it.

At the second meeting all interested adults and high school students were invited. The discussion was broken into three groups, the adults, the high school boys, and the high school girls. One community need that was brought out by all the discussion groups, and especially from the boys, was the great need of suitable recreation within the village.

By the next meeting in Joshua, the workshop members found that the community members had already started work on this recreational problem. The first venture was a field for soft ball. Before the ball field was ready, the community had broadened its efforts to include recreational activities for all age groups.

Through this approach to the curriculum study, the community awakened to its own possibilities. Interests that had only been the concern of the school became the responsibility of the community.

## The Community Cooperates

In Groton, Connecticut, a small town of 5,000, the community agencies joined with the school to improve the recreational facilities for youth.

A civic organisation offered to sponsor a town Hallowe'en party. The superintendent recognised the possibilities for aiding youth and wrote to every agency in the community.

At the first meeting, which had a better response than had been expected, a Youth Council was formed. The superintendent was elected as acting chairman. The school board voted to let the Youth Council use the school auditorium and gymnasium, which made possible a recreational programme or dancing, basketball, badminton, table tennis, wrestling, all under proper supervision.

Other community-wide parties followed. An adult dramatic club was formed which included the mayor, school teachers and civic leaders. Several all-community events took place during the first year, such as a hobby show and an "International Fair" with contributions from descendants of many nationalities.

A monthly calendar that listed all of the community's activities followed later.

Juvenile delinquency has decreased to a great extent. The youth, the parents, and the school have all undergone a change of attitude.

## Mexico's School Made Society

The Mexican government's attempt to better the living conditions of its inhabitants started with the revision of Article 3 of the Mexican Constitution. This revision gives us the background for Mexican progress which is slow but sure.

Article 3. The education imparted by the State shall be a socialistic one and, in addition excluding all religious doctrine, shall combat fanaticism and prejudices by organising its instruction and activities in a way that shall permit the creation in youth of an exact and rational concept of the Universe and of social life.

Only the State—Federation, States, Municipalities—shall impart primary, secondary and normal education. Authorisation may be conceded to individuals who desire to impart education in any of the aforementioned three levels in conformity, in every case, with the following norms:

*(i)* The teachings and activities of private plants must adjust themselves without exception to that indicated in the initial paragraph of this Article and shall be in charge of persons who, in the opinion of the State, shall have sufficient professional preparation and a morality and ideology that is suitable to and in keeping with this precept. In view of this religious corporations, the ministers of cults, the organisations which preferably or exclusively carry on educational activities, and the associations or societies bound directly or indirectly to the propaganda of a religious creed shall in no way intervene in primary, secondary, or normal schools, nor shall they be permitted to assist these financially.

*(ii)* The formation of plans, programmes, and methods of teaching shall in every case rest in the State.

*(iii)* Private plants shall not be permitted to function without first, and in each case, having obtained the express authorisation of the public power.

*(iv)* The State may at any time revoke the authorisation granted (to private individuals or organisations). There shall be no judgment or recourse whatsoever against such revocation.

The same norms shall govern the education of whatever type or grade that is imparted to workers or peasants.

Primary education shall be obligatory, and the State shall impart it gratuitously.

The State may, at its discretion and at any time, withdraw recognition of official validity to the studies made in private plants.

The Congress of the Union, in the interest of unifying and coordinating education throughout the Republic, shall promulgate the necessary laws destined to distribute the social educative function between the Federation and the States and Municipalities, to fix the financial apportionments corresponding to that public service, and to indicate the sanctions (penalties) applicable to those functionaries who do not comply with, of force compliance to, the respective dispositions, as well as to all those who violate them.

## The Highlander Folk School

The Highlander Folk School is located in the community of Summerfield on the Cumberland Mountain. Six hundred fifteen farms make up this community.

The Highlander Folk School was guided by the belief that our economy, which is rapidly becoming collectivised, can be made the basis for a genuine democracy and that the final attainment and protection of the fullest rights of the masses can come only through their own economic and political organisations. With this goal constantly in mind, they set to work. A large house, in which the founder of the elementary school had lived and worked, served as a community centre and residence for two teachers. Social evenings when young men and old gathered to sing familiar songs and to talk and play games were the first organised activities of the school. Only one student from outside the community had come to attend the residence term for workers, later he was joined by others. Scheduled classes did not occur until several weeks after the arrival of the students.

The wife of a neighbouring farmer, in remarking about her unruly child, started discussion about psychology with one of the students and a teacher. As a result of this, a class in psychology for adults was announced. Gradually more and more classes were started.

Out of the first years' experience grew a threefold programme consisting, first, of community work, second, of a residence programme of short courses and week-end conference, and third, or extension work, Members of the community participate as students or co-workers in all phases of the programme.

### Arthurdale

Arthurdale, West Virginia, is one of the better known community schools. It differs from others in that it was started with the vision that the school would be the centre for use and learning of the community. Even in the preparation of the first rooms that were to house the school, the fathers, mothers, teachers and children worked together. At the very outset, before the building was ready to be occupied, the school belonged to the community.

Arthurdale is located in a worn out mine area. The miners for whom the project was built had been out of work from three to seven years. In dealing with people who had so very many difficulties there were many problems to be met. The health of the members of this group was the first to get attention. The school felt this need, and, because there were no other agencies responsible for this, took it up. This health programme included the babies and the older people as well as the children of school age.

The first year of the project included attention to this health situation, provision for recreation facilities for people of all ages, establishment of a night school, a farm cooperative, and a summer programme.

### Shaker Heights

The first venture toward community thinking in Shaker Heights, Ohio, was the establishing of a summer recreation programme. For ten weeks of the summer vacation the schools and playgrounds are open for the children under trained leaders assisted by high school students. Games, sports, swimming, dramatics, story telling and ceramics are offered.

The school plants are used for many adult classes of badminton, table tennis, rifle shooting, ceramics, swimming, study groups. One school has a daily session of Hebrew sponsored by a near-by synagogue. Many church groups use the auditoriums for recreational meetings.

Recently the school joined with the public library in sponsoring a study of books dealing with current world problems.

Several years ago the parents were invited to work with the staff on committees in setting up a new curriculum. These committees had as a basis the answers to questionnaires sent to all children in grades six, nine and twelve, and to their parents. Discussions on the needs of children and the needs of society were followed by conferences on experiences to meet these needs, evaluation of the results of these experiences, and a final one on a programme of studies that could be set up.

Shaker Heights has a Community Council which includes representatives from most of the organised groups of the area. The school has two members, one from the administration and one from the Teachers' Association. This group with other organisations joined in a celebration that commemorated the one-hundred twenty-fifth anniversary of the founding of the original Shaker Colony from which the village took its name.

While there is a rather common social and economic status, there is great need for a more inclusive programme that will bring the entire community into a closer relationship.

**Collins Grove**

Collins Grove, a rural community of around thirty-two families located about ten miles outside of Greensboro, North Carolina, was selected for a community-school programme after a survey of various communities was made by Miss F. Parker, a sociology instructor at Bennett College in Greensboro. It was the most retarded community in the area and needed the most help. Its inhabitants had no electricity, no water close to their homes and very little sanitation.

A door-to-door questionnaire campaign was conducted by the Bennet College group as the first step in its programme. It was found that each family had from two to three children at home; one family with fourteen children lived in two rooms. The family cash incomes were primarily derived from crops plus wages earned by some residents with jobs in Greensboro.

The first problem to be attacked was health. After some progress was made in that direction, demonstrations for cooking and making home furnishings were given. Recreational programmes and educational forums were also set up. Work in this community was conducted in the religious as well as the social and economic spheres.

The people in Collins Grove readily accepted guidance. They dug wells, installed out-houses, remodelled some of their homes, and painted other buildings. They are progressing toward a better life by working with the students and faculty from Bennett College.

## Mr. Tabor

Mr. Tabor, about seven miles southeast of Greensboro, was picked by Bennett College as the second community in which school-community relationships would be developed. Its inhabitants, about fifty in number, would be classified as progressive. At first their attitude was one of indifference to the college project. They felt that for their entertainment and extra activities they would go into Greensboro.

To obtain a true picture of the community, we made a door-to-door canvass and met the people, saw their homes, and received needed information. We did find that most people in the community wanted food demonstrations, sewing information, political information, and other social events. In order to establish such a programme, a place large enough had to be found. Since there was no school, the only building in the community for a meeting of any size was the church. (The children attended a school which took care of a number of communities.)

Here, in the church, the programme was started, and by the end of the year every person in the community was playing an active roll.

## The School Lunchroom

The change in the lunchroom in the nine elementary schools of Orange, Texas, came about through the cooperative planning by the faculty and representative community groups. The lunchrooms have become laboratories for learning and living.

In revising the curriculum, the philosophy agreed upon called for the application of reputable practices in child development to all phases of school life. This made it necessary to include the lunchrooms in the instructional programme. Out of this has come understanding, practices, and personal satisfactions.

The practices included the development of a broader concept of nutrition and education, a better concept of health instruction, a reorganising of the plan of instruction so that the lunchroom would tie in with all areas of learning, and work experiences extending for home-school relations to include the lunchroom.

The only criterion which was set up was that the school lunchroom, as an area of living, should contribute to the child's *total* growth and development. It should be a functional part of school and community living.

The study of foods and food combination led to a study of vegetables and fruits in season, which developed an understanding of some of the problems of production, transportation and prices of food.

To prove that balanced meals were better than lunches bought at hamburger joints led to an experiment with white rats. The rapid decline of rats fed on hamburgers and soft drinks influenced many to eat in the school lunchroom.

The relationship between the home and school has kept pace with this programme. Each Friday the menus for the next week are sent home. This enables mothers to supplement the school meals, and also gives suggestions to mothers whose children do not eat at school.

An attitude of friendliness and goodwill is apparent as teachers, pupils, parents and administrators work on new problem.

## A Community College in Action

The Rochester Community College of Rochester, Minnesota, is a department of the junior college. Up until 1944, what adult education there was, was handled through the senior high school. A few classes were sponsored, mostly in the commercial field.

When the work was turned over to the junior college, the faculty study of the situation was turned over to a faculty committee. After studying the area, this committee came to the conclusion that the community was ready for a much extended programme.

Through the Community College teachers may pursue professional studies while in service. At the close of the war the need arose for helping the veterans made the most of their G.I. rights. One thing that has grown out of this is job training for veterans. Training in the college has been given which relates to this apprentice work.

An economic and social survey of Rochester was made, the expense of which was carried by the Board of Education and the Chamber of Commerce. The results are being used for integrating and improving the economy of that city, and to acquaint people with the city. Several special projects are under way, such as a community canning centre, research projects, lecture series, and study and discussion groups of such questions as the emotional development of the elementary-grade child and home planning.

### Piney Woods School

Piney Woods Country Life School, near Jackson, Mississippi, was founded in 1909 by Laurence Clifton Jones on a pine stump with three illiterate pupils and \$ 1.65 cash. The school now has a \$ 250,000 plant, 1,700 acres of well-tended land, and an enrolment of 440 pupils ranging in age from 6 to 40, drawn from 15 states and one foreign country. It has sent out to rural communities thousands of trained farmers, mechanics, and housekeepers and hundreds of practical competent teachers. In addition, it has carried the gospel of good farming, healthful homemaking, sensible religion, and has stimulated social life for Negroes for miles around.

Piney Woods has never departed from its original ideal of education for poor children. If a boy or girl can pay, the charge is \$ 20 a month including board and room; most of the students pay what they can and earn the rest of their way by working.

Through the extension department of the school, reaching 15,000 Negroes annually, and the influence of its graduates, three fourths of the coloured farmers in two adjacent counties own land, as against less than 5 per cent when Piney Woods was started. Twenty home economics graduates are now housekeepers for well-to-do families at $75 to $175 a month. Others teach in 26 states.

## The Wool Market School

In Harrison County, Mississippi, about eight miles from the Gulf of Mexico and in a typical southern Mississippi rural community, may be found the Wool Market Consolidated School. Three medium sized one-teacher schools were done away with to form this one.

The people of the community felt that a more extensive programme could be carried out with interests all brought together and not divided threefold.

The consolidated school was located near the trading store and other businesses. Extensive programmes of community betterment were inaugurated. People in the community began to take active interest in community gatherings and entertainments. After some time noted progressive changes were seen in this community.

## The Benjamin Franklin High School

This is a school for boys in the city of New York. Established in 1935, it has functioned from the beginning with a determination to become an integral part of its community and to provide ways and means by which the school and community might work together for the good of the children and of the community at large.

As a first move, the school undertook to secure adequate information about the East Harlem neighbourhood in which it is located. All available data on the East Harlem Community were studied thoroughly. Statistical information of all kinds was assembled, and a series of maps showing racial distribution in the community was prepared. Likewise, social maps were drawn showing the location of every school, church, social and civic agency. These provided a background of information for those who were undertaking the task of transforming all necessary details into a programme humanly helpful in which the emphasis is placed not on records, statistics and routine plans but upon human values both in the school and in the community.

A Community Advisory Council was created to bring about effectual cooperation between the various social agencies and the school. Through this council the extramural, or neighbourhood activities of the school, are carried forward. In addition, there are various faculty committees, not ordinarily a part of the routine school programme. Through these committees the regular school programme is linked to the larger community programme, thereby greatly extending the school's sphere of activity and influence.

### Savannah

The Armstrong Junior College in Savannah, Georgia organised in 1935, has maintained the attitude that its responsibility to the city and community does not end with the classroom instruction of the young people. The college has developed many ways of augmenting its programme with activities of benefit to the townspeople. The initiative was apparently taken by the college, but the activities are carried on · through community-college cooperation.

The Forum is one of the most popular features of the programme. The director is a member of the faculty, and he is assisted with arrangements and selection of subjects and speakers by an advisory committee composed of citizens of the community and students.

The Playhouse is another successful activity. It is directed by a Senior Board whose members are chosen from both the community and college on the basis of work done in the theater.

Facilities of the college are available to Savannah organisations at a minimum charge to cover utilities and janitor service.

Other activities include veterans guidance, evening classes, Red Cross service, home economics services, chemical research, and service of faculty members in community organisations.

### Qualifications of Community Teachers

The members of the staff—their attitudes, beliefs, training, experience and skills—will have such a bearing on the possible development of a community school that they deserve some attention at this point. An individual deeply committed to the idea that the teaching of subject-matter and skill represents the basic function of the school, and attainment in such areas a satisfactory end of education, will find himself unhappy in a situation where a community school is being developed. As is the case with the school, no particular pattern can be sketched for successful teachers in a community school. Three or four qualities of successful teachers and leaders in community schools though do seem to stand out in importance. The individual must be at home in the culture in which he finds himself. Such maturity means that the individual understands the environmental forces at work around him. He must have adequate knowledge of the historical development of our nation and its institutions, and of the particular community of which he is a part. Such a worker must have a high level of belief in education and see in it a force for both individual and community improvement. He must have a philosophy of education compatible with the best we know in the fields of freedom and democracy.

Then there are certain things which community teachers in rural as well as urban areas should have.

1. Teachers should develop effective and well-balanced personalities for the enrichment of their own living and for aiding others better to develop well-balanced personalities for themselves.
2. Teachers should become persons rich in firsthand experience and in broader understanding of the many aspects of our culture in order better to advance the experience and understanding of others.
3. Teachers should obtain an expert understanding of the process of human living, growing, learning at all ages, and should become competent in acting upon this understanding in teaching situations.
4. Teachers should obtain an understanding of and practice in the democratic process in all areas of living and should become competent in guiding young people to utilise such democratic process in their own living.
5. Teachers should become expert in utilising their enriched experiences in guiding the process of living, growing and learning in young people.

6. Teachers should develop an adequate working philosophy of life and education.
7. Teachers should be stimulated to desire continuous professional growth.
8. Teachers should become scholars willing constantly to use the resources and methods of critical inquiry in the fields of human knowledge relevant to their responsibilities as individuals and as professional workers in teaching and guiding students to use similar resources and methods in facing their own problems of living.

## OBSERVATIONS AND TENTATIVE CONCLUSIONS CONCERNING THE ROLE OF THE SCHOOL IN THE COMMUNITY APPROACH

1. In every case some one sees a need of the people about which action can be taken.
2. Usually the school takes the initial step. This was true of sixteen of the twenty cases studied. In only four did the original incentive come from outside.
3. There is a wide variety of procedure, but always with the common goal, to fulfil a need.
4. There are records of more small than large communities, of the ones we have observed all but there are of towns and small villages.
5. In the small community the school is often the only formal agency; therefore, it is natural for it to assume some of the responsibility that would be designated to other agencies in a larger community or to a community council.
6. Health and recreation are needs which always clearly require cooperative planning. The activities involve other people or agencies increasingly.
7. The use of the school plant is a common way of beginning.
8. No one kind of physical setting is indispensible to a beginning. The limitations of the situation will, of course, influence the activities undertaken. In planning future

building, space should be provided for educational activities that are to serve all ages.

9. The principal or superintendent is a key figure in the initial steps. Although he may soon relinquish active leadership, any indifference on his part will hinder and may even destroy the vision or enthusiasm of co-workers.
10. Community schools are indigenous; there are no patterns that can be transferred. In the twenty communities reviewed, four showed health as the initial step; four, recreation; three, curriculum planning; and nine could not be grouped at all. Even this classification does not give any indication of the various activities and outcomes. The one common outcome was the improvement of the quality of living.
11. Some undertakings involve only a few people; others involve thousands. Some phases of work are completed in a few days; others go on for years. Some projects arise out of a classroom incident; others require months of pre-planning. Whatever the differences according to size of community or project, however, the ways of furthering work and purpose usually show six major processes: organisation, research, interpretation, publi-city, cooperation, pressure.

These processes vary tremendously in application but they can usually be seen in community action, and it makes for clarity of thinking and future action to recognise them.

*(a) Organization* is a way of giving strength and permanency to ideas and impulses. In the simplest instances, as far as number of people, the organisation may not have actual form. In a one-teacher school the teacher and an interested parent, home demonstration agent, nurse, or the students themselves may be the planners. In a large urban setting organisation may involve community councils, other organisations, and the enlisting of influential persons in the community.

*(b) Research* is the technique of finding facts and rests on the assumption that one must know reality before he can have any well-grounded hope of controlling it. Even the smallest undertakings require careful analysis of the situation first lest

absurd blunders be made in estimating the relative importance of needs.

*(c) Interpretation* is the process of relating evidence to group policy and procedure. Facts do not always reveal their own meanings and care has to be exercised in planning action suggested by the facts. Thus, to use a very simple illustration, the need of children in an isolated school for milk might lead to hasty plans for securing and delivering milk, without proper provision for caring for it (some kind of refrigeration), or without any provision for coordinated educational activities that would extend the values beyond the actual drinking of the milk.

*(d) Publicity* is sometimes described as "a way of reaching the public with the facts." Here the small community has an advantage. Through direct conversation the facts are transmitted. A high proportion of the people know about the plans first hand and are helping develop them. While a city has more avenues of appeal, the spreading of information takes on many aspects of a campaign. At best, it is a case of a few persons trying to tell many people about plans already developed.

## The Role of the Community School Approach

Just as the trends in education have led to the need for a broader concept of the function of the school today, so does an analysis of the social forces at work in the community lead to a similar conclusion. Everett has said, "The potential evils of a technological civilisation can be transformed into human assets only by the cooperative creation of community life patterns within which socially significant growth of personality is guaranteed to all persons."

The community school offers one channel or agency for such "cooperative creation". Through it common concerns can be preserved and developed and experiences that cut across class lines can be shared. Greater community integration can be attained.

Many experiences which children and adults encounter are divisive in nature, setting group against group or individual against individual. Through the community school, however, both children and adults can experience the satisfaction that comes from organising the efforts of many people toward the solution of a common problem. The influence of the community school is cohesive, pulling people together, rather than divisive, and can be, therefore, highly significant in present day society.

Furthermore, there is a growing conviction among many thoughtful people that the democratic way of life is something not merely to be defended and protected but also to be extended by intelligent planning and persistent effort. Important as have been the contributions of the past to democratic living, its full potentialities have yet to be achieved. The extension of the democratic way of life demands a high level of individual initiative and responsibility and a high level of understanding among groups and skill in working together. The community school can aid in this extension since its activities help provide practice in cooperative undertakings, and lead to the development of the very qualities needed for improved democratic living.

## REFERENCES

Mangus A.R., and J.R. Seeley, *Mental Health Needs in a Rural and Semi-Rural Area of Ohio, 1959* (Columbus, Division of Mental Hygiene of the Ohio State Departments of Public Welfare, 1950).

Boyd Bode, a public lecture. For example see *Thirty Schools Tell Their Story,* Progressive Education Publications (New York, Harper, 1943): also The Ohio State University, University High School Class of 1938, *Were We Guinea Pigs?* (New York, Holt, 1938).

Adapted from Willard E. Goslin, "The Characteristics of a Community School," *Forthcoming Developments in American Education,* W. C. Reavis, ed. (Chicago, University of Chicago Press, 1946), pp. 90-93.

Committee members working on this interest were Mildred Swearingen, Katherine Boylan, and Janet White.

R. L. Sharp, "School Public Relations Via a Community Council," *American School Board Journal* (August 1947).

*School-Community Cooperation for Better Living* (Gainsville, University of Florida Press, 1947).

*Parker District School Serves Its People* (Greenville, S.C., 1942).

Edwin Pumala, "The San Diego, California, Community Schook Camp," *The Bulletin of the National Association of Secondary School Principals* (May 1947), pp. 100-105.

Johnie Christian, "Curriculum Planning on a Community Basis, *Educational Administration and Supervision,* Vol. IV (January 1947), pp. 43–48; "Community Participates in Curriculum Building," *Texas Outlook,* Vol. XXXXI, (February 1947), pp. 12-13.

Victor E. Leonard, "The School Cooperates," *The School Executive,* Vol. 66 (December 1946), p. 40.

Booth George C., *Mexico's School Made Society* (Stanford, Stanford University Press, 1941).

Sanchez George I., translator, *Mexico: A Revolution by Education,* The Viking Press, 1939, pp. 102-3.

Horton Myles, "The Highlander Folk School," *The Community School,* Samuel Everett, ed. (New York, Appleton-Century, 1938).

Elsie Clapp, *Community Schools in Action* (New York, Viking, 1939).

Reported from direct observation, 1949.

Essie Young, "The School Lunchroom," *Educational Leadership,* Vol. IV (February 1947), pp. 314–320.

*Lincoln Library of Essential Information* (Buffalo, N.Y., Frontier Press, 1935).

Emil Heintz, *The School Executive,* Vol. 66 (March 1947), p. 47.

Nelson Antrim Crawford, "The Little Professor of Piney Woods," *The Rotarian* (October 1945).

*Lincoln Library of Essential Information* (Buffalo, N. Y., Frontier Press, 1935).

Leonard Covello, "The Benjamin Franking High School," *The Community School* by Samuel Everett (New York, Appleton-Century, 1938).

Leonard Covello, "The Benjamin Franklin High School," *The Community School* by Samuel Everett (New York, Appleton-Century, 1938).

Olson, J.P., "Going Beyond the Classroom," *Junior College Journal* (March 1946), pp. 303-305.

Evenden E.S., and R. Freeman Butts, eds., *Columbia University Cooperative Programme for the Pre-Service Education of Teachers*

(New York, Bureau of Publications, Teachers College, Columbia University, 1942), pp. 29–32.

Lloyd A. Cook, *Community Action and the School* (Columbus, The Ohio State University, 1941), p.9.

Samuel Everett, *The Community School* (New York, Appleton-Century 1938), p. 53.

# 6

# Communication Theories

Notwithstanding the fact that communications has been a subject of study of philosophers, psychologists, sociologists, semanticists, and human relations experts since the first quarter of the century there clearly is *diminishing* communication within organisations and between groups and individuals in society.

As information explodes communication seems to implode in direct proportion. Witness relations between white and black, rich and poor, young and old, faculty and administrators. Contrast these relationships of today to those prior to the introduction of television on a mass scale circa 1950. Modern information systems have made the world smaller, but more hysterical at the same time; it took weeks for the Americans to know what was happening in the Napoleonic wars, and months to learn about a flood or famine in India—now information simultaneously presses down on us in microseconds, and the sheer concentration of disaster makes the media seem so "sensational".

We can vividly see how this information explosion has occurred if we plot the accumulation of information on a historical continuum beginning with the birth of Christ. The first doubling of information occurs in 1750; the second in 1900; the third in 1950; the fourth only ten years later, in 1960; and the fifth in the mid-1960's. In other words, while it took 1,750 years for man to double his knowledge the first time after the birth of Christ, it took only five years for him to similarly double his knowledge from 1960 to 1965! In the past twenty years mankind has acquired more scientific information than in all of previous history. And 90 per cent of all the scientists that ever lived are alive and working today. The information explosion is so vast and so far-reaching that the importance of grasping and keeping up with it at some points becomes indistinguishable from one's career.

Though television has been most responsible for the information explosion, the publishing industry and computers have added their weight to the mass of information that threatens to bury us. Not tat information is not desirable—for it certainly is—but what the abundance of information does is to *increase* the communication problem. It makes communication both more urgent and even less tractable.

The preceding facts point up the imperative for organisations to manage information rather than to be buried by it, to communicate rather than to orate.

Our failure to effectively communicate with one another is poignantly pointed up by the felt need for intensive groups of various kinds (T-groups, encounter groups, sensitivity training, sensory awareness groups . . . ). The popularity of such groups attests to the failure of our attempts at effective communication.

Despite the sorry state of communication in practice, we have nevertheless learned a great deal about it. However, rather than emerging out of studies about communication *per se*, our knowledge of communication theory are largely by-products of studies in other disciplines. Though we may never completely understand all elements making for effective communication we do know some things which are worthwhile will respect to *managerial communications.*

What we know of communication in organisations consists largely of what does *not* work and, sometimes, why it does not work. What seems for blunt truth is that most of what passes for communication in most organizations—whether business, labour unions, government agencies, or educational systems—is based on assumptions that have proven to be invalid—and that, therefore, these efforts cannot have results. Knowing what does not work gives a glimpse at a few things which *do* work.

## Communication Principles

Peter F. Drucker summarises what we have learned about communications through doing mostly the wrong things, in four cardinal principles:

1. Communications is perception.
2. Communications is expectations.
3. Communications is involvement.
4. Communications and information are totally different though totally interdependent.

*Communications is perception*—An old philosophical question posed by the mystics of many religions—the Zen Buddhists, the Sufis of Islam, and the Rabbis of the Talmud—asks; "Is there a sound in the forest if a tree crashes down and no one is there to hear it?" The mystics of old always answered, "No". They knew that there is no sound unless someone perceives it. Sound is created by perception. Sound is communication. Though seemingly trite, the correct answer to this age-old question has profound implications for modern management.

1. First, it means that it is the *receiver* who communicates. The person who emits the communication does *not* communicate. He utters. Unless there is someone who hears, there is no communication. There is only noise. The utterer may speak and write, sing or whistle, but without a receiver he communicates nothing. *No one can communicate anything.* One can only make it possible, or impossible, for a receiver (technically a perceiver) to perceive.
2. We know that perception is experience, not logic. Therefore, one always perceives a configuration, not single specifics, a total picture, not part of a picture. This means that facial expressions, gestures, body posture, tone of voice, cultural and social setting—in short, the total environment—cannot be dissociated from the spoken language. In fact, without such referents, the spoken word has no real meaning and cannot effectively communicate. One cannot communicate a word without the whole man coming with it.

3. We also know that one can only perceive what one is capable of perceiving. Stimulus cannot become communication without understanding. One has to talk to people in terms of their own experience, that is, one has to use an electrician's metaphors when talking to electricians, and so on. One can only communicate in the receiver's language and terms used must be experienced-based. It, therefore, does very little good to explain terms (*e.g.*, electrical) to people if the terms are not of their own experience. Such unfamiliar terms simply exceed their perception capacity.

The connection between experience, perception, and concept formation (cognition) in the learner, whether child or adult, is not separate. We cannot perceive unless we also conceive. Likewise, we cannot form concepts unless we can perceive. To communicate a concept is impossible unless it is within the perception of the receiver. Ergo, in communicating, whatever the medium, the 1st question has to be, "Is this communication within his range of perception—can he receive it?"

The "range of perception" is partly physiological and, thus, largely determined by the physical limitations of one's own body. But when we speak of communications the most important limitations on perception are usually affective and cognitive rather than physical.

That perception is conditioned by what we are capable of perceiving today is well known. Disagreements and conflicts are not so much over answers as simply over incongruities in perception between individuals and groups. One of the best examples of incongruity in perceptions is the old story about the blind men and the elephant. It will be recalled that every one of them, upon encountering the strange beast, felt one of the elephant's part—his hide, his led, his trunk—and each reported an entirely different conclusion to which each tenaciously help. There was no possibility of communication between them until each verified the experience of the other. This old tale illustrates why there is no possibility of communications unless we first know what the receiver, who is the true communicator, understands and can perceive.

***Communications is expectations***—As a rule we perceive what we want to perceive. We see largely what we want to see, and we hear largely what we want to hear. The unexpected and unwanted is usually not received at all. It is ignored or misunderstood, that is, misseen as the expected or misheard as the expected. This *selective-exposure hypothesis,* as it is known, is considered to be the single most important finding of communication research.

Scores of confirming research on the selective-exposure hypothesis have revealed that the human mind attempts to fit stimuli and impressions into a frame of expectations. The mind vigorously resists any attempt to make it "change its mind," *i.e.* to perceive what it does not want to perceive. Thus, the hypothesis implies that as the intended communication becomes increasingly discrepant from the would be receiver's preconception, the more resistance he will put up so as to neutralize or minimize its attitude change effect. To overcome the resistance to expectancy of perception nothing short of a "shock signal" will do. The use of gradual, incremental steps will not work.

Before we can effectively communicate, we must, therefore, know what the receiver expects to see and hear. Only then can we know whether communications can utilize his expectations–and what they are – or whether there is a need for a "shock of alienation," for an "awakening" that breaks through the receiver's expectations and forces him to acknowledge that the unexpected is happening.

***Communications is involvement***—Communication always makes demands. It always demands that the receiver become somebody, do something, believe something. It always appeals to motivation. If the communication fits in with the aspirations, beliefs, and values of the receiver, it is effective. But if the communication goes against an individual's aspirations, purposes and values it is likely to be firmly resisted if received at all. Though it is a rare existential event it is possible for communication to bring about a conversion in personality of an individual through changing his aspirations, beliefs, and values (a vivid example is "the drug scene"). But since this infrequently happens there are few instances of communication unless the message can be keyed to the receiver's own values, at least to some degree.

The most effective communication process to prevent or resolve conflicts and problems, to give purpose and direction, is through the use of *dyádic* groups (groups of two), *e.g.* doctor and patient, lawyer and client, shop foreman and union stewart, administrator and teacher, teacher and student.

Groups of two show markedly *dissimilar* characteristics to *similar* groups of larger size. Dyadic groups are markedly low on showing disagreement and unfriendly behaviour but markedly high on showing tension and asking for information of the other. They appear to take extra care to avoid conflict and to persuade one another gently. In groups of larger sizes, either of two conflicting members can appeal to other persons in the group to combine with them or act as impartial judges. The pressure of a coalition or the pressure of somewhat impersonal group norms can be brought to bear. But in an isolated group of two, each member of the pair is unusually vulnerable to the other. This vulnerability to each other frequently resolves mistrust, leads to mutual understanding, and improves the likelihood of goal realisation. This human phenomenon has extremely important implications for managers. When a manager senses a conflict with a superordinate, subordinate, or peer, with a student or a member of the community, more often than not, a quick arrangement for a tête-á-tête will mitigate, if not resolve, a conflict.

There is considerable merit for superordinates to employ elements of *Rogerian non-directive therapy techniques* in both dyadic and larger groups. The Rogerian method (so named for psychologist Carl R. Rogers) employs all the communication principles summarised by Drucker to varying degrees. In this method the superordinate makes every effort during the discussion to maintain an equalitarian relationship with the other person or persons; to basically be as positive and supportive as possible; to agree without compromising own principles whenever possible; to show friendly behaviour. Such an approach aids the subordinate(s) to see himself and his position more clearly and to cause him to make these adjustments necessary to give himself a positive self-image. This "working through" also tends to make him feel positive about the superordinate because he is constantly accepted and reinforced in his attempts to express his feelings and to work toward a position that is in harmony with both his and the organisation's goals. The superordinate keeps bringing the process back to "early phase of nearly all problem-solving cycles" where friendly behaviour and exchange of information predominate. This subordinate(s) does most of the talking but the superordinate talks a moderate amount. He also provides a sensitive, positive feedback on every remark of the subordinate he non-hyprocritically can.

The superordinate especially concentrates on *repreating back* his interpretation of what a subordinate has said to serve as a mirror for the subordinate and to ensure that his own interpretation of the point presented is accurate. Only in this way will true, mutual understanding occur.

***Communications and information are totally different though totally interdependent***—Communication is perception, information is logic. Information, standing alone, is impersonal rather than interpersonal. The more information is freed from the human component of emotions, expectations, perceptions, and values the more valid, reliable and valuable does it become.

Communications are subject to gross biases and faulty perceptions. The problem, therefore, is how to glean pure and untainted information out of interpersonal relationships. All through history, the problem has been how to isolate the information content from an abundance of perception. Because of the conceptual work of the logicians, especially the symbolic logic of Bertrand Russell and Alfred North Whitehead, and because of technical advances made in automated data processing storage and retrieval, we now have an opposite problem. Now we have the problem of handling information *per se*, devoid of any communication content.

The requirements for effective information are the opposite of those for effective communication. Information is always specific whereas communication is always perceived as a configuration. The best information is economical in content.

Anything beyond what is essential can mask the essence of what is needed. Embellishment does not enrich, it impoverishes.

Information presupposes communication. Information is always encoded. To be received, let alone to be used, the code must be known and understood by the receiver. Therefore, before communication can begin between the emitter and the receiver each must use the "common language" appropriate to the discussion—*e.g.* "pedagese."

The logical implications of the four postulates of communication as perception, expectations, involvement and communication as different from information, though perhaps simple and obvious, are at odds with current practice in organisations. Indeed, notwithstanding the fact that communication is at the very heart of our work as educators our communication skills are among the least developed of all professions.

## Communication in Organisations

What, then, can our knowledge and our experience teach us about communication in organisations, about the reasons for our past failures, and about the prerequisites for success in the future?

1. From time immemorial we have attempted, and continue to attempt, to communicate *downwards*—from superordinate to subordinate. This has not worked, nor does it work, nor will it over work no matter how hard and intelligently we try to make it work. It has not worked nor will this practice ever work for the simple reason that it focuses on what we as the superordinate want to say (*e.g.* superintendent to principal, principal to teacher, teacher to student). This procedure assumes, in other words, that the emitter communicates. But we know that all he he does is utter. *Communication is the act of the receiver.* Past practices in all our formal "management" training programmes (including teaching as well as administration courses) have largely concentrated on ways and means of assisting the "trainee" to become a more effective and capable communicator. But all one can communicate downward are command. One cannot effectively communicate downward anything connected with understanding, let alone motivation. *This requires communication*

*upward,* from those who perceive to those who want to reach their perception (*e.g.* principal *to* superintendent, teacher *to* principal, student *to* teacher).

Managers still need to work on clarity in what they say and write. However, how we say something can only come after we have learned what to say. And this cannot be found out by "talking down to," no matter how well it is being done. Administrative bulletins, faculty bulletins, student bulletins, and the like, no matter how well done, will be a waste unless the writer knows what the receivers can perceive, expect to perceive, and want to do. They are a total waste unless they are based on the receiver's rather than on the emitter's perception.

2. "Listening" is not enough either. Research findings by the Human Relations School of Elton Mayo reveal that listening alone is ineffective as a means of communication.

Certainly, listening is a prerequisite to communication. The superordinate should instead starting out with what he wants to get across first find out what subordinate want to know, are interested in, are, in other words, receptive to. But the classical human relations prescription of being first a "good listener" is not adequate, and it cannot, by itself work. This fact may account for the reason why listening is not being widely used despite the popularity of the slogan—where it has been tried, it has failed to work. Listening assumes that the subordinates can communicate whereas his superior cannot. This he obviously cannot do. Listening can result in as much misunderstanding and miscommunication as talking. Neither talking alone nor listening alone take into account the fact that *communication is involvement.* Listening does not bring out subordinate's desires and preferences, his aspirations and values. Listening may explain the reasons for misunderstanding. But it does not lay down a basis for understanding. These factors account for the fact that extrapolating certain aspects of the Rogerian method of non-directive therapy, previously discussed, to management is soundly based.

The preceding is not to say that listening is undesirable, any more than the futility of downward communications furnishes any argument against attempts to write well, to say things clearly and simply, and to speak the language of those whom one addresses rather than using one's own jargon. Indeed, the realisation that communication must begin with the receiver rather that the emitter is fundamental to the concept of listening. But listening is only the starting point.

3. Moreover, more and better information does not solve the communication problem. Rather, the more information the greater the communication gap is likely to be.

The more effective the information process the more impersonal and formal will it become, the more will it separate human beings. The consequence of impersonal and formal information systems is a dependence upon prior agreement on meaning and application, that is communications. Without communications, information is relegated to mere data. In absence of direct, personal face-to-face relations with other people communication cannot occur. Therefore, an effective MIS manager is even more concerned with the establishment of viable communication links and interfaces than efficient information links and interfaces.

The Information Explosion is the most compelling reason for improving communications. Information is responsible for the widening communications gap all around us—in the academic sector between boards of trustees and their chief executive, between administrators and faculty, between faculty and students (and between both of them and the administration). In other sectors conflicts exist between management and labour, blacks and whites, young and old, and so on. Information flows like a flood out of the television tube and the computer, but without a commensurate increase in communications.

**Communications at Work**

We now know that for true communication to have a chance it must start with the receiver of communication rather than from the emitter. In a hierarchical system communications must start upward. Downward communication cannot, does not, and will not work. Only *after* upward communications have successfully been established will downward communications have a chance.

Downward communications must largely be reaction rather than action, response rather than initiative.

But we also know that it is not enough to listen. Upward communications must first be focused on something that *both* receiver and emitter can perceive, focussed on something that is common to both of them. Moreover, it must be focussed on the motivations, values, beliefs and aspirations of the intended receiver.

One proven example of facilitating the communication process is for the superordinate to request his subordinates to think through and present to him their own conclusions as to what major contribution to the organisation—or to the unit within the organisation—the subordinates feel they should be expected to perform and thus be held accountable for. It likely will be found that what each subordinate comes up with is not what the superordinate expects. But the first aim of this exercise is to precisely bring out the divergence in perception between superordinate and each of his subordinates. The result is a perception which can be focussed on what is real to each pair. To realise that they see the same reality differently is itself communication.

Second, in this approach, the intended receiver of communication, the subordinate in this one-to-one face-to-face interaction with his superordinate, is given access to different levels of experience which will aid him to better understand decision making. Further, the subordinate is aided in better understanding problems associated with establishing priorities, the conflict between what one likes to do vis-à-vis the demands of a situation, and above all also understanding and accepting the need for being held accountable for a decision.

Discussion between subordinate and superordinate on the job perception of the former usually has several favourable results. The subordinate gains an understanding of the complexity of the superordinate's position and the realisation that complexity is not of the superordinate's making, but is inherent in the situation itself. Likewise, the superordinate gains an appreciation and understanding of his subordinate's perceptions and interests which can frequently be capitalised on, especially for ad hoc tasks. Finally, even if a "goodness of fit" cannot be fully achieved so that the perception of the subordinate's job by each is one and the same there is at least a realisation where the differences lie— and why. Thus, greater sensitivity by the superordinate should result in the non-congruent areas of the subordinate's job duties and responsibilities and hence more effective results should be able to be brought forth.

Another example, that has excellent results in an organisational situation, in which communication has been traditionally absent, is the performance appraisal coupled with the appraisal interview. Performance appraisal at the management level today is standard practice in large business and industrial organisations. But is education, formal performance appraisal is sporadically used. Moreover, the kind of performance appraisal used in the economic sector is practically non-existent in education. We know that the most people want to know where they stand. One of the most common complaints of employees in organisations is that they are not being appraised, are not being told whether they are doing well or poorly, or what they can do to be more effective in their work.

Though "evaluation" forms may be filled out and sometimes given to an employee, an accompanying appraisal interview is infrequent. The exceptions are in organisations in which performance appraisals are considered more a communication's tool than a rating device. Where performance appraisal interviews are conducted implicit is, "What has this individual done well?," followed by "And therefore, what should he be able to do well?" The interview then should be able to elicit "And what would he have to learn or to acquire to be able to get the most from his capacities and achievements?" With positive focussing, weakness are then seen as limitations to what the subordinate himself can do well and wants to do, rather than as defects. A proper conclusion to a properly conducted appraisal interview is not on what the subordinate should do so much as on what should the organisation and superordinate do to capitalise on the subordinate's strengths and to minimise the effect of his weaknesses. In short, a successful appraisal interview ends with a communication, which has meaning for *both* subordinate and superordinate.

The start of communication is organisations must be to get the intended receiver himself to try to communicate. To reiterate, this requires a focus on (1) the impersonal but common task, (2) on the intended receiver's achievements, aspirations and values, and (3) the experience of accountability. Research has also revealed that communication will considerably facilitated if the superordinate makes it a point to be seen often by his subordinates informally and in helping ways.

Communication in organisations demands that masses, whether they be employees or students, share in the responsibility of decisions to the fullest possible extent. They must understand because they have been through it, rather than accept a decision because it has been explained to them. Effective communication is only in direct proportion to the involvement of those to be affected by any given decision. To be excluded is to be part of the problem, to be included is to be part of the solution.

The traditional defense of paternalism has always been "It's a complex organisation; it needs the expert, the man who knows best." But paternalism, as research into motivation, learning and perception has revealed, really can only work in a simple world. When people can understand what "Pater" does because they share his experiences and perceptions, then Pater can actually make the decisions for them. However, in our own exceedingly complex society, there is need for *shared* experiences in the decisions, or there will be no common perceptions, ergo, no communication, and, hence neither acceptance of the decisions, nor the ability to carry them out. The ability to understand presupposes prior communication. It presupposes agreement on meaning. The "Father knows best" syndrome, associated with an uncommonly large number of school administrators, is particularly resented by teachers. Since teachers have been entrusted with the professional responsibility of managing from 30 to 300 different young people each week, they feel entitled to full participation in professional decisions. We have seen what has happened since circa 1965 when teachers have not been given the opportunity to meaningfully participate in professional decision-making. Once isolated and scattered, teacher strikes are no longer so isolated nor scattered. The chief issue of these strikes is frequently as much, or more, concerned with teacher involvement in professional decision-making as over "bread-and-butter" issues. Indeed, the danger in some places now is not over the question whether teachers are to involved in professional decision-making but to what extent are *administrators* to be allowed to participate. To exchange one kind of autocracy for another can be no improvement. Instead, mutual respect and cooperation is needed. The theory and principles of communication are designed to facilitate this mutual respect and cooperation.

Exhibit 6.1 shows a communication system that was ratified by the academic staff of Prairie State College—a public, 2-year, comprehensive community college.

> As Exhibit 6.1 shows, the communication system was designed to ensure broad participation by all elements of the college community, and to ensure that communication flowed upwards. This was accomplished by assuring initially that the chairman of each committee be a member of the faculty and to have the majority of members on each committee a member of the faculty. Administrators serve as secretaries to each committee since they have secretarial help more readily available to them; but more importantly, this secretarial role results in faster action by the administration in support of faculty needs.
>
> The Committee on Campus Development and Improvement is not a decision-making body, except as decisions relate to the establishment of standing and/or ad hoc committees to meet the expressed needs of groups or individuals in the College Community. The CCDI will be responsible for selecting Committee members, following up of ideas that have been submitted to committees, receiving the minutes of committees for distribution to the College staff as a whole, assisting in the preparation of academic staff meeting agendas to insure that items which have gone through Committee reach the staff, and other activities which will assist in facilitating communications. The CCDI will insure that each idea or suggestion for campus development or improvement will be considered.
>
> Finally, the CCDI will keep minutes of their meetings and a log of all ideas submitted, date of submission, where idea was considered and final disposition of the idea.

**Exhibit 6.1**

18 September, 67

To: Academic Staff

From: Richard W. Hostrop and Glenn Schmitz

PROPOSED COMMUNICATIONS SYSTEM

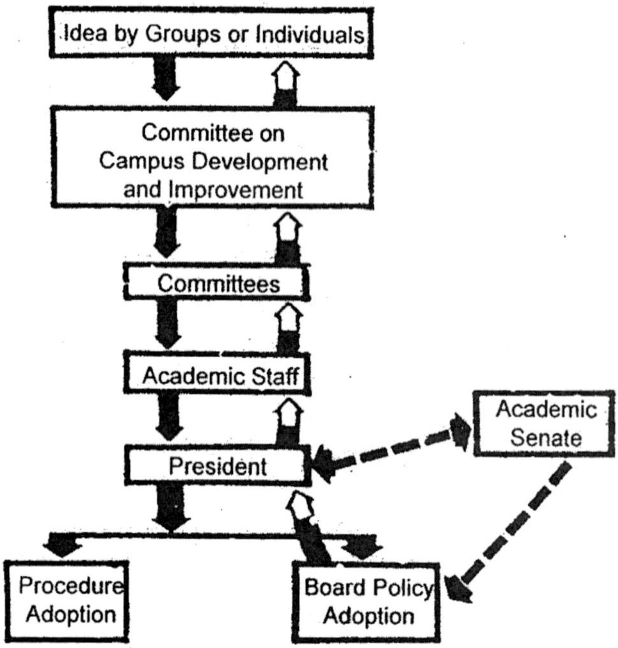


Ideas for campus development and improvement can be submitted by any group or individual in the College Community to the Committee on Campus Development and Improvement.

Committees which are formed will have a majority of faculty. A faculty member will be Chairman and an Administrator will be Secretary. Each committee will have one, but not more than one, Administrator. The foregoing procedures might be changed or modified depending upon expressions received by the Academic staff. The CCDI's final operating procedure is to be approved by the

Academic staff as a whole before the first idea or suggestion is considered by them.

The Committee on Campus Development and Improvement will consist of seven members. They will include the following:

| | |
|---|---|
| 1 Administrator | (appointed by the President) |
| 1 Student | (President of the Student Body) |
| 1 Non-academic staff | (elected by the non-academic staff) |
| 4 Faculty | (selected by the faculty) |

It is requested that each faculty member register his preference as to what the qualifications of the selected faculty should be. The following qualifications have been suggested:

- ❑ Two senators and two new faculty.
- ❑ Three senators and one new faculty.
- ❑ Two division Chairman and two faculty.
- ❑ Three faculty and President of the Academic Senate.
- ❑ Suggestion for some other combination (write in).

Please return any comments you might have on the proposal and your faculty membership preference to Mrs. Webber, non-academic library clerk in the Library no later than 1:00 p.m. on Tuesday, September 19th. Dr Hostrop and Mr. Schmitz will pick up the returns at that time, will review the returns and will report the results at the next Academic staff meeting.

## Comments

Finally, it is noteworthy that the final proposal to the academic staff was sent out under the joint auspices of the president of the college and the president of the academic senate as a *mutually* approved document.

In sum, there will be no communication if it is in conceived as going from "me" to "you". Communication only works from one member of "us" to another. Communication cannot exist without cooperation, cooperation cannot exist without dialogue. Therefore, there can be no communication without dialogue. Communication is not a *means* of organisation. Communication is a *mode* of organisation.

Communication is the most important aspect of managing education for results. As a social instrument, education is wrapped up in the process of communication. Thus, education is communication and communication is education.

What has preceded, and what follows in the remainder of this book assumes the reader's understanding that each topic presented is thoroughly permeated with communication as an integral and viable part of the topic.

# 7

# Operations Research

Delphi helps us to set goals and objectives. PERT helps us to implement them. PPBS shows us what each will cost. And *OR* (operations research) enables us to *analyse and evaluate* our proposed means for implementing them before taking real action.

Though operations research was developed by English scientists and mathematicians as early as 1938, in conjunction with World War II needs, it was not until 1959 that OR techniques were attempted in the field of education. This was some ten years after the economic sector has first extrapolated the war time concepts for peace time use. The Rand Corporation was the group to first see the applicability of OR techniques in education. Some of its members became intrigued with such educational problems as how to optimise the transportation routes of school buses in the interest of cutting costs. Other educational applications of OR procedures are discussed below.

While characteristics vary somewhat between OR models, the following three characteristics are common to most OR models:

1. The models take the form of an equation in which a measure of the system's overall performance is equated to a relationship between a set of controlled and uncontrolled aspects.

2. Users must be able to explicitly state both those variables which may be controlled and not-controlled.

3. All objectives must be quantifiable.

OR tools are of considerable aid in analysing a problem and developing alternative solutions. They can find and bring out the underlying patterns in the behaviour of an educational system and its environment, including those that have hitherto lain beyond the educational manager's field of vision or range of imagination. They can thus bring out alternative courses of action. They can show which factors are relevant (*i.e.*, facts) and which are irrelevant (*i.e.*, mere data). They can show the degree of reliability of the available data and what additional data are required to arrive at sound judgment. They can show what resources will be needed in any alternative courses of action, and what contribution from each component or function would be required. They can be used to show the limitations of each possible course of action, and the risks and probabilities of each. They can show what impact a given action would have on other areas, components and functions. They can show the relationship between input and output and the location and nature of 'bottlenecks". Finally, they can tie together the work and contribution of each function or component part with those of all the others and show this total impact on the behaviour and results of the entire educational system.

In essence the tools of OR are tools of information, and of information-processing, not of decision-making. They focus on possible alternative courses of action. They thus make possible decisions with a high degree of rationality with respect to futurity, risk and probability. This is the kind of information each manager needs as he sets out to achieve the objectives of his department so as to contribute to achieving the goals of the educational system as a whole.

OR are tools of systematic, logical, and mathematical analysis and synthesis. Thus, operations research is a 'system'. They are: *programming, simulation* and *queuing theory.* A library example will particularly be emphasised to illustrate these 3 tools at work. From this focussed example the reader should be able to extrapolate the principles to his own particular situation in any given educational area.

## OR as a System

As the reader continues to read, it should ever be borne in mind that what has preceded, and what follows throughout this chapter and the remainder of the book, is part of a total systems approach. The systems approach can be seen as a framework for organising complex problem situations for readier solutions.

It will be recalled that a system is a collection of pieces or elements which are related or dependent in some way. Consequently, it is useful to consider the whole set as an operational entity. A key word is systems analysis is *connectivity,* or relationships between elements. It is apparent, then, that systems are a fundamental part of any orderly process of thinking, since one must relate ideas in order to achieve a rational framework.

To show that systems analysis is a point of view, consider an ordinary fork. By itself, as a piece of formed metal, a fork is not a system, because no parts or relationships have been defined. A fork is a system, however, if it is interpreted as part of a place setting or when actually in use as an eating tool. Other simple illustrations of systems are children cutting with a pair of scissors or a boy using a fishing pole, line, leader, hook, and sinker to fish. Other complex systems which illustrate the interconnectedness and interdependencies of systems include the limbs and organs of the human body—or the processes in hospitals, schools and libraries.

Using a library as an example of a system, it is clear that a library must function as an integrated whole toward accomplishing goals and objectives which are designated for the total system. Although it is difficult to quantify an all-inclusive performance measure, specific objectives and their measurements should be established. Thus, as one system example, the objectives of library circulation, cataloguing, and reshelving is a subsystem of a library system designed to minimise loss of user time within the limitations of resources available.

As stated earlier, operations research is a collection of mathematical models for the solution of various types of complex problems. Alternate titles, sometimes used interchangeable, such as *management science or decision theory* have slightly different connotations from *operations research,* but all usually share certain important characteristics in common as listed below:

1. The problem is mathematically formulated and uses quantitative measurements for explicit variables.
2. An attempt is made to optimise or improve a set of one or more numerical values which represent the solution to a problem.
3. The scope is sufficiently broad to encompass a significant segment of the total problem environment. Interaction among several important decision variables is included in the model formulation.
4. Models take a systems point of view because they look at the relationship of different variables upon each other; this often implies a team approach or the interaction of several types of expertise.

Among the many different techniques which are collected under the heading of operations research, programming, simulation, and queuing theory are extremely useful to educational managers. Each of these management techniques are described briefly below.

## Programming

A manager must *programme* the resources which he controls in order to optimise the goals of his organisation within the environmental realities of his situation. In programming techniques, quantitative variables or activities are chosen which (1) express a reasonable range of strategic choices, (2) lend themselves to measurement of objectives, and (3) are limited by fixed conditions in the environment. Measurements of activity levels may be in such units as dollars, space, size, weight, or time.

Consider the case of a library which receives a given dollar budget to perform an academic service. The library decides to measure its total service by the amount of annual circulation. Activity variables are assigned to each different class of reading materials and/or customer services. An algebraic expression called the *objective function* adds the various activities in terms of their effect on circulation. Thus, objective functions quantify goal attainment in programming models. A set of algebraic expressions, called *constraints,* relates strategy combinations of activities to environmental limitations. For example, library service activities must be associated with budgetary dollars, supply of trained personnel, available space, and limits of user demand. Among strategy choices within a given budget would be *trade-offs* between more volumes and additional or faster services. If within reasonable ranges, the impact of any activity can be separated out from the impact of other activities (e.g., twice as many books take up twice the space), then conditions are satisfied for an important subclass known as *linear programming* or LP.

The mathematical key in linear programming is the linear equation. This is an equation which is drawn on a graph. The basic idea merely requires that its user know what the problem is and be able to state it in a way so that experts can shape the model. In simple, straight line problems any professional can solve his own problem (e.g., twice as much space will be needed for twice as many books). Mathematicians or systems analysts, with the aid of a computer, can solve the more complex problems.

Since a routine solution procedure is available for LP, but not for most other types of programming, a librarian must attempt to formulate his problem in accordance with the 3 linear conditions cited at the beginning of this section. The library LP illustrated above will determine the quantities of each service activity so as to maximize circulation for given budget, personnel or other limitations.

Linear programming has such further educational applications as scheduling students into classes; determining optimal numbers and hours of counsellors, custodians, cafeteria workers; and where to locate additional educational facilities, etc.

## Simulation

A *simulation* is an OR technique for reproducing or abstracting out, through a computer or role playing, a model of a system, subsystem, component, operation, or environment for predictive or instructional purposes.

Simulations can aid in the very important and frequently asked question by, managers, What would happen if ....? Answers to simulated situations reduce the need for voluminous management reports. Simulating "what if' situations leads to greater contact between line managers at all levels and between these managers and the staff managers.

Simulation, as an OR technique, permits the manager to learn from his mistakes without having to experience the consequences of those mistakes. It provides a means for bringing order and predictability out of seeming chaos of multiple variables. A unique advantage is the ability to forge ahead in time; and if the model is realistic, this glimpse of possible futures permits and educational system to evaluate and choose the most favourable of the many alternatives open to it. We have seen that the Delphi Technique is a means for *setting* goals and objectives. A simulation provides the means for *evaluating* how realistic, or even how desirable, certain goals and objectives may be—given the constraints of available funds, personnel space and time. Simulations make it possible to select *alternative* paths which hold particular promise for achieving system, institutional, and departmental goals and objectives.

Simulation is not a theory, nor is it even a solution technique in the usual sense; rather it is a methodology for experimentation and prediction. The actual definition of the word "simulate," is "to assume the appearance of, without the reality" according to *Webster's Collegiate Distionary.* Webster's definition captures the essence of the technique.

Having captured the appearance of reality in a model we want to "run" the model through time. Usually a large number of "dry runs" can be made in a fraction of the time required for one cycle of the "real thing". From a problem-solving standpoint it is necessary to observe the behaviour of the system over time. Simulation, then, increments time in terms of the variables and relationships of the system. In this way the simulation plays out the scenario which is representative of reality. The decision-maker can thus watch a replica of reality "pass by" and utilise what is learned as a basis for actual decisions.

In our primary example a few hours work on a library financial budget with a piece of paper, pencil, and adding machine may *simulate* many years of actual financial life. All planning is a form of simulation, since the future has not yet taken place. In our library example there is a special problem because the future is uncertain as to both quantities of library materials and relationships. One way to copy with this is to try out different combinations of possibilities by running multiple simulations. Suppose in the preparation of a library budget there are five possible levels for appropriation of funds, three different salary proposals, and five levels of service demand for each of six different classes of books. In order to represent all possible combinations of these factors 234,375 different budgets would have to be calculated. Such calculations would be out of the question by hand, although they might be feasible on a large computer. Even so, this illustration shows that it would not take much variety in combinations of uncertainties to exceed the capacity of even the largest computers. *Monte Carlo* is a simulation technique which can reduce such multiple simulations to a reasonable level.

Monte Carlo is named for the famous gambling casino in Monaco since this type of simulation procedure employs chance methods of selecting particular values for variables. It is a means whereby statistical sampling of value combinations of variable inputs replaces a simulation run for every combination. By accepting some statistical risk of error, a library manager may *infer* behaviour of his variable budgets from a Monte Carlo sample. In our example, the library manager must assign *probability* distributions of values for each of eight variables (appropriation, salary, and six classes of books). The output of his Monte Carlo simulation will show the probability distribution of values for resulting strategies and control items in the budget. The budgeter has succeeded in quantifying and systematising his original uncertainties.

Although Monte Carlo simulation requires a great deal of computation (which can be done by a computer), it is a powerful tool for organising and optimising the behaviour of complex systems.

Another example of the use of the Monte Carlo simulation in an educational setting is the perennial problem of ascertaining in advance the probability of course selections by high school and college students—with all the attendant implications for numbers of teachers needed, class size, location of classes, number of class periods, times to be scheduled, etc.

Other examples of computer-based simulations include such "what if' problems as simulating curricular changes in order to estimate the implications for staffing and facilities, PERTing, preparing budgets in the PPBS format, determining such items as the effect of certain policy variables relevant to decision making, and the functional relationships between policy variables and output variables are other examples of computer-based simulations.

Thus, the use of computer-based simulation techniques by educational systems and individual institutions makes it possible to (1) project future conditions, needs and outputs, (2) test the implications of new policies as related to intermediate and long-term goals, and (3) explore the effects of proposed changes on other components of the system—all in advance of making "real" decisions.

It should also be noted that not all simulations require powerful computers and sophisticated programmers. This is particularly true of the learning manager, *i.e.*, the teacher. Though there are computer-based learner-oriented simulations, particularly for business and economic courses, most *instructional* simulations are non-computer based. Moreover, there are a number of commercial non-computer based simulations appropriate to all levels of education—elementary school through graduate education.

Examples of non-computer based simulations are to be found particularly in history and the social sciences. Most of these simulations require "*role playing*". The participants assume parts and "act out" their roles in accordance with the 'rules' of the game. This is why simulations are sometimes known as *Gaming* or *Game Theory*. Among such non-computer based simulations are the political science games of NAPOLI and INTERNATION, the economic geography game of *Trade and Development,* and the U. S. history game *The Kansas/Nebraska Act.*

Unlike acting role players have no set lines, but instead are usually presented with a complex problem which they attempt to solve. As a result, participants gain insight into the complexity of human relationships (affective domain) as well as acquiring information (cognitive domain). Research has shown that the value of instructional simulations "appears to lie in their ability to clarify abstract relationships by presenting them on a more concrete level which students can experience directly, and in their power to influence students' attitudes."

Role playing simulations also lend themselves particularly well in such real life educational activities as assessing and improving student teaching performance and intern counselling performance. The capabilities of potential administrators can likewise be assessed and improved by simulating problem situations and studying their responses. As Don Bushnell says, "It is a short step from training administrators to the use of simulation for the actual operation of school systems."

Potential and practicing administrators can simulate collective bargaining sessions, student demands of various kind, preparing for trustees' meetings, and the like.

Potential and practicing teachers can simulate the conditions of the "open classroom" by assuming both student and teacher roles. Teachers can assume other teaching roles such as "lecturer' or "systems designer" (teaching and learning via measurable performance objectives), etc. And teachers, like administrators, can use simulation techniques to better comprehend the strengths and weaknesses of collective bargaining.

Besides computer-based and role playing simulations there is one other type of simulation widely used for educational purposes, *psychomotor* simulations. Two brief examples will serve to illustrate: the use of driver education and fight training simulators used in advance of actually driving or flying.

In sum, simulation techniques provide the manager with a means of "seeing' some of the consequences of proposed decisions before taking them. It aids the manager to answer the very important question, "What if . . .?" It provides students with the opportunity to "experience" historical events, notable current events, running a business, or to learn psychomotor skills. It provides a means for administrators and teachers to crawl inside each other's role, as well as their students, in addition to their own. Thus, simulation techniques can provide a means to gain insight and skills without the risk that action in a real situation would entail.

## Queuing Theory

The third, and last, OR technique this chapter discusses is *queuing theory.* The theory deals with the nature of waiting lines, particularly, but not exclusively, as such lines relate to people. It is an important member of a class of models which are used to minimise the total of two sets of costs which move in opposite directions. In education one set of costs generally pertains to financial expenditures, the other to human costs of lost time or learning.

Queuing theory can aid in solving such problems as how to optimise the ration between waiting time of commuters and parking attendant personnel costs at university parking lots; defining optimal levels of storage of food for cafeterias and of custodial supplies for bathrooms and maintenance purposes; defining optimal staffing levels for various hours of cafeteria, custodial, and book store personnel; and other similar situations where queues cause "hurry up and wait" problems.

The important parameters of any queuing system are the average number of *arrivals* for service per time period and the average number of *services* which could be completed per time period. It is, of course, impossible to schedule service to precisely match arrivals because individual arrivals vary unpredictably from the average. Thus, idle costs, as in a school or college cafeteria, cannot be totally eliminated, but rather only minimised. Given a cafeteria (or any other queuing environment) with a particular combination of *average arrival rate* (symbol $\lambda$) and *average service* completion rate (symbol $\mu$), the question is, how many serving stations will result in the least total system cost? In practice this question is answered by calculating costs and income in hourly units and then determining the cost/profit ratio.

For example, in analysing costs of operating a cafeteria it is not enough to just calculate the sum of the cost of a cashier station per hour times the number of serving stations. The cost of waiting customers (and those who leave before getting served!) must also be added per hour. The latter is the cost of lost goodwill plus lost time per customer per hour times the average number of customer in the system (system $\angle$). Customers "in the system" are the sum of those waiting and those being served. If the statistical distribution pattern of arrivals and services is known, it often is possible to compute $\angle$ mathematically from given $\lambda$ and $\mu$.

## OR at the Ohio State University Library

Charles L. Hubbard, Getald Johoda and Robert Torter worked on a problem common to many libraries—public as well as academic – *viz.*, to determine the optimal number of duplicate volumes which should be available for high demand readings. In public libraries this high demand is for 'best sellers," in academic libraries it is assigned readings and reserve books. Alternately, the model developed provides rationing rules for coping with high demand for other library resources, *e.g.*, audiovisual materials and equipment—and personnel.

Multi-channelling queuning was used to determine expected times in a reading programme, and from this a policy for social cost minimisation was developed.

In a library queue, *arrivals* are readers who seek a high demand volume. *Serving stations* are the number of available duplicate copies of a volume in high demand. A *service* consists of reading a desired or required book.

It was found at the Ohio State University Library that $\angle$ (average number of readers in the system) based upon $\lambda$ (average number of readers arriving per hour for a particular high demand reading book) and $\mu$ (average number of non-waiting persons who complete this reading per hour) were not being well served. There was too much waiting for high demand volumes. This fact, in the view of the investigators, resulted in too many lost learning opportunities. They concluded that the "cost of reader time has generally been neglected in library planning, whereas it is actually the most significant decision variable."

In support of the investigations' conclusions they found examples of "impatient' behaviour by readers. Some potential readers would not join a queue if more than X number of persons were also waiting. There is a "discouragement factor" which increases the probability of reader refusal to wait as the length of a queue increases. Then there is "complete reneging" by some potential users who refuse to wait at all if the book desired is not available immediately. "Impatient" readers may return later or never come back. Thus, in the latter instance, there is the serious imperative of how to prevent lost education. If a reader has not had his need met, will he come back at all? Shifting a bit, by way of another illustration, if a student voluntarily comes for counselling help but all counsollers are busy, will he come back? How much learning loss or mental health loss can society afford are sober questions which educators must give serious attention to. The application of queuing theory is one relatively in-expensive way for mitigating potential learning and mental hygiene losses—and other kinds of losses.

At Ohio State University, as a result of the queuing study, library personnel were in a position to better schedule the time of their staff, to make additional purchase of high demand volumes, and to establish closer partnership relationships with the teaching faculty.

The Ohio State University Library queuing study also has important implications for planning new library facilities, and other facilities, where queuing is a factor, *e.g.*, cafeterias and book stores, and location and number of counselling offices.

In this chapter we have discussed three OR techniques: programming, simulation, queuing. These three decision-making models have significant educational implications as well as applications. These three elements of systems analysis will become increasingly important in the immediate years ahead. Educational managers will have to acquire a systems point of view in face of today's traditional 'common sense' view. But as managers shift from the traditional to the new, as they begin to use such system models as Delphi, PERT, PPBS, OR, MIS, etc., present practice should operate alongside new practice until the new practice is clearly understood and accepted as the better way. Old practice serves as a "fail safe" practice even when it is little more than a "rule of thumb" practice.

Finally, a word about the influence of electronic computers is necessary to view the whole subject of systems analysis in perspective. Expensive calculations are required for many useful programming, simulation, or queuing models for large systems. This is why OR sometimes is referred to as a "computer-oriented decision-making system." To make complex OR calculations it thus takes a "systems analyst," a computer programmer and a computer.

Though most academic managers will not require sophisticated system analysts' skills, nor sophisticated programming skills, it will be necessary to acquire a modern systems point of view. The acquisition of a systems point of view is not difficult to acquire once educators become familiar with its logic and its theories, its techniques and its tools.

# 8

# Management Information Systems

*MIS* (Management Information System) can be defined as "an organised method of providing management with information needed for decisions, when it is needed and in a form which aids understanding and stimulates action." From this definition we can see that Delphi, PERT, PPBS and OR are some of the aids which make management information systems possible. But in themselves they do not represent a *total* management information system. MIS strives to integrate these, and other procedures, into a total and unified system.

**Levels of Information**

In an educational environment information is needed at three levels and can be divided thusly: (1) information for operation, (2) information for control, and (3) information for management decisions and planning. These three functions of information somewhat parallel the three functions of management: *administering, planning and leading.*

The lowest level, *information for operations,* consists of the information needed for clerical functions—payroll, financial transactions, student records, and the like. Here good administration is needed.

The middle level, *information for control,* involves information needed to implement administrative decisions and policies. Two examples will serve to illustrate. It is decided that no department shall exceed its supplies budget. Information concerning each department's expenditures for supplies is maintained on a current basis, and controls are established and operate in such a way that orders for supplies in excess of budgeted amounts are automatically rejected. Or student performance minimums are established for promotion from one class to the next with the information used to control students promotion. Effective administration and planning can ensure the adequacy and implementation of information for control.

The highest level, *management decision and planning,* requires the skills of a good planner and, more often than not, a good leader as well. To illustrate, if the chief executive officer determines from planning reports that operating funds will increase the subsequent year by only 3 per cent, but student enrolment is projected to increase by 9 per cent, he and his board are faced with some very difficult decisions—especially, if in addition, the faculty is demanding a 7 per cent increase in salaries and a 5 per cent reduction in class size. The planner must simulate various factors to determine the effects of such constraints and such proposals—including, of course, investigating various possibilities for securing additional funds. This single complex illustration shows the very real need for gathering as much information as possible, and then use such OR techniques as simulation to determine the effects that such inputs will have on the outputs of the total organisation. This will affect such decisions as what is offered to the faculty in the process of negotiations, what alternative "trade-offs" may be put forth, *e.g., increased* class size rather than a reduction of class size, and a salary increase of perhaps 4 per cent rather than the 7 per cent asked.

An information system designed to serve as an aid to management in operating, controlling, and for decisions and planning has two main features:

1. A data acquisition and storage system to maintain orderly records on variables important to the decision-making process and a convenient recall system to make information dervied from the file accessible to the decision-maker.
2. A logical structure to identify what variables are to be maintained in the file, the computations to be made on these variables, and how the results of these computations are to be used in the decision process.

The logical structure, called a *model of the process,* is central to the design of a management information system. Likewise, except for the most simple situations (an enrolment of under about 500 students), a computer is mandatory to retrieve the information management needs.

## ADP

ADP (Automatic Data Processing), a term almost synonymous to the layman for the computer, has revolutionised technological societies. Because of its central importance to MIS we pause to focus on this remarkable "idio-savant". Invented in 1945, introduced for scientific and engineering use in 1951, in a form designed for business applications in 1954, and used for educational purposes beginning circa 1960, the computer, in less than 20 years, now accounts for the dollar equivalent of more than 10 per cent of all new plant and equipment expenditures in the United States!

The electronic computer and, in particular, the information theory and technology that have made it possible, represent one of the most important technological advances of our times. These technologies make it possible to build machine systems for handling information for any purpose we wish. It is this—the fundamental nature of the innovation—that makes the computer such an important example of technological change, profoundly affecting business, industrial, military and educational management decision-making.

Significant improvements of ADP (sometimes also called EDP for Electronic Data Processing) are continually occurring: *e.g.*, pneumatic card-transport systems; improvements in optical scanning devices making it possible for direct machine reading of documents; improvements in voice-input and response devices; more sophisticated visual display device; greater use of electronic light pens on plasma screens for modelling and response purposes; newer peripheral devices expressly designed to facilitate the exchange of information between the computer system and its human users. In short, the computer desk console, with complementary peripheral devices, will become nearly as common by the year 2000 as the manager's telephone is today, Similar consoles will be found in homes not too many years later.

Properly programmed, ADP automatically provides key management personnel not only with exception reporting but with *adaptive dissemination*—a system which has on record a profile of each manager indicating the kinds of events he should know about and the functions for which he is responsible. Adaptive dissemination provides a powerful means for implementing the *situational theory of management*—approaching situations from an orderly and scientific basis rather than from a "rule of thum" basis.

ADP focuses on programmes rather than on traditional departmental boundaries. Decision-makers, thus, are given the opportunity to consider problems in their entirety rather than as segmental pieces.

ADP enables processes from originator to receiver to be reduced cost-wise and time-wese. But one example of things to come is a Japanese newspaper company which now transmits its newspaper directly into the home by television.

What all these new ADP developments mean is work that today seems economically out of reach will, in a very few years, be uneconomic if conducted in any other way.

The MIS manager, heading up the data processing department, must be included in the councils of top management itself so as to ensure that management decisions are based upon the best pertinent management information available.

Educational managers, themselves, will become programmers made possible by ADP languges now available much like every day language.

ADP programmes now incorporate self-correcting features permitting the machine to recognize its own malfunctions, correct them, or to select a different path to solve a problem.

There now are heuristic and self-organising systems that allow machines to develop their own problem solving methods best suited to the management analysis of a given problem at hand. In some instances the decision-making is made by the computer. Increasingly, machines are "thinking" in the accepted meaning of the word.

As has already been suggested, to successfully PERT beyond approximately 30 activities, the use of the computer becomes necessary insurance to assure accuracy and to minimise time required for preparation. To prepare the multi-varied calculations of a budget in the PPBS format, or to computer for an OR model, demands the aid of ADP equipment. To effectively manage an educational system with an enrolment much beyond 500 students also demands ADP aid.

It is essential that every professional educator obtain rudimentary knowledge of ADP systems as a means for making better management decisions. This knowledge is essential not only in order to better understand the nature of PERT, PPBS, OR, and other computer-based management techniques and tools, but to better comprehend the use of the computer in the basic instructional areas as well. Administrators and faculty must become thoroughly familiar with the cost/benefits of CAI (Computer Assisted Instruction) and CMI (Computer Managed Instruction).

The instructional and counselling aspects of ADP systems will become publicly more visible in the years ahead than the planning and decision-making aspects of ADP. Project PLATO, developed at the University of Illinois, shows great promise for bringing instructional costs down via use of the computer to a competitive level with the cost of teachers, and, in some instances, of increasing learning and retention as well.

Though computers are not likely to ever completely replace teachers they, nonetheless, will be able to provide not only highly individualised but highly personalised teaching. Teachers who do not teach like a machine will not be replaced, administrators who do not administer like a machine will not be replaced; but those who do will and ought to be. What has occurred in Palo Alto and Urbana, and what likely will occur elsewhere, is greater cybernation–greater integration of human and non-human resources, working in complementary tandem to achieve system goals and objectives.

Finally, it is to be realized that ADP is the tool of MIS; and PERT, PPBS, and OR are some of its techniques, MIS serves to integrate the theories, techniques, and tools of total information for optimal use by decision-makers.

**Inaugurating a MIS Programme**

It is not possible to develop a MIS programme unless managers themselves are willing to devote time to the effort. MIS cannot be inaugurated by systems and information technologists working by themselves, or only with personnel at the operations level. The development requires a joint effort of management personnel and information specialists. Only management—the decision-makers—know what decisions it must make and what information it needs for decision-making. Indeed, as William M. Zani says, "An effective system, under normal conditions, can only be born of a carefully planned, rational design that looks down from the top, the natural vantage point of the managers who will use it. This means that unless there is interest and participation by the chief executive in developing a management information system there is little likelihood that a viable management information system can be developed in an organisation. This becomes especially evident as one looks at the specific steps necessary for the successful development of MIS in an organization.

1. Objectives of the MIS system are specified.
2. Fixed MIS system requirements are specified.
3. The MIS system is developed as efficiently as possible to fulfil the organisation goals and objectives.
4. Compromises are made as necessary.
5. The MIS system is tested.
6. MIS revision is made as necessary.
7. MIS is implemented.
8. MIS is evaluated.
9. Steps 1-8 are reviewed quarterly.

Though not wholly discrete steps, in general, the tasks should be performed in the order indicated. Figure 8.1 shows how a once inaugurated management information system serves to coordinate the activities of an educational organisation.

Managers at various levels of an organisation require different items of management information even though the actual development of MIS must begin at the very top. The chief executive requires information of a type that is not required of anyone under him for making decisions concerning the educational system, or the institution, as a whole. Yet, *some* of the information he needs is also needed by lower level managers.

**Figure 8.1**
**MIS as System Coordinator**

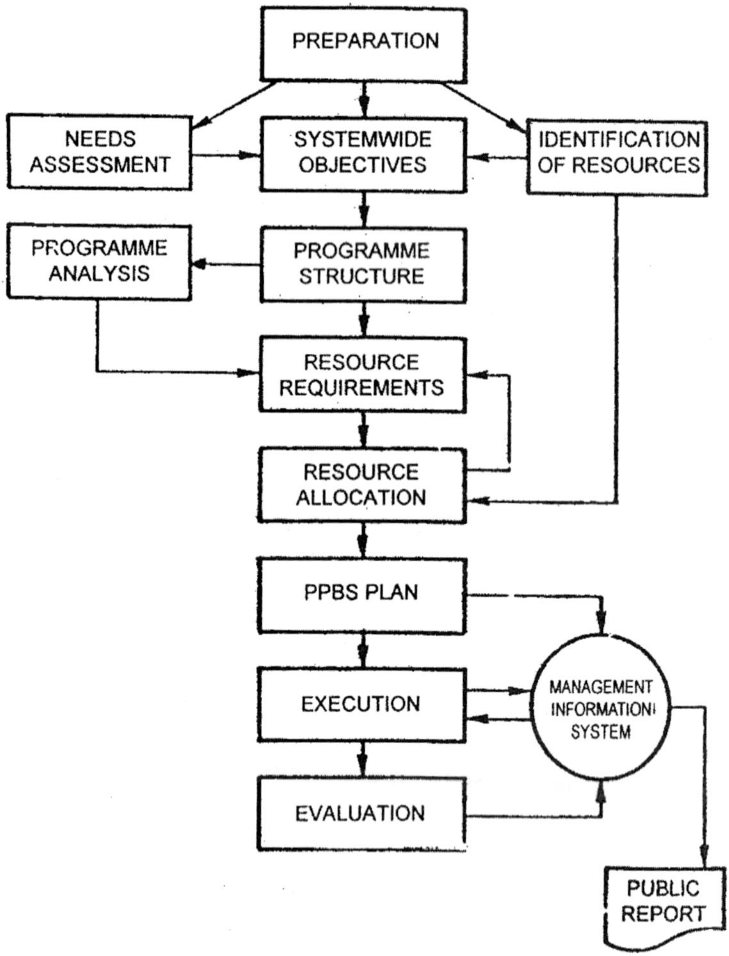

Information which is needed is not always held in common. Still there must be interfacing between all levels of managers so that all information available to an ogranisation can be plugged into as needed. The manager of instruction's information needs are somewhat different than the manager of students, and usually considerably different than the manager of business. Counsellors, educational technologists, librarians, and teaching faculty have still different kinds of information needs even though, obviously, there are close linkages. To ensure appropriate linkages and interfacings each superordinate must insist on MIS summaries from his immedate subordinates.

The fact that there are close associations of information needs throughout an educational structure requires a *unified* management information system. Thus, there must be a common agreement as to data elements with respect to mumbering, titling, summary description, and additional definitions and/or comments. Uniform element numbers are used throughout the system, and the MIS structure typically is organised around six major information areas: Student Related Elements, Staff Related Elements, Curricular Components, Facilities, Finance, Major Equipment. Preferably, the organisation's MIS will tie in to a larger external group, *e.g.,* a consortium so that data gathered can be compared with like educational organisations. WICHE (Western Interstate Commission for Higher Education), headquartered in Boulder, Colorado, is one of the more notable examples of a consortium whose major effort to date has been to introduce MIS among its members. An extract of a WICHE document is shown in Exhibit 8.1. This exhibit is an example of a form designed to assure uniform element numbers, titles, summary descriptions, and additional definitions and/or comments for ready computer retrieval. The "USES" columns simply refers to various consortium needs with respect to reporting. Consortium arrangements aid participants to compare notes so as to help improve one another's MIS. Moreover, it provides a means for highlighting wide deviations from the norm for analysis as to the probable cause of such deviations.

The preceding suggests that an educational system

contemplating a modern management information system would do better to observe developed systems in similar organisations rather than make an extensive feasibility study of its own.

## Data Requirement for Management Decisions

Some further examples of data information banked in a computer will suggest the kinds of information that can aid the decision-maker in making decisions. There are three areas to be considered:

*Data relating input to output* is information needed by every manager. There will be different emphases by the nature of each manager's function. Still, there are certain common input/output concerns by the mere fact of common organisational goals and objectives. Some examples include:

the cost per student per year in particular fields of study or grade levels

the cost per diploma or degree in particular fields of study

the cost of adding students to a particular field of study

the cost of programmer at particular levels of quality

the cost of expanding existing programmes or institutions

the cost of establishing new programmes or institutions

beneficial side effects on the system itself

relationship between inputs and their associated costs and outputs and their associated benefits

reletionship between costs and sources of funding

values added to the student, knowledge and society.

*Information system and subsystems* are identifiable even though an educational system can be considered as a single information system. Subsystems should be developed separately with integration provided where subsystems overlap. The data of all subsystems must be defined with management use in mind, and the data should be stored in such a manner that data in all of the subsystems may be readily retrieved and related to each

**Exhibit 8.1**

*Data Element Dictionary*
*Student Related Elements Section*
*Personal Date*

____________
*(Date)*

*Page: 1*

| *No.* | *Data Element Title* | *Summary Description* | *Additional Definition and /or Comment* | *Uses* | | | |
|---|---|---|---|---|---|---|---|
| | | | | *TU* | *H* | *III* | *IV* |
| 1 | Student Name | Lagal name of student | | T | | | |
| 2. | Student Number | A number to uniquely identify each individual student | The student number will uniquely identify each student in attendance at a given institution. When the student number is coupled with a number uniquely identifying each institution of higher education, it will be possible to uniquely identify each individual student among all students in the nation. The student number may be a social security number. | T | R | R | |
| 3. | Social Security number | | May serve as a student number. Highly preferred. | | | | R |
| 4 | Sex | | | T | R | R | R |
| 5. | Date of Birth | Month, Day, Year of Birth | | T | | | R |
| 6. | Citizenship | An indication of whether the student is or is not a U. S. citizen. | | T | R | | R |

other. The major information subsystems appear to be the following:

Information components related to *output*

Instructional Programme

Research Programme

Community Services Programme.

Information subsystems related to *input*.

Student Records

Personnel Records

Facilities

Major Supporting equipment

Finance.

*Identifying and measuring output* may include such quantitative and qualitative student outputs as the following:

*Instructional Programme*

A.D.A. or F.T. E. students

student credit hours

student contact hours (by level)

academic awards (diplomas, degrees, certificates)

quantitative measures of academic achievement

rate of academic promotion or of employment

peer judgments

characteristics of first employment

degree of success in employment

rate of acceptance of students as transfers to higher institutions of education

rate of participation in academic, community, civic and political affairs

degree of conformance to institutional objectives

rate of salvage of disadvantaged learners

rate of salvage of "unemployables"

rate of admission to apprenticeship programmes

degree of user satisfaction with the institution

rate of graduates placed in national fellowship programmes

rate of elections of graduates to learned societies.

*Research Programme*

Research findings and application (new knowledge and technical advancement)

awards for research findings

social contributions of research

*Community Services Programme*

solutions to community and regional problems: economic, industrial, social (research output can apply here, also)

cultural enrichment programmes (concerts, film series, art exhibits, etc.)

issues programmes (speakers, forums, panels, olebates, etc.)

avocational offerings (hobbies and special interests)

MIS is in its early stages in education, so therefore still "crude." However, even crude analysis provider the promise of being highly beneficial by pointing out probable consequences of alternatives. In other words, it is better to be "crudely right that precisely wrong".

Difficulties with regard to human relations are a greater block toward the establishment of MIS than are the technical difficulties. To resolve the relationship between operating systems and management information systems there must be *communication.*

# 9

# Labour and Leisure

## The Origin of the Opposition

*Exposition*—Labour and leisure were two things in Greece, they still are two things in modern society, but they should be one. The origin of the opposition was in Grecian society composed of the free and the slave.

Of all the antitheses in education and in life, probably the most deep-seated is that between labour and leisure. So we have one education for utility and another education for culture. The values of utility and culture, being first isolated from each other, end by becoming opposed to each other. The initial isolation of values from each other and the final opposition of values to each other reflect, as we saw, a division within social life itself. The very terms, "useful labour," and "leisure," show this. Just suppose the different members of a community equally laboured for a livelihood and equally enjoyed a cultivated leisure! There would not be two educations,—one for utility and one for culture; one professional and industrial, the other liberal. There would be only one education contributing to both ends. The only question would concern how effectively it could be done. Some instructional materials might indeed contribute chiefly to utility, and others to culture, but care would be exercised to secure the maximum of overlapping: the cultural education would contribute also to the efficiency and enjoyment of work, and the useful education would produce emotional and intellectual habits procuring a worthy cultivation of leisure.

Labour is a necessity. It supplies the resources of living. There is nothing about it that should lead to the neglect or attempt of the kind of education preparing for it. Such neglect is due to a division of social classes which should not exist. It may be claimed that getting a living is material and that enjoying leisure is higher; it may also be claimed that material interests are engrossing, insubordinate, striving to usurp the place of higher ideal interests. Let the claims be admitted! Still, the solution would not be to neglect useful education, leading to evil results flourishing in obscurity. It should be to exercise scrupulous care to train for the useful pursuits, while keeping them in their place. But let useful education be identified with the interests of an inferior social class, then it suffers from both neglect and contempt. It is society, not necessity, that rigidly identified work with material interests and leisure with ideal interests.

There is nothing inevitable about such a division of education into two kinds as we have. How it grew up in Greek life as a social distinction and was thence wrought into educational philosophy can be traced. Greek society was divided into two classes; the one had to labour for a living, the other did not. The one class was slave, the other was free. The slave laboured both for himself and for the superior class. The time of the slaves was occupied practically, that of the free was spent intellectually. The social status of the slaves made their training servile, that of the free made their education liberal and intrinsically higher.

The educational formulations made over two thousand years ago to meet social situations have been influential. They deserve special notice. Aristotle's psychology and politics will reveal their nature, and so will be briefly sketched.

In the scale of animate existence, man occupies the highest place. In part he is like the plants and animals, and in part not. He is like the plants in having a nutritive and reproductive soul, and like the animals in having a nutritiue, reproductive and mother soul. He is unlike the plants and animals, and so distinctively human, in having a national soul, existing to behold the spectacle of the universe. The true end of man is the fullest possible realisation of this distinctive human prerogative. The proper life of man is observation, meditation, speculation, pursued as an end in itself. Furthermore, the vegetative and animal soul of man is controlled by his rational soul; the lower elements of his nature, the appetites and the motor impulses, are in themselves greedy, insult ordinate, lovers of excess, aiming at their own satiety; they observe moderation, obey the law of the golden mean, and serve desirable ends only as they are subjected to the rule of reason.

Even among those living a life of reason there is a distinction of inferior and superior. The free citizen is inferior to the pure thinker. The free citizen leads a life accompanied by reason as he devotes himself to the public life of his community sharing in the management of its affairs, and winning personal honour and distinction. His activity in his civic relations retains some of the taint of practice, of external instrumental doing. Civic activity and excellence need the help of others; one cannot engage in public life by himself. But this need for others betrays the infection of the material things of life. All needs and desires imply lack, privation, and dependence on something else for completion. The pure thinker is not so. He devotes himself to scientific inquiry and philosophical speculation. His life makes reason its own medium; he works in reason, not simply by it. Such a purely intellectual life one carries on by himself, in himself. Such intellectual assistance as others afford is accidental rather than intrinsic. In the life of theory, in knowing, in knowing for the sake of knowing, irrespective of any application, reason finds its own full manifestation, is independent and self-sufficing. Such is Aristotle's theoretical psychology.

Turning now to his practical politics, what do we find! The same views are reflected in the classes of men and in the organisation of human society. The function of reason as the law of life can operate in a comparatively few. Vegetative and animal functions dominate the masses; bodily appetite and passion overpower their feeble and inconstant intelligence. Lacking reason, which alone constitutes a final end, such persons are not truly ends in themselves. Like physical tools and plants and animals, they are means for attaining ends beyond themselves, though, unlike them, they have enough intelligence to execute with discretion the tasks committed to them. Thus, some men are slaves by nature, means for the ends of others. These are the class of natural slaves, not made so by social convention, and not necessarily coincident, of course, with the class of actual slaves.

In such a divided society the great body of free artisans are worse off in one important respect than even the slaves. Like slaves, they are given up to the service of ends external to themselves, but, unlike domestic slaves, they do not enjoy intimate association with the free superior class.

Women, moreover, are classed with slaves and craftsmen. They, too, are animate instrumentalities of reproduction, and of production of the means for a free rational life. Slaves, artisans, and women labour for the means of subsistence for themselves and for their superiors. Thus, the latter, being adequately equipped with intelligence, may live the worthy life of leisurely concern with things intrinsically worthwhile. And so, means become menial, and service becomes servile. The worthy life of the few is conditioned by the unworthy life of the many. Making a living unfits for true living, has so inherent rational meaning, and detracts from the time and energy available for ideal interests.

Turning from Aristotle's psychology and politics with their divisions to his theory of education, what do we find? Exact correspondence. As there are two kinds of occupation, or "arts," the servile and the free, so there are two kinds of education, the base or mechanical, and the liberal or intellectual. The base education consists in training persons to do things, to use tools. Thus, personal service is rendered and physical commodities are turned out. Such training is a matter of habituation and technical skill; it is acquired through repetition and assiduity in practice, not through the awakening and nurturing of thought.

But a liberal education aims to train intelligence for its proper office: to know. The less education is concerned with the practical affairs of making and producing, the more it engages intelligence. The less activity has to do with physical things or with the body, the more mental it is. The more mental it is, the higher, the more independent, the more self-sufficing it is. Hence, the only truly liberal or free education is that which makes for power to know as an end in itself, without reference to the practice of even civic duties.

An instructive instance of Aristotle's sharp distinction between mental and liberal education is in his treatment of what we call the "fine" arts,—music, painting, sculpture. The practice, but not the enjoyment, of these he classifies with the menial arts. They all involve physical agencies, constant practice, and external results. Take music, for example. How far should the young be practiced in the playing of instruments? His answer is, enough to appreciate music, but not to produce it professionally. When professional production is the aim, music sinks from the liberal level. "One might then as well teach cooking," says Aristotle. Thus, even the freeman's enjoyment of fine art depends upon the hireling who has subordinated the development of his own personality to attaining skill in mechanical execution.

***Comment***—It would perhaps have capped the climax of Dr. Dewey's argument had he gone on the give Aristotle's conception of God as pure form without any material element at all, pure realisation without any remaining potentiality, the thinker not of the material existence but of his own thoughts, not knowing the world and by the world unknown, yet attracting all things toward himself as end even as the beloved attracts the lover.

One may question at this point Dr. Dewey's genetic mode of refuting a position and his social explanation of psychological and philosophical views. It is suggested that Aristotle held the views he did because he was rationalising the kind of society in which he lived and believed. It is also suggested that views which were the effect of one kind of society are no longer tenable when the social pattern changes. Both of these positions are open to question. A psychologist and a philosopher may hold views independent of the economic and social conditions of which he is a part. Else how would progress through social planning be possible? Else how could the process of thought be free? Else how could a man be ahead of his times? This is not to suggest that a man's thinking is wholly independent of the times in which he lives, far from it; it is only to suggest that a man's thinking is not wholly dependent upon the times in which he lives. Some thinking is rationalising, conformative; some thinking is creative, reformative. Suppose Lincoln, facing modern slavery, had been a rationaliser!

Now thinking that arises under one set of social conditions may be true as representing ideals, and so may carry over to other social conditions unlike themselves. Euclid's geometry has not been proven false by Riemann and Lobatchevski; it has only been supplemented by new conceptions concerning the nature of space; the changing social conditions have had little to do with it; the changing intellectual conditions have had such to do with it. Ideas arising under conditions of slavery say have truth under conditions of freedom. Aristotle's conception of the soul may have validity under modern democratic conditions; many opponents of slavery think that it has. It is no refutation of his psychology to say we no longer believe in slavery.

And similarly concerning liberal and technical education. The distinction between them is not wiped out by the extinction of Greek slavery. A liberal education is no longer that intended for freemen; it is still that which makes men free. A technical education is no longer that intended for slaves; it is still that which enables men to earn a better living. Whether liberal, and technical, education should be two things or one thing cannot be settled by the lapse of Greek slavery. Very likely each man's education should be liberal at the base and technical at the apex, but the conclusion does not follow automatically from the change from Greek aristocratic to modern democratic conditions. Modern conditions themselves may and do need changing!

In this connection it may be recalled that the Greek Sophists were the first Western pragmatists in education. They were "humanists"; they made man the measure of all things; they taught the practical arts of public speaking, domestic economy how to think and how to act, to the noble youth of Greece. They rejected ideal changeless truths and standards of conduct. Their theory was a form of practice. And they arose under social and economic conditions similar to those of Socrates, Plato and Aristotle. And their views too survive and have their modern adherents. Here the original argument, if accepted, would tend to undermine pragmatism itself!

The views here presented are in line with those of both a classical scholar and of a contemporary philosopher. One writes:

"The most important part of the material with which he [Plato] had to deal in his metaphysical or logical investigations does not vary from age to age or from one country to another. The fundamental characteristics of the processes of rational thinker are the same always and everywhere. So are the processes of sense perception. So are the physical processes of the material world; 'fire burns both here and is Persia,' as Aristotle says. So is the nature of numbers and figures, which the science of mathematics investigates. Much more, or course, is known about these things is some period than in others. But the material from which the investigation starts is the same at all times." The same is not true, as Field points out, for moral and political speculation. Aristotle's speculations, of course, embrace both the meta-physical and the political. They partly are and partly are not due to the social conditions of his period.

Likewise, Morris Cohen defends the view that values and historical existence are in a sense independent of each other.

## The Present Situation

***Exposition***—The simple fact is that the present situation in both life and education is a continuation of the Greek situation, despite certain social changes. Let us see.

Aristotle simple described without confusion and with sincerity the life before him. But for this his conception would be just personal, a more or less interesting historical curiosity, in illustration of the lack of sympathy or the amount of pedantry co-existent at times with extraordinary intellectual gifts, and could be dismissed as such. The actual social situation has greatly changed since his day: legal serfdom has been abolished; democracy has spread; and science and general education have been extended, not only through schools but also through books, newspapers, travel, and general intercourse. Despite these changes, however, our situation is enough like his situation to merit criticism. His point of view helps us to see ourselves as we are. We too have an educational cleavage dependent on a social cleavage. We too distinguish between culture and utility in education because our society has a learned and an unlearned class, a leisure and a labouring class, a class concerned with intellectual things and controlling others and a class concerned with practical pursuits, without aesthetic appreciation, with a minimum of self-directives thought, being controlled by others.

Be it said there is a right and a wrong in Aristotle. He has certainly permanently right in holding that whatever activity deprives free persons of excellence is mechanical, or, in his words: "any occupation or art or study deserves to be called mechanical if it renders the body or soul or intellect of free persons unfit for the exercise and practice of excellence." How much more this statement means if all persons are free! If most men and all women are unfree by nature, a mechanical training for them involved for the Greeks neither intellectual confusion nor moral hypocrisy. But we say all are free by nature, and then provide a mechanical training for the many, depriving them of sharing a worthy life. Our mental confusion and moral hypocrisy remain!

In another respect Aristotle was conditionally right. He held that mercenary and physically injurious pursuits were mechanical, or, in his words: "All mercenary pursuits as well a those which degrade the condition of the body are mechanical, since they deprive the intellect of leisure and dignity." He mistakenly held here that all mercenary pursuits are mechanical; they were in his day; they usually are in our day; but they do not have to be so. His mistake was in taking a social custom for a natural necessity. If gainful pursuits do as a matter of fact deprive the intellect of its exercise and dignity, then indeed are they mechanical, as he said. It profits us nothing to improve on Aristotle's theory and continue the Greek practice of enslaving the intellects of the many. We say we have a better conception than his of the relations of mind and matter, mind and body, intelligence and social service; we say, contrary to his view, that the realms of matter, body and society, are the proper fields for intellectual self-expression; but our theory is no better than his if our practice remains the same as his; it is better only if the intellects of free persons are freed by their occupations in education and in life.

What was Aristotle's error? It lay in assuming a necessary separation between the free and the slave, understanding and skill, culture and utility, productivity and self-direction, knowledge and practice. We hardly better matters by correcting his theory while tolerating a social state of affairs which generated and sanctioned his theory. Nay, rather, we lose instead of gain by changing from serfdom to citizenship, if our main prize thereby is the increased efficiency of human tools. What boots it to think of intelligence, not with Aristotle, as the organ of pure knowledge, but as the organ of control of nature through action, if we remain content that workers be ignorant and enslaved while remote scientists and captains of industry alone exercise intelligent control? Train the many for skill in production and the few for ornamental knowledge—this is what we do. If responsible for this practice, we cannot honestly criticise the division of life into separate functions and of society into separate classes. We may think with the moderns but we act with the Greeks.

To transcend the Greek philosophy of education and of life, three things are necessary, the first two of which we have to some extent. One is to change the meaning of the theoretical symbols, "free," "rational," "worthy". Another is to change our emotional attitudes toward "labour" and "service," esteeming them worthy and dignified. But the most important is to develop a truly democratic society, in which all share in useful labour and all enjoy a worthy leisure. For this last an educational revolution is needed. It is here already but it is not complete. The "masses" have been somewhat emancipated, politically and economically; this emancipation has shown itself in the development of a public, free common school system. The idea that learning is properly a monopoly of those few predestined to govern social affairs has been destroyed. But the aristocratic idea still prevails that a truly cultural education for the few has nothing directly in common with industrial affairs and that a useful education for the many has nothing directly in common with the nurture of appreciation and the liberation of thought. Let this solid remainder of Greek practice be destroyed!

What an inconsistent mixture our actual educational system is! It is a consequence of the alleged opposition of labour and leisure, or utility and culture. Some examples: Certain studies are retained in college and in college preparatory courses because "liberal," *i.e.* useless for practical ends; and this view has filtered into and infected elementary education. On the other hand, certain "utilitarian" concessions have been made to modern economic activities and to the masses engaged in earning a living; so we have special schools for the professions, for engineering, for manual training, for commerce, and we have vocational and pre-vocational courses. Even the "three R's" in elementary education are taught in the same spirit. The resuls? An inorganic composite of "cultural" and "utilitarian" subjects, in which the former are not dominated by the purpose to be socially serviceable and the latter do not liberate imagination and the power to think.

Worse confusion remains behind. Subjects labelled "practical" we teach in a useless way as though they were liberal, and subjects labelled "liberal" we teach in a technical way as though they were practical. All this is due to the fact that ours is an inherited situation. The outcome would probably be better if either of the two principles in the mixture were consistently followed. It would be hard to find a subject in the curriculum without the evil results of the compromise between liberality and utility. To illustrate, natural science is both recommended by some and opposed by some because of its practical utility, but it is taught as a special accomplishment without applications. On the other hand, music literature are recommended for cultural reasons and are then taught as though they were practical with chief emphasis on the acquisition of technical skill. A specially instructive case is the elementary studies of the first few years of schooling,—reading spelling, writing and arithmetic. They are popularly supposed to be taught because they are useful; they are instruments for more schooling or for life, so there is much drill to secure automatic skill. But even so the idea of utility is not thoroughly adopted; in that case they would be tied up with situations in which they are directly needed and immediately helpful; instead they are treated as preparatory to remote situations; they are reduced to symbolic devices, they are isolated from practical application. Here is a survival of the idea of liberal training divorced from utility, though in an anemic form. For its ancestor, turn to the Greek schools. There from the earliest years the acquisition of skill was subordinated to the acquisition of literary and musical content having aesthetic and moral significance. We are neither so liberal as the Greek education of freeman nor so practical as the Greek training of slaves; our compromises result in confusion.

What is the educational solution of the problem of culture and utility? A course of study both liberal and useful at the same time. To believe that culture and utility are hostile is only superstition. A useful subject is not illiberal; a liberal subject is not useless. There is a narrow utility, which is illiberal, but there is a broad utility which is liberal. Aim at utility and sacrifice breadth, and you get limited utility. Aim at utility and include breadth, include, that is, the development of imagination, the refining of taste, and the deepening of insight, and you get broad utility, really a cultivated utility. Narrow utility is restricted to routine activities under the supervision of others; broad utility is applicable to new situations under one's own personal control. A culture that is useless and a utility that is uncultivated we reject in a democratic society as survivals of aristocratic Greece.

The same activities that to the Greeks lacked culture may to the moderns have culture. The reason is that these activities themselves through applied science have acquired intellectual, personal and social meaning. The Greeks regarded farming and trading as illiberal not merely because they were useful but because they were rule-of-thumb occupations, pursued for external results, not requiring a trained intelligence, not yielding a personal appreciation of their meaning. Plato deprecated the learning of arithmetic and geometry for practical ends; it was natural for him to do so, for, in his day, the practical uses to which they were put were few in number, lacking in content, and mercenary in quality. But now their social uses have increased, and in so doing their liberalising and their practical value approach each other. And so generally; the most important occupations of today depend on applied mathematics, physics, and chemistry. Science in industry in replacing custom and routine. The understanding of economic production and consumption in modern society involve universal geography and world-wide politics. In our day the cultivated vocationalist is liberally educated.

Why do we not fully recognise this truth? Because of the conditions under which so much work is still carried on. We train, we not educate, our workers. We train them to tend our machines skilfully, automatically, mechanically. We do not furnish their minds for the enjoyment of the leisure our machines allow both on and off duty. Their preliminary years in schools are spent in acquiring rudimentary symbols of learning, not in the study of science, literature and history. Worse yet, they do not work for themselves, they work for their employers for wages; they are means, not ends; they lack insight into the social aims of their pursuits; they lack personal interest in what they do; they do not act freely and intelligently; they are our modern industrial slaves. Their activities are illiberal, not because of the inherent character of the activities but because of the limited character of the education they have received. Such education, aiming simply at skill in performance, is not only illiberal, it is immoral.

The solution? Democracry in education and in industry as well as in politics. Democracy will give us at one stroke both a better education and a better economic order. Education in a democratic society will reconcile liberal nurture with social serviceableness; all will share efficiently and happily in productive occupations; men will have a vital concern in the ends controlling their activity; they may thus continue to do the same work, but now as free men. Democracy provides for direct participation in control; we have democracy in politics we lack it in industry; in industry control remains external and autocratic; whence comes the split between inner mental action and outer physical action, of which the traditional distinction between a liberal education and a utilitarian education is the reflex. Let education unify the disposition of the members of society; in so doing it will help unify society itself. The problem of education in a democratic society is to heal the dualism between the inner and the outer man, between thinking and doing, by constructing a course of studies which makes thinking a guide of free practice for all. Leisure should be a reward of labour, not exemption from it.

*Comment*—There are several things to note here. The first is that Dr. Deway is revolutionary in his aim but not in his method. He aims at an industrial democracy but his method is that of education reform. He is a pedagogic Fabian. We are in the thick of these economic problems today. An education that could give us an industrial democracy might mean either a modified capitalism or the overthrow of capitalism. With industrial democracy as an aim there is no need to quarrel; something of the kind is already here and growing; profits are being shared, workers are participating in control increasingly, workers are becoming joint owners of the business; the personal relations in industry are being established and emphasised.

Going as far as he does toward the economic reorganisation of society, one can understand how Dr. Dewey is criticized by the economic radicals for not going further and by the economic conservatives for going so far. For the economic radical it may be said that the logic of Dr. Dewey's position seems to demand that he go further. Historically he holds that society has made our schools; but he recommends for the future that our schools made our society. What hope is there that they can or will? The schools work with the young generation; they are supported by adult society; they reflect the adult society that supports them. How then can they do other than continue the type of society in which adults believe? The adults live where the economic problems are, where the changes are going on. If not the expectation that the school will change society the use of education as "preparation" after all? Should not an adult society reform itself instead of expecting the school to do it? If it is a problem of education at all, is it not a problem of adult education? So might a radical reformer turn the argument.

Two things are to be said there. One is, that the ideals acquired in progressive schools and colleges are sometimes actually lost in the maelstrom of our competitive economic order, and in this respect Dr. Dewey's prescription for a reformed society is faulty. The other is just the opposite, that one in life stands by the reforming ideals of his youth and becomes a conscious centre for social improvement, and in this respect Dr. Dewey's prescription is valid. Which is the more frequent outcome is hard to say. Just to what extent the schools can become an agency of social reform is consequently uncertain. But it is certain that the proposed remedy would operate slowly and without social cataclysm. The objectives of Dr. Dewey are similar to those of Soviet Russia; his "ideology" and methodology are different. While the reformed schools he proposes might slowly reform society, a transformed society in Russia has quickly transformed the schools. If America ever chooses at all between Dr. Dewey and Russia, it will probably choose Dr. Dewey. And the reason will be the economic one that the American working man has a high standard of living.

Turning from the social and economic to the educational aspects of the problem of labour and leisure, what shall we say of Dr. Dewey's proposed union of culture and utility? This, it is a one-way union. Much culture may be attacked to any utility but utility simply cannot be attached to all culture. By utility is here meant what Dr. Dewey means,—earning a livelihood and social serviceableness. Every occupation of man may and should have its meaning culturally extended through social, geographical, and historical associations. But the culture to which utility cannot be attached is the set of personal interests an individual may have over and above his useful occupation or occupations. Such interests are his avocation, perhaps his hobby. He may collect stamps or coins, do cabinet work in wood, read Latin epigraphy, compose poetry nobody sees, commit classic selections to memory, study the Chinese ideographs, read ancient Egyptian history, sight the stars with his own telescope, dig into Einstein, and so on. Utility in the sense defined? No. Useful only in the sense that thereby is a personal interest gratified and leisure time enjoyed. That such interests make one a larger personality, more interesting, more intellectual, perhaps more aesthetic taste, is undeniable. But this is culture. All utility may acquire some culture; not all culture can acquire utility. Some branches of mathematics are liberalising without being socially useful. Life is for enjoyment as well as for service. If one still insists that enjoyment is use, then the reply is that "use" has ceased to have a useful meaning. A useful activity sends one beyond itself for its significance; an enjoyable activity is its own excuse for being. Dr. Dewey's proposal can succeed in making all utilitarian education more liberal; it cannot succeed in making all liberal education utilitarian. This defect is inherent in the pragmatic philosophy itself which holds all ideas are only tools, allowing no knowledge to exist for its own sake, and maintaining that the human intelligence, responsible as it is for all theories of education and of life, is only "an organ for the control of nature through action".

# 10

# Intellectual and Practical Studies

## The Opposition of Experience and True Knowledge

*Exposition*—On way of regarding experience and knowledge is to oppose them to each other. In this case experience is regarded as changing and knowledge is regarded as changeless. This is the Greek way of regarding the two. It accounts for the corresponding opposition between the practical and intellectual studies. The practical studies were based on experience and the intellectual on knowledge. But in truth this Greek way of opposing experience and knowledge is mistaken, the notion that true knowledge is changeless should be given up, and the practical and intellectual studies should not be two but one. We will go somewhat more in detail into these views. Just as we saw labour and leisure were mistakenly opposed to each other, so also are practice and theory, execution and intelligence, activity and knowledge. The same Greek social conditions are the fountain of these false oppositions. The alleged separation of doing and knowing is connected so directly with certain educational problems that we must discuss it explicitly.

The notion is that knowledge is derived from a higher source than practical activity, and so possesses a more spiritual worth. The notion is false, but it has a long history. Plato and Aristotle first consciously opposed experience and reason. Though differing in many respects, these thinkers agreed in identifying experience with practical concerns, whose purpose was material, and whose organ was the body; experience always involved lack, need, desire, and was never self-sufficing; it was a perpetual flux.

But knowledge was free from practical reference; is existed for its own sake; its sources and organ were an immaterial mind; it dealt with spiritual or ideal interests; it was complete in itself; it was concerned with eternal truth. What a contrast!

Plato said that philosophers should be kings in the ideal state. This is a social statement. It means that rational intelligence should regulate human affairs, securing unity, order and law. Negatively it means that human affairs should not be regulated by habit, appetite, impulse, and emotion, signifying multiplicity, discord, and irrational fluctuations from one estate to another.

Experience at its best to these thinkers is represented in the various handicrafts,—the arts of peace and war. The discipline of experience leads to skill. So with the cobbler, the flute player, the soldier. The senses, and other bodily organs, have had repeated contact with things, whose results have been preserved and consolidated as ability to foresee and to practice. Such knowledge and skill were "empirical"; they were not based on insight into rational and universal principles; they were the result of a large number of separate trials,—what we call the "method of trial and error," with special emphasis on the accidental character of the trails. The ability to control was a matter of routine, a rule-of-thumb procedure; if the new situation was like the old, it might work well enough; otherwise, failure was likely. The common craftsmen of Athens mistakenly assumed that, because they could do the specific things of their trades, they could manage household affairs education and politics.

Experience thus has a definitely material character; it deals with physical things in relation to the body; it is an affair of the senses; the senses are connected with the appetites, wants and desires; they lay hold on things which give pleasure by satisfying the wants of the body; the body itself is but the substratum of a higher life; the senses do not lay hold on the reality of things. Moreover, there is something morally dangerous about experience, suggested by such words as sensual, carnal, material and worldly. Further, experience is ineradicably connected with the changing, the shifting, the manifold, the desires, the variable, the untrustworthy, the unstable, the anarchic, the "many". Experience is not dependable, changing as it does from person to person, from day to day, from country to country. From experience come warrings, conflicts, both within the individual, and between individuals. Local customs vary, so no standard of belief can issue from them. The logical outcome was drawn by the Sophists: that is good and true which to each individual at each time and place seems good and true.

In contrast, true knowledge, reason, "science," are not so. They lay hold of the immaterial, the ideal, the spiritual, the morally praiseworthy, the single, the uniform. They assure coherence and harmony.

All this opposition between experience and true knowledge comes to a head in the contrast between doing and knowing. Practice falls within experience. Doing proceeds from needs and aims at change. To produce and consume are to alter. All the obnoxious characters of change attach to doing. Knowing, on the other hand, having a permanent object, is itself permanent; it grasps a thing intellectually, theoretically; it is out of the region of chance and change; its object, truth, has no lack, it is calm and untouched by the perturbations of sense; it is universal and eternal. Only the law of reason can properly subject the world of experience, giving it control, steadiness and order.

Whence came this sharp antithesis? In part from the fact that philosophy in Athens began as a criticism of custom. Tradition and custom as providing standards of knowledge and conduct proved unsatisfactory. They held men in bondage. What should replace them? Athenian philosophy hit upon reason as the answer. It was to be the only adequate guide of belief and activity. But custom and tradition were identified with experience. So reason, the new authority, and experience, the old authority, declared war on each other. Reason held itself superior to experience as unstable and in adequate; experience in turn refused to acknowledge the authority of reason. So what began in the historical criticism of custom ended in the philosophical opposition of experience and reason.

But why identify experience with custom? The grounds for the identification are not far to seek. The condition of things was unsatisfactory. But this state of affairs was itself due to custom. The customs and beliefs of different communities were found to be different. Increasing trade, travel, solonizations, migrations, wars, broadened the intellectual horizon, bringing the knowledge of different communities. Civil disturbances had become one of the customs in Athens; the fortunes of the city fluctuated with factional strife. The increase of leisure accompanying the broadening horizon brought new knowledge of nature, with new curiosity and speculation. The questions arose, What is constant in Nature? That is universal in Society? And the answer came: the universal principle and the constant essence are apprehended by reason; the changing and the unstable are perceived by the senses. The work of the senses was preserved in memory and imagination, in habit and in skill,—and this was the world of experience. Thus, because customs were matters of experience and were unsatisfactory, experience came to be debased and reason exalted.

Not that all the sharp distinctions thus portrayed persisted in their fullness. Nevertheless they did profoundly influence men's subsequent thinking, especially about education. Here are some examples: the contempt for the senses, for sense observation, for physical science; the contrasting high regard for mathematical and logical science; the disesteem of knowledge of the concrete; the contrasting feeling that the knowledge which deals with ideal symbols is high and worthy; the scorn of all particulars not deductively subsumed under a universal; the disregard of the body; and the depreciation of arts and crafts as instruments utilising intellectuality. All these things found sanction in the opposition of experience and reason, the practical and the intellectual.

Mediaeval philosophy accepted, continued and reinforced the same tradition. To it experience dealt with mundane, profane, and secular affairs; these were indeed practically necessary but relatively unimportant when compared with supernatural objects of knowledge. All action was subordinate to the knowledge of supreme reality, whose contemplation was the ultimate end to man. Such knowledge meant relationship to God, and the enjoyment of the eternal bliss of that relation. It was the beatific vision.

Take an illustration from medicine in our own day. If a physician is called an empiric, it is discreditable; it implies be lacks scientific training; that he has learned only from practice; that there is no reason in what he does; he does not know where his knowledge begins or ends; in new situations he must pretend; he makes claims without justification; he trusts to luck; he imposes on others; he "bluffs"; he degenerates into the quack. Thus, we still discredit experience and practice,—the real source of all our true knowledge.

All told, take the Greek philosophic tradition, add the literary character of Roman education, add again mediaeval otherworldliness, add still again the aristocratic social preference for the alleged higher studies, and you have four great forces tending to subordinate the practical to the intellectual. Small wonder that the higher schools and educational philosophies were drawn into their train.

*Comment*—Again, let it be noted that Dr. Dewey is utilising the genetic mode of refutation. The practical and the intellectual should not be opposed to each other because the social conditions under which the opposition arose have changed. Thus, he holds that problems are not solved, they are outgrown philosophies are not refuted, they are shelved. The river of time carries all its sons away.

But this mode of refutation is emotionally unsatisfactory and intellectually unconvincing. What we want to know it whether there really is a world of reality, changeless in character, which is grasped by the intellect, which remains despite man's denial and social change, which is implied even by the process of change itself.

Now thought does possess just such a world, and it can be shown to do so. In general, it is the realm of concepts, essences, universals. The very notion of change implies the changeless. Without the permanent there is no impermanent. The only constant may be change, yet there is a constant. If there were only change, we might not be conscious of it, as we are not conscious of the weight of the air which is always present but never sensed. Certain characteristics even of changing phenomena do not change, for example, all phenomena have both form and content, both figure and stuff. Here is a formal changeless truth about our changing world. There may be many changing shades of blue, but the truth of the proposition that all sensory blues have some extension does not change. There are many pairs of twos but the truth that two pairs of twos is four does not change. The illustrations are many of the fact that there is a changeless realm of truths, grasped by thought. The changeless conceptual order is one thing, the changing perceptual order is a different thing. And the changeless conceptual order permeates the changing perceptual order as changeless space permeates changing matter. These views remain in any actual or conceivable form of human society. Educationally, they mean that there is an intellectual which is concerned, as the pragmatic philosophy says, with the changing practical; and also that there is an intellectual, denied by the pragmatic philosophy, which is concerned with the changeless order of things. Our education should adjust us to the changeless as well as the changing. That is the kind of world we live in.

Two quotations will be order at this point, one from a psychologist, and one from a mathematician. Says the psychologist: "Each conception thus eternally remains what it is, and never can become another . . . The paper, a moment ago white, I may now see to be scorched black. But my conception 'white' does not change into my conception 'black' . . . Thus, amid the flux of opinions and of physical things, the world of conceptions, or the things intended to be thought about, stands stiff and immutable, life Plato's Realm of Ideas."

The other quotation: "Transcending the flux of the sensuous universe, there exists a stable world of pure thought, a divinely ordered world of ideas, accessible to man, free from the mad dance of time, infinite and eternal."

Our conclusion here must be that the opposition between changing experience and changeless reason cannot be entirely rejected. Many things change in our practical world; with these man's intellect may be concerned. Some things do not change in our conceptual world; with these man's intellect may also be concerned. Our debt to Plato remains.

## The Modern Theory of Experience and Knowledge

*Exposition*—By "modern" is not here meant "contemporary"; the term is used to refer to the post-Renaissance theories of the seventeenth and eighteenth centuries. In brief, this theory is somewhat like the Greek, just considered, in identifying experience with sensation, but it is unlike the Greek in making knowledge dependent on sensation. These views too, as we shall now see, provide an unsatisfactory basis for a philosophy of education. They made experience entirely too passive.

These modern reformers like Bacon, Locke and Helvetins held views concerning reason very different from those of Plato, and much less appreciative. To Plato, as we saw, reason meant the principle of reform, or progress, of control, devotion to whose cause meant breaking through the limitations of custom, and getting at things as they really are. To these modern reformers reason meant either blank mental forms or prejudices. In the one case reason was not self-sufficient, and in the other case it was evil. Reason as blank forms, *a priori* notions, universal principles, had to be filled in by experience, by sensation, to become significant and valid. Reason as prejudices were dogmas imposed by authority, masquerading and finding protection under august names. The need, as Bacon felt it, was to break with reason and resort to experience. Conceptions which "anticipated nature" and imposed human opinions upon her were bonds to be broken. Experience would tell us what nature is like. This Baconian appeal to experience meant a break with authority; openness to new impressions; eagerness to discover and invent; the irruption into the mind of things as they really are, free from the veil of preconceived ideas. Men's minds were no longer absorbed as in the mediaeval days of tabulating and systematising received ideas and "proving" them by means of their own mutual relations.

The effect of the change from the Greek to these modern views was two-fold, both lamentable. Experience ceased to be practical and became cognitive, and the mind ceased to be regarded as active and became passive. (1) Experience teased to mean ways of doing and being done to; it came to mean apprehending material to balance and check reasoning; a way of knowing. How good a way is it? That was the only question. If "intellectualism" designates an emphatic interest in knowing isolated from doing, here is intellectualism beyond even that of the Greeks. Practice was indeed subordinated to knowledge by the Greeks but it was not treated as a kind of tag-end, or aftermath, of knowledge as by these modern philosophic empiricists. (2) As "experience" now was a means of basing truth upon objects, upon nature, the mind was looked at as purely receptive. Objects can truly impress themselves only upon a passive mind; for the mind to be active in knowing would vitiate the process, would defeat its own purpose. The ideal for the mind of man was a maximum of receptivity!

The most influential of the empiricists was John Locke (d. 1704). The empiricists derive all knowledge from impressions made upon the mind by objects. Locke allowed two sources of knowledge, *viz.*, sensation and reflection. The sensation came from the object; the reflection from the mind. At birth the mind, he held, is like blank sheet of white paper, or like a wax tablet without any engraving on it (*tabula rasa*). Still, the mind, though blank and empty at birth, has powers it exercises on the material received. Such powers, or faculties, are discrimination, comparison, abstraction, generalisation, etc. These faculties work up the sense-material into definite and organised forms. They even evolve new ideas on their own account, such as the fundamental conceptions of morality and mathematics.

In crossing the channel, British empiricism became French sensationalism (cf. The writings of Baron Holbach, Lamettrie, Condillac and Helvetius). The impressions made upon the mind by objects were generally termed "sensations," whence the name, "sensationalism" which, of course, has other distinct meanings. The doctrine of sensationalism identifies knowledge with the reception and association of sensory impressions. It belongs to the latter part of the eighteenth century. What if the faculties allowed the mind by Locke were themselves only sensations? Peculiar sensations, indeed, made in us by the conjoint presence of other sensations. Thus, even discernment and judgment became effects in us of prior sensations. The French successors of Locke razed away the faculties from the mind, deriving even these from the sensations received. Thus, the doctrine of mind as passive and sensational experience as cognitive reaches its limit.

What were the educational effects of the view that experience is a matter of sensation upon which knowledge depends! These were several, *viz.*, (1) greatly to increase faith in what education could accomplish; (2) the rejection of bookishness; (3) the rejection of tradition; (4) the introduction into schools of real things, "object-lessons"; and (5) the exclusion of active pursuits from the school. The second alone of these was an unmitigated good.

1. It was a time when education was fostered as a method of social reform. The "sensationalists," who advocated a first-hand contact with things, found the harmony in nature which was lacking in society. The emptier the mind at the beginning, the more it can be made into anything through its educational environment. Helvetius was perhaps the most extreme and consistent sensationalist. He proclaimed the omnipotence of education.
2. Empiricism protested against mere book learning in school. This was its directly beneficial office. Without objects to impress the mind, no knowledge. Things before words! Without prior objects, words are symbols. Words without objects give a knowledge of the symbols themselves, not of the realities symbolised. The knowledge of symbols is not instructive.
3. Sensationalism combated mere tradition. Doctrines resting merely on authoritative opinion it repudiated. It set up its own test of knowledge: What are the real objects of sense from which these ideas, beliefs, opinions, and doctrines are derived? If these basic objects could not be produced, the ideas in question were pronounced untrue; they were the result of false associations and combinations of sensation. Such crude psychology!
4. With the rejection of bookishness went the demand for instruction by means of objects. The object must make its own impression upon each individual. Empiricism demanded a first-hand contact with things. The impression must be made upon my own mind. The object itself is the direct first-hand source of knowledge. The further we get from the object, the vaguer the ideas and the more the error.

5. Practice, which we have taken as the source of knowledge, was excluded from the school. Active pursuits had no place in the schools. If allowed at all, they were brought in for purely utilitarian ends,—to acquire habits by drill.

What shall we say of these effects of sensationalism on education? They were better on the negative than on the positive side; better in the elimination of bookishness and unsupported opinion than in the substitution of object-lessons. The full use of a good thing was here vitiated by a false theory. It was good to have first-hand acquaintance with natural objects in the schoolroom. The theory did not allow anything to be done with the object; it allowed only an impression to be made by it on the mind. The object was isolated, its sensory quality was isolated, so that the sense-impression as a unit of knowledge might be the more distinct. Sense-activity became an isolated end in itself. Instruction was reduced to the physical gymnastics of the sense-organs, thinking was neglected. Strictly speaking, the theory did not allow thinking in connection with sense observation; thinking came after the impressions had been made in properly sorting and combining them.

Because of the bad theory of sensationalism, it has never been widely put into practice educationally, except in early infancy. Instead, it has been modestly used to lend greater "interest" to barren symbols, and to give point by illustrations to "rationalistic" knowledge, such as, definitions, rules, classifications, and the use of symbols. It did inject the new factor of natural objects into the older curriculum; it brought about a greater regard for pictures and graphic descriptions; it reduced the importance attached to verbal symbols; thus, it incidentally modified older studies and methods. But it required supplementation; its scope was too limited; the resources of direct sense-perception are too meager; and there are important matters which do appeal more directly to thought. Because of its inadequacy, sensationalism left practically unimpaired the reign in the curriculum of informationism, abstractionism, and the "rationalistic" studies.

We may sum up under three heads our objections to sensationalistic empiricism as an educational philosophy of knowing. In doing so, our own views will become clearer.

(*a*) The work of education is constructive, not critical. Education needs to build up new experiences into intellectual habits. Everything should be as correct as possible from the start. Mind denotes responsiveness to meaning. Meaning exists only in a context. In contrast, sensationalism was critical; it destroyed hard and fast dogmas; it presupposes the existence of old beliefs needing to be revised or eliminated; the historical value of the theory is in its negative attitude; it is unfitted for the constructive task of education. If falsely regarded mind as response to direct physical stimuli; it falsely identified knowledge with a combination of sense-impressions. The theory led in the schoolroom to extolling physical excitations, or else to heaping up isolated objects and qualities.

(*b*) Direct impressions, though having the advantage of being first-hand, have the disadvantage of being limited in range. Some illustrations will make the point clear. Home-geography is all right as far as it goes, but it does not go far enough. Children should be directly acquainted with the natural surroundings of their homes; thereby ideas about portions of the earth beyond perception are made real; and thereby intellectual curiosity is aroused. But geographical knowledge cannot be limited to the home environments; that would be a fatal restriction. Again, in realising number relations, it may be helpful to utilise such things as beans, shoe pegs and counters. But they should not arrest growth on the low plane of specific physical objects, thus becoming an obstacle to arithmetical understanding; they should aid in the apprehension of meaning. In the historic growth of our number system, the use of the fingers as numerical symbols got in the way; so especial symbols were developed as tools of mathematical calculation. Just so, the individual must develop from concrete to abstract symbols whose meaning involves conceptual thinking. This desirable development is hampered by unique absorption at the outset in the physical object of sense.

(*c*) Sensationalistic empiricism has a false psychology of mental development. Children grow not by being impressed by physical objects but by trying to use them. Experience is not passive reception; it is active initiation; it is instinctive and impulsive activities; it is interaction with things. The experience of an infant consists of what he does to things and what things in turn do to him. He handles, throws, pounds, tears, an object; what happens to the object directs his subsequent activities. The traditional empirical philosophy neglects the deep-seated motor factors of experience; it is a fatal defect. A scheme of object lessons leading to passively received sensory qualities is as uninteresting as it is mechanical. On this point the Greeks knew better; their notion of experience as a practical matter is closer to fact than the post-renaissance notion of it as a mode of knowing by means of sensations. Because of these three defects, sensationalistic empiricism cannot furnish a satisfactory philosophy of the learning process.

***Comment***—Undoubtedly the school of sensationalism provides an inadequate philosophy of knowing and experience. It is too bare, too mechanical, too deterministic, too naturalistic. Still, the discussion of it in the text leads us to make three suggestions. The first concerns the real importance of sensations. They may not be important enough to provide an adequate basis for a philosophy of knowing, but no philosophy of knowing can dispense with them. The sensory qualities of experiences can be directly known to us only through sensations, of course. All the colours, all the sounds, all felt physical contacts, all odors, all tastes, all muscular and joint movements and strains, are first of all sensations. Without them to awaken the mind into activity, we should not only lack knowledge of the sensory qualities of the world, we should probably be without knowledge altogether.

This leads, second, to the recognition of the importance of passivity; not that passivity is an adequate foundation for an educational philosophy, but that it is indispensable. It is one phase of our experience. We are active when we do things to our environment; we are passive when our environment does things to us. What is done to us is probably as significant as what we do. Sensations themselves are received passively as stimuli; they are not actively created without stimulation. The nervous system may be tensely set for their reception as a tiger stalks its prey; still one must wait for the stimulus to arrive from without The educational uses of quiet and silence have not been adequately recognised.

Third, we may note the importance of sensory activity for its own sake, apart from the use to which the things sensed are put. One may lie on his back on the ground and enjoy looking at the blue sky overhead. He is not trying to do anything with the sky, he is seeing it with pleasure on its own account. So with harmonious sounds, sweet tastes, pleasant perfumes, smooth surfaces, and the like. When a sensory experience develops pleasure in itself, apart from the uses of the object sensed, we have one form of aesthetic enjoyment. Such sensory experiences do not lead on to further activity in any practical way; they tend to continue themselves, they are worthwhile on their own account. Thus, while agreeing in rejecting sensationalism, we would emphasise the importance of sensation, of passivity, and of certain sensory experiences on their own account.

## Experience as Experimentation

*Exposition*—Experience is experimentation. This is our own view in contrast with the rationalism of the Greeks, which put reason above experience, and with the sensationalism of the early moderns, who put experience as sensation above reason. Our view will put reason in experience.

This view of experience as experimentation will stand out more distinctly if the reasons for rejecting sensationalism are held clearly in mind. These are two, *viz.*, (1) it is contradicted by modern psychology, and (2) it is contradicted by modern scientific method. To each of these we will devote some consideration.

(1) As already intimated, sensational empiricism omits the primary position in experience of active response. Children learn about things not by being passively impressed by them but by putting them to use. Five minutes of unprejudiced observation in a nursery is enough to refute sensationalism. The infant does not passively receive impressions of such qualities as sound, colour and hardness; he makes motor responses to sensory stimulation, he reaches and handles, he learns from the results of such

responses. He does not learn isolated, ready-made, sensory qualities of things; he learns, the changes in the behaviour of things and persons including himself, produced by his activity; in brief, he learns connections between acts and consequences. Even sensory qualities, like red colour, high pitch, hard and soft, are learned through the activities they stimulate and the consequences of these activities. Children learn about persons in the same way; they respond to persons, and persons respond to them. What things and persons do to us and what we in turn do to them is experience; they further and check our action, we produce changes in them; it is all a process of experimentation. Sensory qualities are not impressed on a passive mind; experience is by an active organism responding to stimulation.

(2) The methods of science teach the same lesson. These methods have to their credit the revolutionising of our knowledge of the world since the seventeenth century; they are the refinement of the methods of leaning in the nursery; they are only experimentation under deliberately controlled conditions. The infant with his ball; the cobbler with his leather awl, needle, thread and wax; the scientist with his acid and metal; these all are learning in the same way; they are all experimenting; they all are using the only method to acquire in adequate knowledge of the world. Of course, the purpose of the cobbler is trade, not knowledge. Science is the extension of the child's method of learning; more sense data are had, by the aid of microscope, telescope, and other experimental apparatus; the data arouse new ideas, hypotheses, theories; general ideas as tools, like those of mathematics, are required; such tools aid in conducting experimental inquiries and in formulating their results.

This scientific procedure was a stumbling block to the Greeks and foolishness to the early moderns. The Greeks looked for true knowledge to reason above experience, not to a cobbler punching holes. The early moderns, like Francis Bacon, looked for true knowledge to sense perceptions, supposed to contain within themselves some universal "form" at "species" in a disguising mask which reason could strip off. In contrast the scientific method neither puts reason above experience, nor experience above reason, but puts reason in experience,—

defining problems, collecting data, forming hypotheses, drawing and testing conclusions. This is scientific experience, and this is experimentation.

There results in our day a new philosophy of knowledge and of experience. Rational knowledge and experience are no longer opposed to each other as with the Greeks. Experience is no longer a mere summarising of the more or less chance results of the past, as with the early moderns. Experience cases to be a matter of chance, impulse and custom. Experience becomes experimenting, inspired by a purpose, guided by an aim, conducted by method, leading to consequences. Such experience is reasonable, rational, significant, enlightening, instructive. When experience thus becomes rational and reason becomes functional in experience, what happens to the old antithesis between empiricism and rationalism? It vanishes, like the human situation of master and slave which once lent it meaning and relative justification. A new science gives us a new epistemology to match a new society.

Returning now to our main topic of the intellectual and practical studies. What happens to their opposition? It may and should vanish too, it is not intrinsic and necessary, it is dependent upon modifiable conditions. Practical activities and studies may be intellectually narrow and trivial, a matter of routine, pursued under authority, aiming at some external result. But they do not have to be so. Childhood and youth,—the period of schooling, allow practical activities to be carried on in a different and more liberal spirit. Our discussion of thinking showed it deals effectively only with practical situations. Our discussion of subject-matter showed it develops finally into logical form out of childlike work and play. Our previous chapter shows leisure as the true spirit of labour. Our present chapter shows the intellectual is a function of the practical. These conclusions all indicate the continuity of all the valuable phases of education and of life.

We will have for convenience sum up our now familiar results concerning experience and the school in three propositions.

(*i*) Experience primarily consists of the active relations between a human being and his natural and social surroundings.

These relations are reciprocal. Either the individual or the environment may initiate the activity. When the environment initiates, the individual undergoes stimulation, checking, or deflection of activity. When the individual initiates, the environment causes him to succeed or fail; he undergoes the consequences of his own efforts. Through connecting these initial acts with their consequences, both his own deeds and things and men acquire meanings. He and his world become intelligible and meaningful.

What then is the business of schooling? The purposeful providing of an environment, interaction with which involves acquiring important meanings. Such meanings become is turn instruments of further learning, as we saw when discussing the role of reflection in experience.

But are not children out of school in most active relations with their environment? Yes, and the results are vital and genuine as far as they so. But, as we have repeatedly seen, such activities are limited in many ways. The environment is not deliberately planned; it is not always adapted to promote understanding; some powers are left undeveloped, being undirected; others are stimulated only occasionally or whimsically; others grow into habits or routine skill at the expense of resourcefulness and inventiveness; the chance activities so stimulated bear an accidental relation to insight and thinking.

No, the business of the school is not to transport youth from an active to a passive environment, requiring a cramped study of the records of the learning of others. Rather is it to transport from an environment of unregulated to regulated activities, regulated to guide learning. "Intellectual" studies are not opposed to practical pursuits, they intellectualise them. The progressive schools have laid hold of this principle, more or less consciously; it remains to grasp it more firmly and a practice it more widely.

(*ii*) The practical pursuits of modern man are of a kind to allow intellectualising. Play and work in the modern school, reflecting the content of modern social life, may be intellectualised. Modern occupations—domestic, agricultural, manufacturing, transportation, communication, are instinct with applied science. It has not always been so. Practical activities in the Greek and mediaeval periods were mostly matters of routine, external, even servile; this was due to the social environment of master and slave or the noble and the peasant. Small wonder that educators rejected such practical pursuits as unfitted to cultivate intelligence. True enough it is that many modern workers are unaware of the intellectual content of the activities in which they engage. This, however, is only another reason why the schools should utilise these pursuits, thus allowing the coming generation to acquire what the present generation lacks, and to carry on labour not blindly but intelligently.

(*iii*) The progress of experimental science has given the most direct blow at the traditional prestige or purely "intellectual" studies, at the traditional separation of knowing from doing. This progress has demonstrated many things, among them the fact that all genuine knowledge, all fruitful understanding, is the offspring of doing. When men wish to find out something about things, they have to do something to things, they have to alter conditions. The growth of knowledge, of the power of explanation, of right classification, involve the analysis and rearrangement of facts which cannot be done purely mentally, just inside the head. This s the lesson of the laboratory method. All education has to learn it. Etymology suggests that in the laboratory one discovers labour: the conditions under which it is not merely externally productive but intellectually fruitful. In too many cases at present even the use of the laboratory results only in acquiring an additional mode of technical skill. For this evil result these are several reasons, *viz.*, the laboratory still remains too largely an isolated resource; it is not resorted to until pupils are too old to derive full benefit from it; it is still surrounded by other studies where traditional methods isolate intellect from activity.

The Greeks were right; experience is primarily practical, a matter of doing and undergoing the consequences. The sensationalists were wrong: experience is not primarily cognitive. But the Greeks were wrong too in separating knowing from doing. Doing should be so directed as to take up into its context all fruitful ideas and so to result in securely tested knowledge. In this way experience ceases to be empirical and becomes experimental, and reason ceases to be a remote, ideal faculty and becomes all the resources of fruitful, meaningful, activity. Educationally, this change denotes the plans of studies and methods developed in the preceding discussions.

*Comment*—Dr. Dewey has dropped the liberal New England theology of his upbringing, and all Puritan social conventions, but he has retained his New England conscience concerning work. Every thought must be harnessed to labour. There is to be no intellectual interest which does not guide a practical activity. Following Kant's famous phrase, we may say that in Dr. Dewey's system action without thought is Mind, while thought without action is empty. There is to be no occasional daydreaming, no intellectual idling, no playing with concepts, no mental fooling around, no joy of thinking for its own sake, no revelling in bare intellectuality, no sheer speculation, no probing beyond the practical, no vacation for mentality, no philosophising in the region of the unprovable guess, no thinking where there is no experimental testing. Life a laboratory! Shades of an intellectual prison house! Here is indeed a drab intellectual Puritanism.

There are two propositions involved here. One is, all practical pursuits should be intellectualised. The other is, all intellectual pursuits should be practicalised. Both are involved in the proposed functional unity of the intellectual and the practical, of knowing and doing. The first of these propositions is unexceptionable, bearing in mind that some practical pursuits, like steel-riveting, have less intellectual content than others, like designing a skyscraper. The second proposition is objectionable. It keeps the intellect of man in working clothes.

Educationally, the school should have a laboratory, true enough; but it should not be only a laboratory. There are problems for the laboratory, but there is a place for the thought-provoking classroom, for the stirring auditorium, for the quiet library, and for the noisy playground, in which one may enjoy beauty, read for pleasure, listen to a good story, see a good movie, hear good music, play for fun, and even formulate unprovable hypotheses. There is an intellectual element in each of these, but it is not tied down to practical pursuits.

Dr. Dewey's doctrine of learning by doing, found also in Rousseau, Pestalozzi and Froebel, is a good one for elementary education, but it has never fully grown up. Adolescent and adult education involve also learning to think by thinking. Some problems worth thinking about are not matters of practical pursuits. It is well enough to liberalise with thought our professional schools; it is highly objectionable to professionalise our liberal schools. If the educators surrender the cause of liberal education, the professions will take it up. In the broader sense of practicality,—perspective, range of knowledge, joy in knowing, cultivation of a refined personality, a liberal education is the most practical. "Image the whole,"—that's liberality; "then execute the part,"—that's practicality.

The conception of experience as experimentation is inadequate. Experimentation is indeed one phase of experience, but experience is much more than experimentation. Experimentation is trying out an hypothesis under controlled conditions. It is strictly intellectual and practical. But there are emotional factors of experience over and above experimentation; we do not experiment with the love of family and friends. Munsterberg said we should not take the experimental attitude toward our pupils. Besides, in experience, there are the elements of intellectual curiosity on its own account, of custom, of impulse. No one of these is primarily experimental. The dentist may engage in experimentation, while the patient gets the experience.

Difficult as are the distinctions between pure and applied research, they nevertheless exist. The difference is not so much in the field studied as in the attitude of the student. One engaged in pure research is trying to find out the truth for its own sake; it satisfies his desire to know; it may or may not lead to practical use; he is not concerned with that aspect of the question. One engaged in applied research is trying to find out the truth for the sake of the use he can make of it. The World War greatly stimulated applied research. Most of our industrial research today is applied, some of it is pure. Most of our graduate school research to day is pure, some of it is applied.

It would hamstring research all along the line to limit it to application. Pure research is basic to all applied research, as

Maxwell and J.J. Thomson preceded Marconi in the field of wireless telegraphy. Those who want to know have regularly provided the materials for those who want to do. Those who want to do have often "drawn the circle premature". It is not yet clear whether the theories of cosmic rays of Millikan are true or not; or, if true, what the practical effect will be on living. But who would say to Millikan that his intellectual studies should confine themselves to practical pursuits? It is not yet proven and may never be proven experimentally that gravitation is electro-magnetism, as Einstein says; the equations seem not to fit the facts exactly as yet (1931). Neither is it clear what practical use could be made of this theorem if it were experimentally proven. But who would limit Einstein's intellect to practical pursuits? It is not yet experimentally proven and may never be so whether Millikan is right in saying the universe is winding up or Eddington and Jeans are right in saying it is running down; or what practical pursuit would be different if it were. But who would say to these astro-physicists that their intellectuality should be limited to practicality? If one replies that what these men are doing is practical and so justified, then do Plato and Aristotle come among us again as real teachers, though they did separate some intellectual knowing from some practical doing. If all intellectuality is practical, then there is no issue. The intellect of man is broader than doing, while including the directing of doing, and always will be so. Our philosophy of education must not clip the wings of intellect; it need not keep it always on solid ground; it needs only to assure it a safe landing.

## REFERENCES

James, W., Psychology, pp. 239-240.

Keyser, C.J., *The Human Worth of Rigorous Thinking,* Columbia University Press, New York, 1925, p. 57.

# 11

# Physical and Social Studies: Naturalism and Humanism

Physical studies deal with nature; social studies deal with man. There has been conflict between these two groups of studies for a place in the curriculum. It is the conflict between naturalism and humanism. The solution of the conflict hitherto has been only a mechanical compromise: the curriculum was divided between the two. This is only another instance of the external adjustment of educational values, another dualism to be overcome. Are nature and man two things or one? How is nature really connected with human affairs? The compromise between the physical and social studies suggests that nature and man are two; that the world and mind are two independent realms, though having certain points of contact with each other; that each realm has its own separate group of studies. With such an objectionable division between nature and man, it is natural that the growth of the physical, scientific, studies of nature should be suspected of marking a materialistic encroachment upon the domain of the spirit. If our education is to be unified, then nature and man must somehow be unified.

We will study the problem from three angles, *viz.*, the historic background of humanism before the great renaissance, the post-renaissance scientific interest in nature, and the resulting present educational problem.

### The Historic Background of Humanistic Study

***Exposition***—The Greeks are not the ones responsible this time for a dualism. The isolation of man from nature took place in the

Roman days and continued in the mediaeval period. Plato and Aristotle did not follow their leader, Socrates, in neglecting the study of nature and centering on the study of man. Socrates seems to have thought that the knowledge of nature was not attainable, and not very important, while the knowledge of the nature and end of man was the chief thing, for upon this knowledge hang all moral and social achievements. Cicero praised Socrates for bringing philosophy down from heaven to earth, that is, for shifting attention from astronomy to ethics.

Plato made the study of nature indispensable for the study of man. He connects the good of man with the good of nature. The knowledge of nature is not an end in itself but a necessary means of bringing man to acknowledge of himself. Through studying nature man comes to realise that his law is one with the purpose of all existence. Thus, his chief work, the *Republic,* deals both with morals and metaphysics. He agrees with Socrates that right action depends on knowledge, but he disagrees with Socrates that all we know is our own ignorance. The end of man cannot be determined apart from the knowledge of the end of nature, whence come law and unity. He consistently subordinates the studies of man (Called music") to the studies of nature,—mathematics, logic, physics and metaphysics. He found the study of nature indispensable to the interests of man. There was no conflict in Plato between naturalism and humanism.

Plato's greatest pupil, Aristotle, goes even further, if possible, in recognising the study of nature. Unlike Socrates, to Aristotle the proper study of mankind is not man but nature. The things of man are transient but the things of nature are permanent, universal, necessary. As we saw before, Aristotle subordinates citizenship to philosophising. The highest end of man is not social but cognitive, not human but divine, not being a citizen but being a thinker. Pure thinking, said he, is the essence of divinity. So Aristotle too felt no conflict between the literary studies of man and the scientific studies of nature. Plato and Aristotle were interested in the free inquiry into natural fact, they enjoyed nature aesthetically; and they were conscious that human society was rooted in natural law. These things kept them from bringing man and nature into conflict with each other.

But a change came in the Alexandria and Roman days. The literary studies, those dealing with man, got the upper hand. The reason is two-fold: culture became increasingly reminiscent and borrowed, and the bent of Roman life was not scientific, but political and rhetorical.

Athens achieved civilisation and culture for itself; it looked out directly upon nature and society. Alexandria and Rome inherited their civilisation from alien sources. Instead of looking out, they looked back. They took the short road to culture. The administrative talent, the practical genius, of the Romans was directed to the conquest and control not of nature but of men. The educational effect was the study of literature, not the study of nature. The study by Hatch has well shown this result. He holds (taking much succeeding history for granted) that it is the influence of the later Greeks which couses us still to study literature rather than nature. And the later Greeks did so because, though having lost their state, they kept their literature, and devoted themselves to it, and so paid attention to cultivated speech; and the Romans employed Greek teachers to educate their sons.

Mediaeval Europe was literary too rather than scientific. As Rome was taught of Greece, so the barbarians were taught of Greco-Roman civilisation. They too borrowed their culture, they did not evolve it; they borrowed their general ideas; they borrowed the artistic mode of presenting these ideas; they borrowed even their laws. They relied on the records of alien peoples; they depended on tradition. Furthermore, the dominant theological interests of the period increased the dependence on tradition; the authorities appealed to by the Church were literatures in foreign tongues. Learning became identified with linguistic training and the speech of the learned was not the mother tongue but an alien literary language.

What was the effect on education of such subject matter? It compelled recourse to the *dialectical* method of scholasticism. By scholasticism is meant simply the method of the Schools or the School Men. Their method was appropriate to their problem. Their problem was to transmit and authoritative body of truths. Contemporary society and nature were not studied; the literature of the past was studied. Inquiry, discovery and invention were not required; defining, expounding, interpreting were required. Scholasticism developed as the method of transmitting, not discovering, truth. Since the close of the middle ages and the revival of learning, it has been used as a term of reproach, and justly so. The mistake has been in not recognising that this mediaeval method is still used today, and not used so will. The body of authoritatively Received literature has indeed been increased by the addition of geography, history, botany, astronomy, etc., but schools still generally teach from textbooks and rely upon the principle of authority. Pupils are led not to inquire but to acquire. This is Scholasticism continued, minus mediaeval accuracy and plus modern laxity.

So the Greek tradition of humanism was lost; the knowledge of nature was not made basic to the progress of man; life became interested in authority; the very study of nature was suspect: it drew men away from the documents already containing the rules of living. Moreover, nature could be studied only by means of the senses which were material and hence opposed to the immaterial interests of the spirit. Furthermore, the knowledge of nature was utilitarian, physical, secular, temporal; but the knowledge of the authoritative, traditional literature led to man's spiritual and eternal wellbeing. So the Greek unity of man and nature gave way to their mediaeval disunity. Thus, the matter stood at the time of the Revival of Learning.

***Comment***—How is it that the Greeks are now dualists and now monists? They gave us the dualism of labour and leisure, and the dualism of experience and true knowledge, but now they give us the unity of man and nature? The answer is that Dr. Dewey has here probably overdrawn the doctrine of unity between man and nature in the Greek thinkers. Socrates is admittedly an exception, depreciating the knowledge of nature and appreciating the knowledge of man. Plato made up his curriculum from the study of man rather than the study of nature; it was composed of gymnastics and music till twenty, mathematics as a discipline till thirty, and philosophy till thirty-five, after which the philosopher ruled the state with his eye on the eternal pattern of justice until fifty, when he was released again for the study of philosophy until his soul at death rejoined its kindred heavenly essences whence it had once come. Plato allowed the study of mathematics as a discipline in thinking the abstract; he allowed the study of nature, for example, astronomy, as embodying, the idea of harmony. Man was not in his essence a child of nature at all but of heaven; "man is a creature not of earthly but of heavenly growth." Plato regarded nature as a mixture of being and non-being; he did not despise it; but he allowed man to transcend it. He was a quantitative dualist but a qualitative idealist, that is to say, ideas and matter both exist but ideas are the reality; in no sense was he a naturalist, unifying man and nature. Like Socrates, he can hardly be cited as a precedent for unifying humanism and naturalism.

Neither can Aristotle. The dualism remains between form and matter, between entelechy and *energia.* So far from the soul of man being one with nature, it gives form to the body; it is an active principle. It has in it a rational element which is immortal at one with the pure thinking of thought which is God. True enough, Aristotle is the father of most our sciences. And doubtless the lost portions of his educational theory included the biological sciences as a part of his curriculum, supplementing the gymnastic and musical training be describes. But the characteristic excellence of man, his rational soul, Aristotle did not find in the realm of nature, plants and animals. The forms and essences that were in nature were also in man but man had an additional trait that their natural types lacked. Aristotale too is a dualist, not a humanistic naturalist. There is warrant for citing him as a precedent for studying natue but not as a precedent for man's continuity with nature. The Greek thinkers were dualists with emphasis on the intellectual as the more real, to whom no scientific study of nature was equal in educational value to philosophy.

One additional point. One might conclude from the text that the dialectical method, to which exception is taken, first arose among the mediaeval Schulman. They took it from Plato. It is the method of the rational analysis of concepts with a view to securing logical consistency. It is not yet outworn as one phase of method; the other phase is the admission of new data not found in the initial concepts. Plato admitted new data, thus widening concepts; the cholmen did not.

### The Modern Scientific Interest in Nature

*Exposition*—Following the great Renaissance the scientific interest in nature widened the breach between man and nature, and thus widened also the breach between the humanistic and the physical studies. From the Renaissance till now we have had centuries of dualism between man and nature, between the humanities and the sciences. Such dualism is as regrettable as unnecessary. How it came about we are now to see.

The period of the revival of learning and the great Renaissance ushered in modern times. The trouble began not during the Renaissance but following it. During the Renaissance the science of nature was a daughter of humanism, as interest in has said. The scholars of the Renaissance were interested in man's present life, and so in his relations to nature; they were not interested in mediaeval supernaturalism; they turned from divinity to humanity; they are called 'humanists'. This change in the centre of man's interest was due to the contemporary conditions, new inventions, new geographical discoveries. It was not so much the revival of interest in Greek literature sending men to observe nature as it was a revival of interest in nature sending men back to Greek literature for congenial sustenance and reenforcement. They were seeking not so much the Greek literature as the Greek spirit, the spirit of mental freedom, the spirit of joy in the order and beauty of nature, the spirit of untrammeled observation. The content of Greek literature inspired the dawning physical sciences of the sixteenth century. They sought in nature the macrocosm of which man was the microcosm; the big world of nature and the little world of man were one.

How then did man and nature come to be divorced! Whence the sharp division between the humanities and the sciences? There were four causes of this result.

*(a) The institutional cause*—The old authoritative tradition was firmly intrenched in the educational institutions of the day. Politics, law, diplomacy and history were still rooted in bodies of

authoritative literature. Effective methods of language teaching were already developed and possessed the field; these profited by the inertia of academic custom. Greek itself had to fight its way into the scholastic universities; it was the "Greeks against the Trojans" over again; the Greeks finally won, but having won, they joined the forces of their erstwhile foes against the newcomer: experimental science. The teachers rarely knew science; the scientists rarely taught, but worked in private laboratories and held membership in scientific academies. And the mighty aristocratic tradition still looked down upon material things, the senses and the hands.

*(b) The revolt of Protestantism*—North of the Alps the Renaissance affected religion. The Protestant Reformation resulted. The interests of men centered in theological controversy. The appeal of the disputants was to authoritative literature. Men were trained to study and expound the literary records; the respective faiths must be defended and propaganized By 1650 the gymnasia and universities were tools of linguistic training, religious education and ecclesiastical controversy. The prestige of Latin, Greek and Hebrew in education today is due only indirectly to the revival of learning and directly to the theological controversies of the information period.

*(c) The misconceptions of natural science itself.* Men did not follow Francis Bacon; he taught the progress of science in the service of man. We do not follow him yet; we practice the progress of science in the exploitation of man. Thus, science has been misused to war on the interests of man. And so the physical and social studies are not unified.

Francis Bacon ideally unified naturalistic and humanistic interests. He rejected the mediaeval learning and logic as controversial and agrumentative; it did not discover the unknown. Men should cease the futile effort to dominate each there and should join in the cooperative task of dominating nature in the interest of man. Scientists should give up "participating" nature by imposing their own preconceived actions upon her and seek instead humbly to interpret her. Intellectual obedience would lead to practical command:

"knowledge is power". The old logic of deduction should field place to his new logic of induction, whence would come expansive discoveries and fruitful inventions. Bacon was a prophat of a new scientific knowledge and a new social order. The former has come, the latter not yet.

The new science has regrettably, not necessarily, been worked in the interest of the old order of human exploitation. It has given man not new ends but new means to old ends. The revolution in science has been followed by the revolution in industry; the revolution in industry has bot been followed by the revolution in society. It is taking the scientific revolution many centuries to produce the new mind. It doomed feudalism to transfer power from the landed noble to the urban manufacturer, but it has led to unsocial capitalism instead of to social humanism. Capitalism in self-interest uses science in the economic production and distribution of goods; it misses the moral lesson of the new science, which is that man has human interests beyond making, saving and spending money. This untoward and unwelcome situation played into the hands of the professed humanists; they claimed that science was materialistic, and that languages and literature represented the moral and ideal interests of humanity. So the gap was further widened between man and nature.

*(d) A mistake philosophy.* This post-Renaissance philosophy purported to be based on science. In form it was either dualistic or mechanical. In either case the breach between nature and man was widened. Dualistic philosophy made a sharp division between mind and matter. It was represented by Descartes. Mind was *res cogitans;* matter was *res extensa.* Man had mind; nature had no mind. Men would, of course, regard human affairs as of chief importance. The effect on the curriculum was to exalt the humanities and to debase the sciences.

**Mechanical philosophy**—Lamettrie, Baron d'Holbach) had the same net effect. It reduced the signal features of human life to illusion. It thus threw suspicion on physical science, giving occasion to treat it as an enemy to man's higher interests. Some explanation is desirable here.

The mechanical philosophy gave a new slant to the new science, treating nature as having only quantity and lacking in quality. This was contrary to both Greek and mediaeval views, which accepted the world in its qualitative variety and regarded the processes of nature as purposeful, teleological. Not so to the mechanical philosophy. Sounds, colours, purposes, good, bad, were regarded not as objective but as subjective as mere impressions on the mind. All qualities being thus withdrawn from objective existence, only quantitative aspects remained. Objective existence was mass in motion. The only differences left in nature were that in some places there were larger masses and faster motions than in others. Lacking qualities, nature lacked significant variety. Uniformities, not diversities, were emphasised. The grandiose scientific ideal was thought to be the discovery of a simple mathematical formula explaining all the variety of the universe. Though Einstein is not a philosophical mechanist, his mathematical formula seeking to unify gravitation and magnetism illustrates this ideal. The effect of the mechanical philosophy was, of course, to separate the physical and social studies from each other.

We pause to indicate that a mechanical philosophy misses the genuine purport of science. It is true that science is mechanical and quantitative, that it ignores the qualities of events, that it confines itself to the prediction and control of events. But in leaving qualities and ends out of account, it does not exclude them from reality; neither does it relegate them to an ineffective mental region; *it furnishes the means for realising ends.* A mechanical philosophy takes the technique, the apparatus, the terminology, for the reality; it substitutes the method for the subject-matter; it thus reduces the rich world of possibilities to a barren and monotonous redistribution of moving matter in enveloping space. The new science, in fact, increases man's power over nature, enables him to realise his legitimate cherished ends, and allows him to diversify his activities almost at will.

Looking back at the modern scientific interest in nature we see how various reasons have combined to separate man from nature, destroying the unity he once had with it in the Greek days, and splitting the curriculum of his studies into two contending parts, the physical and the social. This leads us to consider the resulting educational problem.

***Comment***—The title of this section refers to only over of the points made in the argument. A more descriptive title might be: The Post-Renaissance Separation of Nature and Man.

Francis Bacon is shown to have been mistaken in supposing a scientific revolution would usher in a new social order. Science did not have in it the motivation Bacon supposed it to have. Three centuries have made this clear. Yet Dr. Dewey is still trusting science to give us a new social mind. This seems fatuous.

One might gather from the discussion that all modern philosophies of science have been either dualistic or mechanistic, and that all modern educators have opposed the sciences to the humanities. No monistic philosophy of science is mentioned and no educator advocating science is named. However, these two conclusions would both be mistaken. Among such philosophers should be mentioned Spinoza, Leibniz, Kant (?), Hegel, Fichte, Schelling and Schopenhauer. Among such educators should be mentioned such early sense realists as Ratke and Comenius. These philosophers all found man and nature at one with each other either directly or through some deeper synthesis. And these educators, while espousing the cause of Latin, Greek and Hebrew, also found a place for the science of their day, and urged its place in the curriculum on the grounds both of utility and training. It would take us too far afield to show the validity of these statements in detail but reference may be had to the histories of philosophy and to the histories of education, or better, to the sources.

Not, of course, that these statements contradict the views of the text, but that they are needed to supplement the position in the text. It is true that the sciences have had to wage a mighty war against the classics for a place in the curriculum, but we are not to think that they have not had their proponents among some of the educators and we are not to think that all philosophy of science has been either dualistic of mechanistic.

There is another reason that might be added to the list to explain the long conflict between the languages and the sciences. It is that the languages were old and perfected and the sciences were new and perfecting. For this reason the languages were better taught than the sciences,—they probably still are. The study of the languages develops powers of expression; the teachers of the languages express themselves well; they have a developed feeling for speech. Thus, the humanities, being older, being taught better, being in possession of the educational field, naturally resented sharing the field with the somewhat rude and obstreperous youngster.

## The Present Educational Problem

*Exposition*—That is, as regards the physical and social studies. The present problem is to unite them. This can be done, as we shall now see, by making proper educational use of industries. In following through this argument, the following points will be noted: (1) the real unity of nature and man, (2) the proper way to teach the sciences, (3) the limitations in Greek humanism, and (4) the educational use of industries.

(1) Our experience shown us no division between a human non-mechanical world on the one hand and a physical mechanical world on the other. Man's home is nature. All human purposes depend for execution upon natural conditions. Separated from nature, the purposes of man are empty dreams and idle fancy. Any justly made distinction between man and nature rests on the difference between purposes and the means for their realisation; the purposes are man's, the means are nature's. This distinction is a matter of experience. Educational endeavour should recognise it, but allow no dualism between human concerns and a mechanical world.

This philosophy of the unity of nature and man is vouched for by two things, *viz.*, biology, and the experimental method of science. Biology teaches us its doctrine of development that man is continuous with nature, that he is a higher animal, that he is not a transcendent alien entering the processes of nature from without. And the experimental method of science shows that knowledge results from directing physical energies toward social uses. Man derives his knowledge from a naturalistic source. This experimental method of inquiry, as now repeatedly indicated, consists in defining a problem arising within experience, collecting data upon it, formulating an hypothesis about it, and then testing out the hypothesis. This process of manipulating material is the source of man's knowledge. This is the method of knowing, and the only method. It arose with the natural sciences.

And progress in the social sciences depends on using both the method and the results of the natural sciences. These social sciences include history, economics, politics and sociology. Social welfare is intelligently promoted only as the scientific method is used in handling social questions and only as the technical knowledge ascertained by physics and chemistry is utilised. Among such perplexing social problems the following may be mentioned: the conservation of natural resources, insanity, intemperance, poverty, public sanitation, city planning, and the use of government for the public welfare without weakening personal initiative. So, man's organism is one with nature, man's knowledge is one with nature, man's progress is dependent on his using the means provided by nature. Hence, we conclude man is one with nature; his whole being is naturalistic.

Such being the case, the humanistic and naturalistic studies are really interdependent. Let education take notice! Science should not be kept apart from literature; the study of nature should not be isolated from the interests of man. The sciences are more than technical forms of manipulation and technical bodies of information; they are the condition of man's, progress, from which the humanistic studies should not be isolated. It is artificial for the school to separate what life unites. Outside of school, there is no separation between natural facts and human action; the understanding of natural facts, principles, and processes are necessary for social activities to go on. For the school to rupture this intimate association of the natural and the human breaks the continuity of the student's mental development, deprives his of the normal motive for interest in his studies, and makes him feel and indescribable unreality in them. Instead, education should aim at cross fertilising the sciences and the humanities. And the pedagogical problem of doing so is simpler than that of keeping the two apart, as we shall see.

(2) The way science has been taught has tended to keep man and nature apart. Science has been taught as a body of logically arranged subject-matter distinct from the interests of life. The reason for so doing has been blind tradition, not a conscious

dualistic philosophy. The colleges introduce their students as would be experts into segregated scientific subject-matter, and the high schools imitate the colleges. The student beginning science should begin with his daily experiences; instead, he is offered a choice between "nature study" and "science" as a body of technically organised subject-matter. The "nature study" is miscellaneous, is presented haphazardly and leads nowhere in particular. The "science" is cut off from daily life. And so it results that a large part of the teaching of science is comparatively ineffective.

There are two classes of students of science, the few who will be specialists and the many who will not be. The many are concerned with the effect of science upon their understanding of their daily environment and upon their mental habits; they need to be more alert, more open-minded, more inclined to accept ideas only tentatively until they are tested in the crucible of experiment. For all such students it is certainly ill-advised to start them off with technically organised subject-matter. They achieve only a smattering which is too superficial to be scientific and too technical to be practical. But how about the few who will be experts? Even here the procedure described is questionable. They would probably make a better finish if they had a better start. Of course, all who have the disposition and the ability to become scientific experts should have the chance to do so. They may end by learning what other experts already know and by adding to such knowledge, but they might better begin by experiencing science.

So to begin is easier today than ever before. Ordinary experience should be utilised to secure and advance into science. Scientific material and method should be kept connected with familiar human interests. This is easy to do in our day because the usual experience of everybody in civilised communities is now intimately associated with industrial processes and results, which, in turn, are so many cases of science in action. Illustrations of science in action within the experience of most persons are the steam engine, both stationary and traction, the gasoline engine, the automobile, the telegraph, the telephone, the electric motor, the radio and the airplane. Children may see scientific achievements in both the business occupations and the household pursuits of their parents, in the maintenance of health, and in the sights of the street. Such experiences can be utilised to stimulate interest in scientific principles. What is the starting point in scientific instruction? Obviously not to teach things labelled "science". Rather to utilise the familiar in directing observation and experiment. Let pupils learn to know some fundamental principles in their familiar practical workings.

Here the old question meets us, is it better to study "pure" or "applied" science? Pure science is held to be cultural, while applied science is held to be practical. This view is mistaken. A subject is cultural in proportion as it has meaning; the more meaning the more culture. And meaning is a matter of connections; you see the meanings of a thing is proportion as you see its connection. Pure science deals with physical, technical, connections. Applied science adds the human and the economic connections. Thus, the cultural value of science is enhanced when it is both pure and applied. And the more important thing is that the fact is grasped in its human, social connections, that is, in its function in life. This makes the study of science humanistic, and bridges the gap between the physical and social studies.

This is the place to note too that there is a "humanism" that is not humanistic. The right sort of science is humanistic; the wrong sort of "humanities" is not humanistic. The wrong sort is that which pursues its interests apart from social well-being. The true humanism is inbued with an intelligent sense of human interests. Social interest is in its deepest meaning identical with moral interest, and this social-moral interest is necessarily supreme with man. Any study, whether physical or social, deserves to be considered "humane" only when it increases concern for the values of life, produces sensitiveness to social well-being, and develops ability to promote the public good. Instead, a specious humanism gives a knowledge *about* man, such as his past, his documented records, his literature, and his languages. Such a store of facts readily degenerates into a miser's accumulation, and the pedant, missing the meaning in the affairs of life, comes to pride himself on what he has. Such pedantic occupations as his have the letter without the spirit of real activity; they are on the level with the "busy work" of children; they are as technical as any accumulation of scientific details; they do not enlarge the imaginative vision of life. Physical and social studies have alike to learn the lesson of genuine humanism.

(3) We may point a contrast here by referring to the limits of Greek humanism. Not even the culture of the Greeks, could we attain it by studying our "humanities," would give as the true humanism. Despite the acuteness of the social observations and speculations of the Greek thinkers, they regarded Greek civilisation as self-inclosed and self-sufficient; they did not suspect that its future was at the mercy of the despised "barbarians!" Within the Greek community the humanistic spirit was native and intense, but narrow; there was higher culture but it was based on the labour of slaves and economic serfs,—classes necessary to the state but not genuine parts of it, as Aristotle declared. This ancient Greek humanism failed to consider economic and industrial conditions. It was thus one-sided. Its culture inevitable represented the intellectual and moral outlook of the ruling class. Such culture is aristocratic, emphasising class distinctions, and the conservative standards of the past. It does not represent common fundamental interests, it does not aim to extend the range of human values.

(4) The industrial revolution has given us a different world from that of the Greeks, necessitating a democratic culture. This revolution is due to applied science. It has brought different peoples in close contact through colonisation and commerce. One nation may still look down upon another but it can no longer harbour the delusion that its career is decided wholly within itself. Further, agricultural serfdom has been abolished. A new class of more or less organised factory labourers with political rights has been created; this class claims a responsible role in the control of industry; these claims receive sympathetic attention from many of the well-to-do; economic class barriers are breaking down. The new democratic culture is to be conveyed through the educational use of industrial activities. This is not so much an attack upon the narrow culture of the past; it is a wider way of making the culture of the classes more solid and the culture of the masses more genuine. Technical scientific studies

and refining literary studies are opposed to each other today because an industrial democracy and a literary aristocracy are opposed to each other. If society is to be unified in a true democracy, education must unify the physical and social studies.

***Comment***—We pause not for praise but for appraisal. The matters not specifically mentioned receive our tacit support.

Studies are here held to be usually divided into the physical and the social. This is the historic division into the sciences and the humanities. It falls in with the distinction between nature and man. This division can be profitable sub-divided. Among the sciences there are the physical and the natural. The physical sciences include physics and chemistry. The natural sciences include biology and related studies. The social studies may also be sub-divided into the humanistic and the social sciences. The humanities include languages and literatures. The social sciences include history, sociology and economics. A division into these four groups is carried out in the new reorganisation of the curriculum at the University of Chicago. At the very time that Dr. Dewey proposes a monism of studies to overcome the dualism of the physical and the social, a new pluralism appears on the scene, Here are two counter tendencies in the curriculum,—toward greater unification, and toward greater diversification. The advance of science favours specialisation and so diversification of studies. Yet a mental unification is necessary for a large life of adjustment to one's world. And certainly a social unity is gradually being atained by a zig-zag course. It is philosophy that says unify; it is science that says divide.

What will the educational outcome be? Probably the curriculum will continue to be divided in Junior High School, High School and College, where the project method meets increasing difficulty. Possibly the curriculum will be much more unified in the lower grades where the project method works best. But to offset the disunion of the higher curriculum, more stress will be laid upon the inter-connection of all subjects, and the unifying study of philosophy will receive more attention. That all subjects may be cross-fertilised to mutual advantage is perhaps obvious. The British scientists, like J. Arthur Thomson, often show a wide literary background.

The text argues for the unity of man and nature as a basis for the unity of the social and physical studies. This unity may very well exist but hardly on the naturalistic ground advocated. The two arguments adduced are evolution and pragmatism. The doctrine of evolution is still a doctrine, an hypothesis, or, at most, a theory, accepted it is true by most leading scientists today. Still, it is not yet a principle or a fact, the demonstration of which would be convincing to all. Furthermore, as a theory, it still requires a philosophy beyond biology. Biology as a science tries to answer the question whether man came from some pre-existent animal, and, if so, how. Philosophy tries to answer the question *why*. Whatever biology says, its answer is not final, though it may be true as far as it goes. The text goes no further than biology on the question of the origin of man. But all the typical philosophies have their answer as to the why of evolution. Among the variants there is a theory of theistic evolution which does not make man a child of nature except as nature itself is a dependent child of a Supreme Person.

The experimental method of inquiry, which is the same as the pragmatic method of Dr. Dewey, does not really make man one with nature, though it claims so to do. It is admitted that the means are nature's, but the ends are man's. If nature has means without ends, and man has ends without means, here is a dualism indeed. A real unity would assign ends also to nature and means also to man. This Dr. Dewey does not do. Until it is done, dualism remains. It can hardly be done on a naturalistic basis. It has been done on an idealistic basis which regards both nature and man as having both ends and means in themselves. Nature realised an end in the appearance of man, and man has some physical means in his own physique as well as in his powers of both practical and abstract thinking. We conclude on this point that the dualism between man and nature has bot been overcome on the grounds indicated but might be overcome on a different basis.

We may refer also to the possible danger of applying the experimental method to the social questions. With gravest difficulty can we experiment with the marriage rate, the birth rate, the death rate, and the fundamental virtues of truth speaking and respect for personality. Some social questions are already settled in principle. There is no occasion to call every social virtue and attitude into question. The race has learned much by unconscious experimentation. Society can ill afford to start afresh in testing by conscious experiment what the race has already will established by unconscious experiment.

A last point concerns the distinction between pure and applied science. That made in the text is between the technical and the practical, meaning by "practical" the human and the economic. In this sense applied science may will have the richer culture. But there is another distinction possible, as seen before. Pure science is disinterested, applied science is interested in consequences. In this sense the pure scientist is not thinking of applications, he is in love with the discovery of truth for its own sake; the applied scientist is not thinking of advancing human knowledge, he is thinking of making use of what is already known. The pure scientist is following an intrinsic interest, the ultimate results of which for society are extrinsic to him. His is the culture of truth. The applied scientist uses the results of the intrinsic interest of the pure scientist; these become instruments to his ends. Some industrial companies, practical, money-making, man-serving concerns, employ some high-salaried men just to do pure research, not to solve practical problems at all. Some of the most striking recent discoveries have so arisen. While some of these discoveries are immediately useful, some are not. Here is a type of pure science that fully justifies itself, because it satisfies the intrinsic interest of the investigator, and because it furnishes as supply of knowledge greater than the practical demand for it. Our conclusion on this point is that there is a form of pure science, and so a form of culture, that does not have to be harnessed to solving practical problems and that nevertheless justifies itself.

# 12

# Pedagogical Orientation–Classical Studies Foundation

## THE CLASSICS AND NATIONAL LIFE

**Livingstone**

The title of my chapter is vague and I must define its subject more precisely. The classics include Latin and Greek; am I dealing with both of emphasising one? They may be regarded as fields of scholarship, as instruments of education, or as influences on the mind and the character; which aspect have I in mind? Let me take the second question first and say that these three aspects are a trinity which cannot be divided. Classical scholarship is the earth from which our studies grow and on whose condition they ultimately depend; not all the products of either the earth or of scholarship are fit for ordinary human consumption and most of them need treatment and transformation before they reach the family table but as humanity would perish if the earth was destroyed, so the classics would vanish if scholarship disappeared. Classical teaching in schools and universities brings the products of scholarship to digestions with very various powers of assimilation, and needs perpetual thought and revision of that the maximum quantity of food may be healthily absorbed and so that the technique of teaching may not become mechanical routine. But there is another aspect of the classics besides scholarship and teaching. Such names as Goethe, Shelley, Mill, Matthew Arnold, Robert Bridges can hardly fail to suggest the classics, which were a chief formative influence on their minds. But they suggest neither classical scholarship nor classical teaching. They remind us of a further aspect of the classics, apparently unknown to many critics of a classical education and certainly often forgotten in controversy on the subject—the influence of Greek and Latin on the national mind, partly through poets and thinkers whose view of life has been moulded by them, partly through men of action whose early education was predominantly classical. It is with this aspect of the classics and this argument for their study that my address deals. It is the root and centre of the controversy about Greek and Latin, for the question that we discuss when we argue as to the place of the classics in education is whether we wish this influence to persist in national life or whether we feel that it can be dispensed with and discarded; whether their disappearance from our educational system would make little difference or whether it would be a disaster.

Approaching the classics from this angle I must talk chiefly of Greek. That is not to underestimate Latin. There are many arguments for its retention as a staple subject in secondary education, but there is one overwhelming reason. The majority of English words are Latin in origin, and without some knowledge of Latin no Englishman has an educated man's grasp of English. Even if a pupils takes Latin only to School Certificate standard, he can get some idea of the fineness and depth of tone in his own language and learn to strike some of its notes more accurately. And, linguistics apart, what intellectual stimulus he can get from being shown the descent of words like "civilisation," "liberal", "urbanity,' "society". Still, though Latin is indispensable to higher education, Greek is more important in the formation of the mind.

In a world of flux and mortality Greek seems to be one of the few imperishable things; humanity apparently cannot afford to let it die. Latin has survived for historical and practical reasons; it has been in continuous use from the Roman Empire to the present day, first as the *lingua franca* of educated men, then as the international tongue of scholars, and throughout in the services of the Roman Catholic Church; without it no scholarly study of European law and history, of the Romance languages, or even of

English and Irish, is possible. But there are no such reasons to keep Greek alive, and it has had no such steady and continuous existence. The stream of Latin has been perennial unbroken. Greek, like one of the rivers of its own land that vanish in seasons of drought, almost wholly disappeared in western Europe for hundreds of years, till human thirst drew its waters again from their deep cisterns.

There have been three Greek revivals in European history. The first came when Greece lay prostrate in the ruins of its lost independence, and Rome, though mistress of the world, turned to her to learn literature, thought, civilisation; a paradox which no one felt more keenly then the Roman who wrote:

*Graecia capta ferum victorem cepit*

Then the language, the outlook, an most of the influence were lost in western Europe and a new organisation and new ideals took its place. Yet the Middle Ages found these insufficient for its life and turned to the Greeks as if they were the possessors of a great secret, who perhaps could not by themselves save the world but without whom it could not be saved. And this second Renaissance involved something which is unique in history—the revival in western Europe of a language which is those lands was to all intents and purposes dead. There is no more arduous task than to revive a dead language and men will only undertake and succeed in it when they feel a great need, a great hunger. It is characteristic of More's Utopians, who had so little to learn from Europe the "when they heard me speak of Greek literature and learning (for in Latin there was nothing except the historians and poets that they seemed likely strongly to approve) it was wonderful how enthusiastically they urged me to allow them to learn it under my instruction. So I began to teach them, at first more because I did not wish to seem to refuse the labour than for any results that I hopes from it. But when we had advanced a little, their diligence at once convinced me that mine would not be given in vain..." Sixteenth-century Europe did, in fact, what more imagined his Utopians doing.

The third revival of Greek, less recognised but no less real, began with the opening of the last century and may, and should, continue and increase. I shall say something of it and of some of its leading figures later. It is not comparable with the Renaissance, for its makers had not to revive a lost language, and turned to Greece not for actual knowledge, with which they were better provided already, but for something rarer—wisdom. Their need was spiritual (it is essentially a spiritual need that has caused all these three Greek revivals), and they saw that this two-thousand-year-old literature possessed something indispensable to human life, and wanting in the civilisation of their day. They felt, long before the world felt it, the barrenness of the civilisation created by the Industrial Revolution, and the need for a life which would embody the virtues for which the Greeks cared most—truth, beauty and justice. The need is not dead nor the movement. Nothing is more remarkable than the interest in Greek and the appetite for it shown in this country by persons of all types and classes who know no Greek but happen to have come across Greek thought in translation. It is further evidence of the indispensability of Hellenism to a full human life, so that men will not let it die.

A study of these returns to a civilisation apparently dead and gone would reveal much of the deeper needs of human nature, which continually deserts the path of its peace but is never permanently contented in error. In each of these Greek revivals there is a search for, and recovery of, some element without which spiritual health is impossible, a quickening and enriching of life. Glance for instance at the influence of Hellenism on the nineteenth century. What would you have expected England to become when the Industrial Revolution transformed it into a manufacturing nation and the Reform Bill of 1832 put the middle classes into power? You would have expected it to become the modern Carthage, all its thoughts given to industry and commerce, its motto.

*Rem facias, rem,*
*Si possis recte, si non quocunque mode rem.*
*("Make money, money; honestly if you can, if not,*
*by any means, money.")*

How easily wealth, or the less ignoble but equally moral ideal of power, might have become the ruling principle of the nation!

And there is that element in the history of nineteenth-century England. But manufacturers and markets are not the only words on its lips. Britain is a great mercantile power and a great imperial power. But she is something more, and that is due to two forces in the age which were hostile to materialism in English life and politics. One was Charistianity, the other was Hellenism, both equally hostile to the rule of Mammon or of the Miltonic Satan. The former, which was much the stronger in the Victorian Age, is obvious in Shaftesbury, Bright, and Kingsley, the latter in J. S. Mill, Matthew Arnold and Walter Pater. The two combine in Gladstone and Ruskin. Charistianity and Hellenism were and are the bases of our national culture, so far as we have one. If a nation possesses a culture, its life flows on through deeps and shallows, past obstacles, eddies and backwaters, in a steady current. Such a flow English life has so far maintained, though at the moment this current of our culture is in danger, for the two streams which form it. Hellenism and Christianity, are both weaker than they were. In the nineteenth century they flowed strongly. Christianity was far the most effective and influential, for it touched and coloured the whole nation, while Hellenism only affected an *elite*. But it was a very important *elite*. For, with certain exceptions, it was the educated classes of the country.

I doubt if everyone realises how important an influence Hellenism had on nineteenth-century England, or how much of what we admire in it is due to Greek, which counteracted its besetting sins. Without that element its pattern would have been broken, its texture threadbare and mean. Take only the field of political and social thought, and consider some men of the age whose minds and outlook were largely formed by Greek influence; utilitarians like Mill and Grote, idealists like T. H. Green, Matthew Arnold and Ruskin and lesser but influential men like John Morley, L. T. Hobhouse, Graham Wallas, Henry Sidgwick, Lowes Dickinson, C. E. Montague, R. H. Tawnev, Arnold Toynbee. Innumerable living names will occur to my audience; I will only mention two eminent present-day representatives of poetry and thought—T. S. Elliot and Professor Whitehead. Take from these men what Greece taught them, and how completely they would have been changed! Take them out of the last century and how you would have impoverished the thought and action of England!.

For one thing English Liberalism would have lost its chief source and most enduring quality. The influence of Greece is not confined to the Liberals. It is as powerful in Newman who hated their creed, in Ruskin who mistrusted it, in Pater who was wholly uninterested in it, in Bridges who was a poet and not a politician. Yet Greece is one of the chief makers of English Liberalism, if we are thinking not of that thin wine associated with the names of Cobden and Bright, but of the rich cordial, which, far back in English thought, is found in More and Milton, who also learnt it from Greece, and of which the grapes were pressed in a brighter land and in days when Manchester was an uninhabited swamp. I am thinking of the Liberalism of Mill and T.H. Green and Gladstone and Morley. It is clearly no accident that they and so many of the most characteristic Liberals of the age we brought up on the classics and drank deeply of the springs of Greece. One of the most famous of them has traced his creed to its origin. "Oxford,' said Gladstone, "laid the foundations of my Liberalism. In the region of philosophy she had initiated if not inured me to the pursuit of truth....... The splendid integrity of Aristotle....... conferred upon me an inestimable service."

Certain Greek beliefs reappear in the best English Liberalism: the acceptance of reason as a guiding light in human conduct and affairs; the belief that truth is not a ready-made article, retailed by governments or even by churches, but something to be pursued and painfully won; the conviction that liberty is neither a privilege nor a luxury but a necessity in whose absence the human spirit contracts, withers and finally dies.

But Hellenism is something more than a belief in reason and liberty. These words do not exhaust the contribution of Mill to English political thought, or of Gladstone to English political action, or of Greece to the ideal of human life. They are only part of a wider creed. Gladstone's statement of it is the more interesting, because he was an ardent Christian and churchman and because in him the two spiritual forces of the age, Christianity and Hellenism, combined. His address at Edinburgh University "On the Place of Ancient Greece in the Providential

Order' may sometimes be old-fashioned in phrasing but its general conception is sound. He argues that Hebraism teaches the relations of man to God, but he sees clearly that it is not enough; it did not supply "the Christian ages with laws and institutions, arts and sciences, with the chief models of greatness in genius or in character". That was the function of the Greeks who created the ideal of civilisation, "a thing distinct from religion but destined to combine with it." "Christianity meant for him a tradition of art, letters and politics, chiefly Greek and Roman in achievement and experiment, illuminated by the Christian revelation and itself contributing to its power."

Hellenism by its influence on the educated class and through it on the national life, did much to save the soul of the nineteenth century. What of its uses to our own age?

Anyone who studies it has the inspiration of supreme achievements in art, architecture, literature, thought, politics, human character, and life, and of living with the men who created these and also created, in a world where they did not exist, science and philosophy and, something even more important, the scientific spirit. Further, he has seen most of the fundamental problems of life, not in the complicated forms which they assume in modern society and thought, but in their simplest shape. Take Plato for instance. Each age discovers some new attitude to life: how often Plato has been before it! We have conceived the idea of a planned society. Plato, living in free Athens, drew the first sketch of such a society. In his philosopher-king he anticipated Masaryk and Smuts; and—less heppily—in the Nocturnal Council of the *Laws,* the purpose and methods of the Inquisition. If not of the Cheka. The early twentieth century saw the emancipation of women; Plato, in a world where women had neither liberty nor education, argued that they should have the same education and the same spheres of work as men. Hitler has taught and practised the gospel that might is right. In the *Gorgias* Callicles expounds the same doctrine and is answered by Socrates. In the *Laws* the materialist asserts that matter alone is real, and that religion, morals, law and art are mere human inventions without a basis in nature; and Plato's retort is still the best summary reply to his view.

But to study Greek is to see more than permanent problems and elements of human life. It is to see them fitted into a coherent design There is nothing more characteristic of the Greek mind than their use (to which we have no equivalent) of two common and recurrent words, *kóσμos* and *àρμovia* "order" and "harmony" or "fitting-together." Those words reveal the Greek passion for an "ordered," harmonious" existence, in which all the elements and possibilities of human nature are "fitted together," find their place, and work without jar or clash. It is the artistic instinct, applied not to words or stone or marble but to life; a salutary correction to the English temperament which thinks in particulars and not in wholes, and to our age, in which there is so little order, so little "fitting together". The Greeks called the universe *kóδμos*—a far profounder word for it than "universe"—and they sought to make human existence a *kóδμos* in side the *kóδμos* which is its theatre.

Hence to study Greek is to study a great picture of human life; a picture which is not complete, but is the most nearly complete yet painted; which is essentially modern, for reason directs and controls its design; which is human, for its subject is man in his relation to the material universe, to religion, to knowledge and art, to politics and society. A man brought up on Greek is more likely to know clearly what he thinks, because he has lived with men who knew what they thought, and who formed a clear and consistent view of life. At least he will feel the need for such a view and be uncomfortable without it. Because he has seen this Greek picture of life, he will have a pattern with which to compare his own time, a standard by which to judge it. And he will have seen the world not as an Englishman or a Frenchman or a German or a Rusian but as a human being. For Hellenism is a universal and supernational culture which each nation can adapt and modify as its own genius and tradition may suggest, but which, like Christianity, remains a common bond between all its children.

I am not, of course, suggesting that the Greeks spoke the last word about life—no view could be more untrue to their forward-looking spirit, eager, even is their decadence, "either to tell or to hear some new thing"—or that the study of Hellenism is a complete equipment for the modern world. But it is an unrivalled base from which to go forward: partly because the Greeks were so great, partly because they were so simple, partly because they saw life as a whole and within their limits saw it completely. Greek is no substitute for modern studies, but it is a correction and assistance to them. An American scholar, brought up in his own country on sociology, once told me that he never realised what it was all about till he read Plato. The world of modern studies in so vast and complicated that the student almost inevitable fails to orientate himself in it. He is like a man who begins his study of a continent on a six-inch-to-the-mile map—intimate with details, never fitting them into a whole, unaware even that there is a whole. That perhaps is why Professor Whitehead wrote: "I will disclose on private conviction…that, as a training in political imagination, the Harvard School of Politics and Government cannot hold a candle to the old-fashioned English classical education of half a century ago." And in this place I may add another testimonial. "The Oxford School of *Literae Humaniores* seems to my mature judgment the best scheme of education that I have ever heard of. … The subjects discussed are the eternal problems of thought, of conduct and of social organisation. These are discussed, not by means of contemporary catchwords but by translating them back into another world and another language.

These and other reasons explain the place which Greek has taken in education and its fascination for very different men and ages. But it has a special value and importance for us. In 1914, there was a tendency to look to science for salvation. Science is obviously one of the most powerful forces in the modern world and an indispensable element in higher education, but few people today would argue that by itself it can make or save a civilisation. In 1941 that role is assigned to economics or sociology. They too are indispensable to the health of the body of civilisation, but they are not concerned with its soul, and have no answer to our deepest problem. As Plato said in the *Charmides,* "It is not the life of knowledge, not even if it includes all the sciences, which creates happiness and well-being, but a single branch of knowledge—the science of good and evil. If you exclude this from the other branches, medicine will be equally able to give us health, and shoemaking shoes, and weaving clothes. Seamanship will still save life at sea, and strategy win battles. But without the knowledge of good and evil, the use and excellence of these sciences will be found to have failed us." Of the truth of these prophetic words we are becoming aware. Our science has not created for us "happiness and well-being". It fulfils its function and bears its amasing fruits, but their "use and excellence" is "found to have failed us" and even to turn to our destruction, because our age, so strong in other ways, is weakest in that "science of good and evil" of which Plato speaks, and which we call a sense of values. Eric Gill, writing of English intellectual and artistic circles years ago, said: "The thing that strikes me most is the absence of any clear leading or sense of direction. R. himself, in the middle of his intellectual salon, sat profoundly on the fence, and all the other people seemed to be balancing themselves nicely in the same way... They all believed in beauty, were interested in truth, and had doubts about the good." Fifty years have not made this description less applicable to us.

Ours is a very good age on the technical side; there is nothing wrong with its physics and chemistry, its biology, its mining and metallurgy; its political administration, considering human nature, is not bad. But it lacks that clear purpose which is prosperity guides men to use their resources and opportunities nobly, and in adversity keeps them steadfast and undismayed on their course and sustains them which the certainty of a better day which, if not they, their posterity will see. We live in a world clear, efficient, and creative in the realm of means, but almost wholly at sea about its ends. And our education suffers from and aggravates this weakness. At the best it teaches admirably isolated subjects, mathematics, languages, science, history, literature, technology; but they remain isolated. No common purpose informs and directs its processes. It provides its pupils with the means of living but leaves them in the dark about ends. That is the modern form of putting the cart before the horse what wonder that the cart jolts so much and progresses so little!

We cannot have too much science, technology, economics, but they lose their usefulness unless we see clearly the ends for which we intend to use them, and unless those ends are worthy of man. They deal with means and not with ends, and the more we have of them the more we need to strengthen, in both education and life, those studies whose subject is the "knowledge of good and evil". Education, we are often told, should be related to a social background. But a social background includes a spiritual element as well as economics, technology, and political machinery; and these exist for the sake of the spiritual element and not for their own. To ignore that element is to make life material and mechanical, and—what is not always realised—to deprive the machine of its chief motive power. In the modern world it is too often ignored; and part of the greatness of Plato and Aristotle as political and social thinkers is that they never forgot it. There are truths of economics and science: but there are even more important truths in which the mind needs to be dipped so deeply that it never wholly loses the dye—such, for instance, as Aristotle's words, "The state originates for the sake of life; it continues in existence for the sake of the good life." "The chief task of politics is to produce a certain character in the citizens and to make them good and capable of noble actions." "Man, when perfected, is the best of animals, but when divorced from justice he is the worst of all … Justice is the principle which brings order into political societies.." "The study of what man should be and what he should pursue is the noblest of all studies". It is also the most important. That study fascinated the Greeks and pervades their thought on politics and life. Their success in it may be judged from Goethe's saving that of all men they have dreamed the dream of life best. Their literature is the record of that dream. That is why the world has continually recurred to it, and that, for any age and above all for our own, is the greatest argument for reading it.

How incomplete is any serious study of literature without a knowledge of Greek liteature—not because of specific debts which later writers may owe it, but because it is the greatest European literature except perhaps our own, and because it is so unlike our own! To study literature seriously, yet remain ignorant of Greek literature, is like studying religion and remaining ignorant of Christianity. But, however successful our efforts, only a small minority in this or any country will learn Greek. Must the great mass of educated persons remain untouched by Greek thought? The answer is "Yes, unless they study it in translation."

Those who object to translations for such purposes have a case on paper; but only on paper. The Old Testament in the English version is not the Hebrew Scripture; yet we read it with profit. English translations of *War and Peace* and *Peer Gynt* are far form what Tolstoy and Ibsen wrote; yet are we deterred from reading them? Plato in our language is not the same as Plato in his own; yet undeniably the thought and even the eloquence of Plato do stir the reader in a translation. It is, of course, absurd to go to the opposite extreme and say that nothing is gained by reading the original, if we have a good translation. That is untrue for good prose; it is still more untrue for poetry. It is untrue for modern languages; it is much more untrue for Greek. Those who care for great poetry, great prose, great thought, will always wish to learn the Greek language so that they can read the actual words written by Homer and Aeschylus and Plato and many others. If the Greekless reader missed nothing else, he would miss the most lovely and subtle instrument of expression ever devised. But there is such a thing as a ὕδετερος πλοῦς ; and sensible people do not refuse to be saved from shipwreck in a cargo boat, on the ground that they never travel in anything less than a liner. No same person who can read great literature is the original prefers a translation. But our choice is not between the great majority reading Greek literature in the original and their reading it is translation. It is between their reading it is translation or not reading it at all. Who can hesitate between these alternatives?

Assuming that we prefer a knowledge of Greek thought in translation to entire ignorance of it, I would like to make three suggestions. First, the attention should be directed to Greek authors rather than to books about them. No discourse on the Greek ideal of liberal democracy will make the same impression as the statement of it in the second book of Thucydides, any more than a sermon on the Beatitudes can equal the words of St. Matthew. So begin with the Funeral Speech of Pericles, with the speech of the Laws in the *Crito*, with Plato's'*Republic* and Aristotle's *Politics,* and go on to Zimmern's *Greek Commonwealth* or Barker's *Political Thought of Plato and Aristotle.* Bring the reader at once face to face with genius itself, and do not let us repeat without any justification a defect of some school teaching of the classics, in which the pupil spends two or three years in preparing to read two great literatures, but never gets a glimpse of them; like a man who goes lion-hunting through a jungle, and instead of lions sees only tangled vegetation in which the lions are supposed to live.

(May I suggest, in passing, a method of avoiding this defect of school teaching? It is worth putting on a blackboard once or twice a week something memorable in the language studied; a phrase from Horace of Tacitus or the Vulgate, a Latin epitaph ancient or modern, a Greek epigram, a line from a tragedy, a sentence from Plato. The class has something to look at in its moments of boredom, is reminded that its labours have a goal, and perhaps stores in memory something to delight and inspire.)

The Greeks then, before books about the Greeks. But if an English reader is thrown straight into Plato or Aristotle or even into Thucydides, unsupported and unhelped, he may crawl to the bank as quickly as he can and avoid the water in the future. This has been the cause of many failures to interest people in Greek. Even more than those who read the classics in the original, the Greekless reader needs an introduction and brief notes. Jowett did a great service by his translation of Plato, but it would have been greater if there had been explanatory notes and rather different introductions. The notes and introductions to Professor Murray's translations of Greek plays are models of what is needed. So are many volumes in the Bude series, especially those of Plato. The Claredon Press, which has already published the *Apology, Crito* and *Phaedo* and Aristotle's *Poetics,* in translation, with notes and an introduction for English readers, has published a similar edition of the *Republic* by Professor Cornford. One feature of this edition is the brilliance of Professor Cornford's translation. This takes me to my third point. For our purpose good translations are essential, and by good I mean translations into good English. Most of our readers will know nothing of Greek literature or Greek thought and will come to it with uncertain if not suspicious minds. They will not get far with these new studies if their first impression of Plato (for example) is of a writer without imagination or style who, had he been English, would have used words like "wherefore" and addressed a jury as "O my judges" and a friend as "O my blessed Simmias." The ideal translation of the *Republic* would sound as if Plato had composed it in English, writing somewhat as Newman wrote; certainly it must not appear to be the work of an Englishman unfamiliar with English idiom. Such translations give a far more erroneous impression of Plato than actual errors in interpretation. Some scholars have perhaps too much knowledge and too many scruples to be good translators for our purpose; with a little more ignorance or lack of conscience they would do better.

I would put translator roughly into five classes. Some have done the work so well, that it need never be done again: for instance, Bigg's *Confessions* of Augustine, or Phillimore's Philostratus done into trilliant English, yet reproducing exquisitely the manner of the original. After these I should put such renderings as Rice Holmes's Caesar, Jackson's Marcus Aurelius A. E. Taylor's *Laws* of Plato, Rackham's Aristotle's *Ethics* and Butler's Quintilian, which on the whole read like original English. (There are, of course, may others.) The close behind come a number of translations that will do till we get something better; Jowett's Plato for example. It has many errors, it shows genius in avoiding difficulties, it is uneven—clearly much less pains were taken with the *Laws* than with the *Republic*—and it only resembles Plato as champagne which has been standing for some hours in a glass resembles champagne. Yet it was a great attempt: it has introduced innumerable people to Plato; and it is far better to read Plato in Jowett than not to read him at all. But Plato still awaits his translator. The late Professor Phillimore suggested Mr. Compton Mackenzie for the task. I suspect that so far as the *Republic* is concerned, Professor Cornford will be found to have done it. In a fourth class I put translations, like North's Plutarch, which are works of literature but reflect the translator rather than the author. Plutarch was not an

Elizabethan; he was an enlightened Victorian with the outlook of Dr. Hammond or Professor Trevelyan, and North's English gives a wholly false idea of him. In the fifth class I put translations which have no reason at all for existing—but think it wiser not to give examples.

So far I have spoken only of prose. Poetry is a more difficult problem, for a Greek play in translation must read not only as if it had been written in English but as if it was poetry. Except for Shelley's *Cyclops,* how many Greekless readers had any reason to suppose that Euripides was a poet till Professor Murray translated him? It is arguable that poetry cannot be translated. Yet even here there are degrees of approximation to the original. I should put the *Agamemnon* of Mr. McNeice and Mr. Day Lewis's translation of the *Georgics* very high. The *Oxford Book of Greek Verse in Translation,* which covers the whole field of Greek poetry, shows what can be done in this kind. Prose translations of poetry are not so suitable for our purpose, but. Dr. Mackail's renderings from the Greek Anthology show how effective they can be; and though Lang, Leaf and Myers is open to criticism. I have heard a good judge of literature, who is not at all impressionable, say that the death of Hector in their translation was too moving to read aloud.

There are two fields in which this study of Greek in translation can be developed. The first is the school. Shortly before the war a syllabus was drawn up for an optional subject in Group I of the General School Certificate, including Greek Literature and History in Translation, and was submitted to the Matriculation Council of London University. Such a subject would not only enable pupils to learn something about Greek but also give those teachers up and down the country, who at present teach no classics except School Certificate Latin, opportunities in different and perhaps more interesting field. It is to be hoped that the project may be revived. But subjects can be studies apart from examinations and some masterpieces of Greek literature in English should normally be read in the highest forms of schools, so that it may be impossible for any boy or girl, who is capable of interest in such things, to leave school in total ignorance of what are probably the greatest intellectual and literary achievements of

European man. Some acquaintance with them is an essential element in a liberal education. Equally important, the necessary books should be in the library of every secondary school. A subject can be encouraged by its inclusion in the curriculum; but also by its appearance on library shelves. Translations from, and books about, the classics should be included in the books recommended in schools for private reading. This is especially important in the lists for higher forms.

But outside the schools there is an equally important and even more neglected field for the study of Greek thought through translations. There are, I am sure, an immense number of persons who have never learnt anything of Greek or Greek thought in early life but who, if they came across it later would find it "a possession for ever". Let me give two instances. A scholarship in Greek was recently founded at an Oxford College by a lady who in middle life became an invalid, learnt Greek in her enforced leisure, and finding in its literature strength and solace in illness, left her fortune to promote its study. My second instance is contained in an extract from a letter written last Christmas by a Lieutenant in the Navy to a relation who had sent him a volume of selections from Plato. "I must confess when I opened your parcel I was considerably shaken when I saw the title of the book. But I settled down after dinner last night and for about three hours I was fascinated. I had always held the view that a classical education was out of date and that a scientific education was of more practical use to the schoolboy in after life...Well, after reading quite a portion of this little book, which only professes to be a small selection from one man's work, I find it so very true to life now-a-days and so very much to the point, that I feel I have missed something. Thank you so much for this present which has opened new fields for me." It would be easy to multiply instances.

I happen sometimes to broadcast to schools about Greek, and I am struck by the number of letters I get from adult listeners who ask where they can read more about Greek thought. Such adults have and advantage over school and university students just because they are adults, and bring to their studies that knowledge of men and affairs without which literature never comes fully to life. The student gets much from reading history and great literature at school and university; but, limited by his lack of first-hand experience of its theme—life and men—he sees its vision of them is a glass darkly. Fuller comprehension comes later, when, having learnt from living what life and its problems are, we read or re-read the masterpieces of poetry and thought.

Here surely is a fertile and untilled field for this Association which was founded "to promote the development and maintain the well-being of classical studies"—a chance to carry out these objects by bringing some knowledge of Greek and Latin in translation to educated persons who have never learnt the languages. It can be done by the private enterprise of members, and, where these exist, by branches of the Association. These are apt perhaps to confine themselves too exclusively to the reading of papers, and might organise play–reading and circles for reading and study, designed for the unconverted as well as for the elect. I believe that this will add in the next generation to those who wish to learn the classical languages. Show the parents what they have missed and they will be more anxious for their children not to miss it. But in this generation it will have results perhaps even more important. It will bring classical thought into channels which otherwise it could never reach. The more successful such efforts are, the more influence the classics will have in moulding the national mind. And that is the real issue. For, as I said earlier, in discussing the place of Greek in education, we are discussing the future of English thought, and perhaps of western civilisation. We have a missionary task, deserving missionary fervour. And, as with all missions, it is a task for the individual as well as for the society.

## REFERENCES

Livingstone, R. W. "The Position and Function of Classical Studies in English Education" in *The Rainbow Bridge and Other Essays on Education* (London: Pall Mall Press, 1959).

Hammond, J.L., *Gladstone and the Irish Nation,* pp. 54f.

Logan Pearsall Smith, *Unfortotten Years*, p. 159.

Eric Gill, *Autobiography,* p. 172.

# 13

# Psychological Dimension

## LITERATURE AND THE NATURE OF MAN

**Theodore Spencer**

...If we think of it as a whole (Shakespeare's picture of man's nature), we can see that his work embodies, more completely than that of any other artist, the primarily artistic vision. To see it as a whole is essential. As T. S. Eliot remarks, "the standard set by Shakespeare is that of a continuous development from first to last, a development in which the choice both of theme and of dramatic and verse technique in each play seems to be determined by Shakespeare's state of feeling, by the particular stage of his emotional maturity at the time. What is 'the whole man' is not simply his greatest or maturest achievement, but the whole pattern formed by the sequence of plays; so that we may say confidently that the full meaning of any one of his plays is not in itself alone, but in that play in the order in which it was written, in its relation to all of Shakespeare's other plays, earlier and later: we must know all of Shakespeare's work in order to know any of it."

And as we look at all of Shakespeare's work, and try to derive from it his view of the nature of man, two facts emerge. In the first place there is the "continuous development" of which Eliot speaks, the development that begins with a period of experimentation—what we might call Shakespeare's "external" period—a development that continues with an enormous increase in dramatic scope and that presents the evil in man's nature with tragic force, a development that ends with acceptance, with regeneration, with a vision that sees human life as it is and sees it redeemed.

The second fact that emerges from our picture of Shakespeare's work as a whole—and this is something at which I have previously only hinted —is that though he drew very largely on what he inherited of the conventional concepts of man, and though his picture of man's nature would have been very different without them, nevertheless Shakespeare's vision of human life transcends anything given him by his time. The inherited concepts represent; of course, one particular codification of what is permanently true about humanity, and when a civilisation lacks such codification, that civilisation is in danger. But Shakespeare's presentation of Hamlet, of Lear, of Cleopatra, of Imogen and Miranda goes deeper than any codification: it is the individual human life, the thing itself underlying codification that Shakespeare gives us, and which makes him, in Ben Jonson's familiar phrase, "not of an age but for all time."

If we keep these two aspects of Shakespeare's vision of man in mind we may perhaps be able to accomplish the last of the three aims with which this discussion began. We have so far tried to see Shakespeare in relation to his time, and we have tried to see how his craftsmanship enabled him to use what his time gave him. The final problem remains: we must try to judge Shakespeare's work in relation to what we believe to be true of human experience as a whole. For the conflict between order and chaos, in the world, the state and the individual, the difference between appearance and truth, the search for what is most natural to man—these are the central problems of human thought; they were as pressing in the age of Aeschylus as they were in the age of Shakespeare and as they are today. The greatest writers have, directly or indirectly, always been concerned with them, and though these problems may take on different forms in different periods, it is only their accidents that change; the essence remains the same.

Since art, Aristotle says, is an imitation of life, the individual artist is necessarily compelled to imitate the life of his own period, and it is clear enough that certain periods are more favourable to good art than others. It is also clear that there are different kinds of imitation, even is the same period, and that a writer like Ben Jonson, who is concerned with the surface of experience, who describes social vice rather than spiritual evil, whose characters, unlike Shakespeare's, never look inward or experience an inner division—it is clear that a writer like Jonson will give us a different picture of his period from that of a man who probes more deeply and resolves more conflicts. It is not with Ben Jonson, or others like him—admirable in their own sphere though they may be—that Shakespeare should be compared. He should rather be compared with those writers, and they are not many, who used the views of their time to see human nature in its broadest terms, and whose imitation of life is an imitation not only of man in relation to society, but also in relation to himself and to the larger forces by which he feels himself controlled.

The periods in which the greatest writers have flourished have been those which, like Shakespeare's, have enabled the writer to use all three relationships; and this means that they have been periods when the writer's medium has been close to the life of the people. In such periods the artistic form has been traditional in the sense that it has been taken for granted, as the drama was taken for granted in the time of Aeschylus and Shakespeare, the allegorical vision in the time of Dante, and the novel in the nineteenth century. And in each of these periods there seems to have been a heightened consciousness of the precarious balance in human affairs between order and chaos, with varying emphasis on religion, the state and the individual.

The *Oresteia* of Aeschylus, more than any other dramatic unity, represents a completely fused relationship between literature and society. As Professor Thomson has recently shown, it was produced at a time when the drama had an intimate connection with religious and with social forms, and hence we find in its magnificent conception as interweaving, a fusion, of the three realms of man's being, the religious, the social and the individual; in the *Oresteia* an essential problem of man's nature is solved in relation to the gods, to the state and to himself. Orestes, the central figure of the trilogy, has killed his mother Clytemnestra because she had previously killed his father Agamemnon, and the moral problem he faces is whether or not he should be punished for having tried to avenge one crime by committing another. The situation is similar in many respects to that of Hamlet, but it is treated very differently. The play of *Hamlet* is equivalent, as far as the action is concerned, only to the second part of the trilogy of Aeschylus, and if Shakespeare had wanted to treat Hamlet's story as Aeschylus treated that of Orestes, he would have had to write an introductory play about the murder of Hamlets father and a concluding one which would have assumed that Hamlet's revenge had been successful, but that he was now himself on trial before a court of supernatural powers. We can imagine the first play easily enough, but the last one is inconceivable in terms of Elizabethan drama. In the *Oresteia* of Aeschylus, on the other hand, the last play, the *Eumenides*, is the essential culmination of the whole story. When Athena solves the problem of Orestes' individual guilt she at the same time solves the problem of man's relation to the supernatural by appeasing the Furies, and she solves the problem of justice in the state by establishing the court of the Areopagus. The three realms of ethics, religion and government are all brought together in one solution, in one reconciliation. The intimate relation between drama and the life of the people in fifth-century Athens, combined with his own extraordinary genius, enabled Aeschylas to create a work which fused into a single unity the three essential aspects of the nature of man.

The other Greek dramatists accomplished nothing so grand as this. Yet if we think of the plays of Sophocles in chronological order—though general speculation about them, since only a small percentage of them has survived, cannot be very securely based—we can see that the view of human life which they present also ends in a reconciliation, like the end of the *Orestela* and like the last plays of Shakespeare. *Oedipus at Colonus,* the play of Sophocles' old age, shows us Oedipus after his terrible ordeal, exiled and blind, stern and awe-inspiring, but no longer the proud and self-willed man whom Fate had so 'dreadfully punished. His death is miraculously calm:

It was a messenger from heaven, or else
Some gentle, painless cleaving of earth's base;
For without wailing or disease or pain
He passed away—and end most marvellous.

His death also is surrounded by wider implications, for it is heralded by a thunderstorm sent by Zeus, and, because he dies on Athenian soil, Athens will be forever preserved from her enemies. The death of the individual hero is related to the gods and to the state.

The use of the *deus ex machina* by Sophocles in the *Philoctetes* and by Euripides in nearly all his plays may be seen as another method of giving universality to the individual action, and of relating human concerns to the supernatural powers that control them. But in the hands of Euripides this device becomes only too often merely a mechanical trick, and we feel that Euripides, here as elsewhere, is unscrupulously manipulating his plot in order to give his audience a false satisfaction that has no basic relation to a view of human experience in general; he is striving for results that will surprise his audience rather than fulfil their expectations. There is a great difference between the Athena of Aeschylus, who solves the moral problem of Orestes with such rich social and religious connotations, and the Castor and Pollux of Euripides who appear at the end of Euripides' version of the story. The *dei ex machina* of Euripides merely describe what will happen to Orestes as a result of the murder, there is no weight of social implication; the effect, as usual with Euripides, is not an effect of grandeur but of pathos, and we think chiefly of Orestes himself, not of a world restored to order.

There is a striking parallel between Euripides and the dramatists, such as Webster and—on a lower level—Fletcher, who immediately followed Shakespeare. In each case we find a kind of irresponsibility, an emphasis on the unusual, a fondness for solving the problems of plot by some external means, like a *deus ex machina*—all of them characteristics which may be immediately successful on the stage, but which illustrate a view of man's nature that tends to disintegration, to a divorce between literature and the essential concerns of man. In each case we feel that individualism is glorified, instead of being made, as it is in

Shakespeare, one of the attributes of villainy, and when this happens in the thought and literature on an age, that age is on the road to decadence. For it means that one of the three realms in which man lives is being emphasised at the expense of the others, and that the proper balance between the individual, the state and the forces behind Nature has been lost. The part—and the same thing is true of all romantic literature—becomes more important than the whole, as it never does in Aeschylus, Sophocles or Shakespeare.

Nor does it, of course, in Dante. *The Divine Comedy* is the most perfectly ordered poem ever written, and the chief element in its order is Dante's use of the medieval view of life to present man in relation to the three realms of his being. In fact, it would be possible to use the poem as an illustration, perhaps the best illustration, of the orderly view of the cosmos, the state and the individual as so important a part of Shakespeare's intellectual and emotional inheritance. In *The Divine Comedy* the spheres of the Ptolemaic heavens correspond to various states of intellectual being and of moral purity they control everything on earth, and, in Dante's words, "direct every seed to some end according as the stars are its companions" (*Purgatorio* xxx). To Dante man's worst sins are those by which his special faculty of reason has been corrupted. And throughout the poem man's function as a citizen receives equal emphasis with his function as a rational animal; his duty to the state is as much a part of his nature as his duty to God. And after Dante has described the whole orderly universe, disordered only by man's wrong use of his free will (and even that disorder is taken care of by the ordered punishments of Hell and Purgatory), at the end of the poem he finds beneath the order the unity that is its soul, and in the final vision he sees all the individual accidents and substances which are scattered in leaves through the universe "bound up by love in one volume".

In its final emphasis nothing could be more different from Shakespeare than this; though to Dante man's behaviour in time may determine his place in eternity, Dante is primarily concerned with the eternal rather than the temporal world. His subject-matter is as different from Shakespeare's as the form of the allegorical vision is different from the form of the drama. Yet though Dante may describe order and the life that begins with death, while Shakespeare in his tragedies describes chaos and the life that *ends* with death, nevertheless Dante and Shakespeare have one thing in common, for both use the same views of man's nature for their very different purposes, and like the greatest of the Greek dramatists, see man's situation in relation to the three realms in which his thought and action move.

The greatest novelists treat human experience in the same way; we have only to think of Tolstoi's *War and Peace* to realise that if the nature of man is to be fully presented in literature, the same fundamental relationships must inevitable be included. Tolstoi's account of Prince Andrew and of Pierre, of their relation to peace and war, includes a description of their relation to the external forces that move them and to the society in which they live, as well as a description of the various ways in which they try to find a moral basis for action. It is because *War and Peace* contains all these things, these central relationships in which man sees himself, that it is a touchstone by which other fiction can be judged. By its side the work of Dickens, even the work of Flaubert, takes on a smaller dimension, for Dickens and Flaubert do not describe so much of what we believe to be true of human nature. In the long run the criterion of literary greatness must be not only qualitative but quantitative as well; quanity, or scope, as far as the vision of human life is concerned, being itself the final quality.

Tolstoi's description of man's nature differs, however, from those of Aeschylus, of Dante and of Shakespeare. For in the earlier periods of human history it was much easier than it was in the nineteenth century to take a positive attitude toward man's primary relationships; in fifth-century Athers, in the Middle Ages and in the Renaissance thought on the subject was far more clearly formulated than in Tolstoi's day. The earlier periods gave the writer a set of beliefs, the nineteenth century gave him as set of questions, and in no respect does Tolstoi more clearly reflect his time than in the way he presents Pierre Bezukhof, his main character, as *seeking* for answers to the meaning of life. Aeschylus, to be sure, is more original, more a creator of his own belief, than either Dante or Shakespeare, but Aeschylus could rely much more firmly than Tolstoi was able to do on a community of belief, just as he could relate his dramas much more closely to the social concerns of his audience, grouped together in a theater, than Tolstoi could relate his novels to his nineteenth-century readers, miles away from each other, scattered in a thousand arm-chairs.

Yet Tolstoi's questioning, so far as *War and Peace* is concerned, does produce an answer; an answer that is closer to Shakespeare's, perhaps, than those of Aeschylus and Dante. He also comes back to the individual experience, to the simplicity of the facts, to the marriage of Pierre and Natasha, to their life in their children, to that which is. The end of *War and Peace* lacks the exaltation of Shakespeare's last plays, because the medium is not poetry, but the meaning is the same. It is richer than the conclusion of Voltaire's *Candide,* whose hero shrivels into the restricted conviction that the only thing to do is to cultivate one's garden; it has a warmer human truth than the end of Goethe's *Faust,* whose hero self-consciously reclaims a swamp for the impersonal benefit of mankind.

When we think of the literature of the past in such general terms as those which I have been using, and which are universally applicable both to the life of action and to the art which interprets it, we are bound to have in our minds the thought of our own literature and our own lives. What strikes us at first is the contrast between the past and ourselves.

At the height of the Italian Renaissance, when, toward the end of the fifteenth century, the tradition of humanism was being felt with a new vigour and man's crucial position in the world of created nature was being re-stated with new force, Pico della Mirandola summed up the traditional thought of his time in his famous *Oration on the Dignity of Man.* To Pico, as to his contemporaries, man was in the centre of things, since by the right use of his reason and his will, he could choose whether he would live the life of the angelic intellect or the life of the brutish senses. Heaven and hell were on either side of him, and, as the chief inhabitant of an ordered universe, his responsibility was to see that he played a conscious and rational part in the marvellous structure which the divine architect had created for him, so that he could praise the God who made him. Out of that view, that dramatic tension of responsibility, grew the drama of Shakespeare.

What has our own time to say that would be as typical of the twentieth-century view of man's nature as Pico's view was typical of the Renaissance? What can we say of the dignity of man?

At first sight it would seem that we could say very little. We see ourselves today as living on a minute satellite of a tiny solar system that is of an almost infinitesimal size compared to the hugeness of the galaxy to which it belongs, a galaxy that is itself only a small part of the material universe. We can comprehend our universe only in terms of mathematical formulae, we cannot see it. And our existence on this unthinkably small planet seems to have come about by accident. A set of apparently chance events started the peculiar biological process called life of which we are the temporary products. Both the space and the time which have produced us are incomprehensibly huge. And, to shift the focus, we owe what we are, not to our wills, but to a set of predetermined forces, the accidents of birth and environment, which decide what sort of beings we will be long before we are conscious of being. Our unconscious desires turn as this way and that, like weathervanes, and if we are to be happy, we are told, we must let the wind blow us where it pleases. "I think I could turn and live with animals," says Walt Whitman, "they do not make me sick discussing their duty to God." We pay a kind of lip-service to reason, but we trust our instincts more than we do our brains. We have lost any real belief in the capacity of intellect to dictate our actions, and our prevalent theory of education persuades us to adopt as our principle of behaviour the motto which Rabelais put over the entrance to his Abbey of Théléme, "Fais ce que voudras"—Do what you please—without any of the Stoic principles of order which Rabelais had assumed the inmates of his Abbey to possess before they went there.

Believing ourselves to have no necessary relation to the cosmos, and to be at the mercy of our unconscious impulses, and hence finding ourselves in an unsatisfactory relation to two of the three aspects of our situation as human beings, we are in danger of ower-emphasising the importance of the third aspect, and of seeking in our relation to the state a compensation for the impersonality of the universe and the impotence of our wills. In some countries this over-emphasis has already gone almost as far as it can go, and the countries that remain are being forced into temporary imitation in order to destroy their rivals so that the balance may be restored.

In other words, as we look today at man's relation to the three aspects of his world, we seem to be facing a depressing and belittling situation, and our concept of the insignificant nature of man seems unlikely to produce any permanent expression of human life, in literature or elsewhere, that can compare with the expressions of the past.

And yet, if we consider more deeply, and take into account the possibilities of the future, this gloomy picture, which was given in such different terms at the beginning of the seventeenth century, represents only a partial truth. Though some aspects of science—which bears the same relation to the thought of our day as religion did to the thought of the sixteenth century—seem to make man hopelessly insignificant, other aspects present him as occupying a more favourable and important position. From one point of view contemporary scientific thought about man is even parallel to the religious thought of Shakespeare's day. For example, Mr. Julian Huxley, in his essay on "The Uniqueness of Man," after discussing the differences that science observes between man and animals, remarks that "biology. . . reinstates man in a position analogous to that conferred on his as Lord of Creation by theology. There are, however, differences," he continues, "and differences of some importance for our general outlook. In the biological view, the other animals have not been crated to serve man's needs, but man has evolved in such a way that he has been able to eliminate some competing types, to enslave others by domestication, and to modify physical and bilogical conditions over the larger part of the earth's area. The theological view was not true in detail or in many of its implications; but it had a solid biological basis."

If man's importance can thus be formulated by the impersonal and long-range view of science, can we derive similar convictions by examining the more immediate and local situation? Biological science describes man in relation to Nature; is there any evidence at the present time that man's relation to his own consciousness and to the state promises anything more satisfactory than psychological or economic determinism would pessimistically describe?

If an awareness of the problem indicates the possibility of a more hopeful answer, we can, I believe, say "Yes." Of course, it is far more difficult in our own time than it was in Shakespeare's to say that any one view is typical of the age or predominant in it, for variety of opinion is much greater with us, but there can be little question that serious thought about man's nature is at the present time moving away from determinism to a view that re-establishes some psychological hierarchy in man's structure. The old emphasis on reason and will, the division of man's mind into faculties, is not likely to be re-accepted, any more than what Mr. Huxley calls the theological view of man's relation to the other animals is likely to be re-accepted. But just as that theological view is recognised to have had "a solid biological basis," so the old concept of an element in man's nature which can know and can direct is recognised as having a solid psychological basis. "There is nothing is the intellect which was not first in the senses," said Locke. To which Leibniz replied, "Only the intellect itself." And modern psychology returning to the central problems of man's nature, is trying to describe that "intellect" in terms consistent with scientific knowledge. "Mental life at its best," says one of the most distinguished of contemporary psychologists, "exhibits a consistency, a coherence, and a hierarchy of values." And it is on this fact that emphasis is now being laid with increasing force; the higher, rather than the lower aspects of man's nature, are being re-examined and re-defined. What is chiefly lacking (and it is a very large lack indeed) is an intellectual and emotional sanction—a conviction of truth like that which the Christian system gave in the sixteenth century—which will make the higher impulses of the mind seem the right ones to obey.

Certain people, as we know too well, have found a sanction in the state, but the sanction they have found is evidently not the kind that demands the use of man's highest faculties. And that is why, in government as in psychology and in science, fresh thought is being given to the old problems; necessity is forcing us to re-define our concept of the relation of the individual to the state. Here, as in natural science and in psychology, a change is taking place, and just as materialism and determinism have had to be abandoned because they do not fit the facts, so our unthinking acceptance of the nominal form of democracy, where the average citizen has had little or no relation or responsibility to the state—this also has had to be abandoned because it does not fit the facts. Upon the new order that may result, all our lives depend.

In other words, the gloomy picture of man's present relation to the three aspects of his world, the picture which seems so easy to paint, need not, and, if our civilisation is to survive, *must* not, be the right one. It gives only half the truth, just as the pessimism of the early seventeenth century gave only half the truth. And if we think of ourselves in relation to that period, and in relation to the two different views of man's nature which that period expressed, it would seem, as if a three-hundred-year cycle were coming to a close. What brought about the essential conflict in Shakespeare's day was the fact that the old views of man were being broken by new discoveries which widened the split between what man should be and what he was, and which made the reality seem evil under the appearance of good. Order was breaking into chaos. And in the course of the three-hundred-odd years between that time and our own, the consequences of those new discoveries have been pushed, it appears, as far as they will go. Galileo's confirmation of Copernicus has become the cosmology of Einstein, Montaigne's comparison of man to animals has become a philosophy is which impulse and determinism are seen as the masters of behaviour, Machiavelli has helped to produce what may be only the first of a series of Hitlers. Those one disruptive forces have almost created a new world of their own. But, as I have tried to indicate, their mastery is perhaps an appearance, and when the first half of the twentieth century is regarded three hundred years from now, as in this discussion we have regarded the early seventeenth century, our situation may perhaps be seen as the reverse of Shakespeare's, and our time may be described as a time when the new forces were not disruptive but collective, and when man's orderly relations to the three aspects of his world were not broken, but restored in a new shape.

If this is to happen—and enormous resources of thought and activity will have to be used to make it happen—literature will inevitable reflect the situation. Prophecy is, in such matters, rash, but we can safely say that if a first-class writer is to appear in our century he will have to present, in an artistic form that is taken for granted by his audience, the individual experiences of human beings in relation to themselves, to society, and to the larger forces that control them. The best writers of our generation have already recognised this responsibility, and any future historian of our time, is considering the work of Thomas Mann, of Proust, of Eliot, Yeats and Joyce (and there are others besides these), will see that each of them, in various ways, has been seeking for that ordered pattern of relationships which is the only true universality. Perhaps, for a complete expression of our age, we shall need a writer greater than any of these. Or we may, as seems likely, find that our time will be expressed in another form than that of the merely written word; the movies and the radio are closer to our lives than anything on a page. But whatever medium he may use, it is clear enough that the great interpreter of human life in our century, if he appears, will have to be in as intimate touch with the central problems of our thought and emotions as was the dramatic art of Shakespeare with the Renaissance conflict about man's nature.

But Shakespeare was in touch with something more than his age, and if we are to come back to our starting-point and try to arrive at a final view of his work as a whole, we must see it as a reflection of deeper truths than any that can be described by a local and temporary picture of the cosmos, of psychology, or of the state. Beneath any view of man's nature, at the very basis of human experience, are the elementary facts of birth, of life and of death. The rhythm of their sequence and renewal lies behind all our knowledge and emotions, and it is the rhythm that we share with all of living nature, with animals and grass. The earliest known religions are based on it, and so is the earliest literature.

Birth struggle, death, and that which is beyond death—these, as Gilbert Murray says, are the subjects of that primitive dance and song "which is the fountainhead of ancient classical poetry." They have been the essential subjects of all great literature ever since, as they were the subject of the morality plays which were so important a part of Shakespeare's technical background. And if we think of Shakespeare's work in relation to this essential pattern, this fundamental rhythm, we shall have, perhaps, a view of the sequence of his plays that will both underlie and transcend any view that we can obtain by thinking of his work merely in relation to the ideas of his time. "Shakespeare," said Keats, "led a life of allegory; his works are the comment on it," and we may interpret this somewhat puzzling remark by remembering that Shakespeare's career was divided into three stages: a period of experiment and adaptation, a period of tragic vision and a period of affirmation. Birth, struggle, death and renewal; these are not only the themes of the individual final plays, they are the themes which describe the course of Shakespeare's work as a whole, from his earliest plays through *King Lear* to *The Tempest*. Such, we may say—as we think of art and life together, so that historical description and technical analysis merge into an understanding of the symbolism of all men's lives—such was the allegory of Shakespeare's life: to have illustrated in his own work more richly than any other writer, that rhythm, that sequence, that vision, which all human being must recognise and accept as fundamental to the nature of man.

## REFERENCES

T. S. Eliot, *Selected Essays,* (New York, 1932), p. 170

George Thomson, *Aeschylus and Athens,* (London. 1941). Mr. Thomson writes (p. 297).

Murray, Gilber, *The Classical Tradition in Poetry,* (Cambridge Mass., 1930), pp. 205††

Huxley, Julian, *The Uniqueness of Man,* (London, 1941), p. 5.

Köhler, Wolfgang, *The Place of Value in a World of Facts,* (New York, 1988), p. 411.

Sherrington, Charles, *Man on His Nature,* (Cambridge, England, 1940); F. T. Stace, *The Destiny of Wetern Man* (New York 1942).

# 14

# Social Concepts Dimension

## The Aims of Education

....In what I wrote about education several years ago, a critic finds an inconsistency. He says, "Mr. Eliot's chief complaint of other writers on education is that they seek to use the schools to achieve social purposes they have at heart. Then he falls into the pit he has digged for others: he wants to use the schools to advance social purposes of his own." Now, I do not think that anybody can think seriously about education who is devoid of social purposes of his own; and I am sure that these social purposes will guide him towards some of his conclusions about education. For anyone who denies that education should have a social purpose will be omitting something without which it is not education. But I think that anyone who considers education in relation to social purpose should try to be quite clear as to what social purposes guide his own theory of education: which are peculiar to himself, or to a group whose views are not shared by some other group; which he believes to apply to the society to which he and his sympathisers belong; and which, if any, apply to every society.

What I have been saying before, therefore, was intended to elicit the fact that the meaning of the term "social purpose" is subject to a good deal of variation. In a liberal democracy it should mean something discernible in the mind and temperament of the people as a whole, something arising out of its common ethos, which finds expression through a variety of intellectual leaders holding varied and sometimes conflicting opinions. In a totalitarian society, it may mean something formulated in the brains of a few persons in power, deduced from a particular political-social theory, and imposed by every means of compulsion and indoctrination, so that it may in time become integrated into the common ethos. This is a very different kind of social purpose. In a liberal society every writer on the subject will have some social purpose of his own; something he wishes to retain, restore, or introduce through the means of education. Therefore, he should know himself how far his assumptions are his own, and how far he is justified in assuming that they are shared by all intelligent men of goodwill. He should, in short, examine his premises.

Now as education, it has been agreed, has several aims, the social purposes have to be guarded from interfering with the other aims; and also, we have to allow for the possibility that we may have several social purposes which have to be reconciled to each other. I remind you of the sage words of Gustave Thibon and Simone Weil, which I have already quoted. I shall take as an illustration "the ideal of equality of opportunity," because my previous reservations on the applicability of that ideal seem to have provoked especially strong dissent. This ideal certainly expresses a social purpose, and is equally applicable to other things than education: education is merely one of the benefits to which men and women should ideally have equal opportunity. This ideal has two very strong grounds of appeal, which must be distinguished. One is that ability is wasted, of which society has need, through our failing to recognise and train it. This is a utilitarian argument; it has force, but of a very different kind from the second. This is, that it is not just that any person should be prevented, by our failure to educate him, from the full development of his latent powers and faculties. The second seems to me the more universal and compelling, because it is a *moral* ground. Now as this ground at least, the assertion that every child should have equal opportunity for education is one which nobody will deny. The only difficulty comes when we proceed, from cherishing this ideal, to attempt to realise it; and when we give it priority, in our educational schemes over other ideals of education.

If we pursued the ideal of equality of opportunity rigorously we should, it seems to me, have to see to it that no educational institution was superior to any other professing to supply the same grade of education. We should certainly have to see to it that no institution gave a better education simply because it could charge higher fees, and select its pupils for any other reason than intellectual promise. To what extent do the pupils at expensive private schools get a better education? What is it that their parents are paying for? I know that the motives from which affluent parents choose a school are often motives which have nothing to do with education. There is the desire that their children should mix with other children of the same economic status and social type; there is also the calculation that their children will make the sort of friends who will be "useful" to them in later life; there is also the simple snobbism attached to the name of a particular school or university. But there are better reasons than these: there is the attraction of a foundation with traditions, and a long list of distinguished alumni. And there is the best reason of all, especially for the private school—for it is in school days that this reason is the most cogent: the parents know that their child will be member of a small group, that he will be taught in a class of fifteen or twenty instead of in a class of forty or fifty. Anyone who has ever tried to teach young children knows that the larger your class is, beyond fifteen or twenty, the less you can teach.

It is certainly desirable that every school in the country should have enough accommodation, and enough teachers, to be able to teach children in smaller groups. I thought, in 1944, that the Education Act of that year—an attempt, certainly, to improve state education—put the wrong things first. Instead of extending immediately the years of compulsory education, and thus adding to the number of pupils, we should in my opinion have aimed first at the supply of more teachers and accommodation for those already in the state-supported or aided schools; and undertaken to give better teaching than we do, to those under fourteen. But when will we, in any country, provide the money for this reform? Again, before we train more teachers, we ought to consider whether we are paying our present teachers adequately. I have never worked in a coal mine, or a uranium mine, or in a herring trawler; but I know from experience that working in a bank from

9:15 to 5:30, and once in four weeks the whole of Saturday, with two weeks' holiday a year, was a rest cure compared to teaching in a school.

I am told that "no American advocate of equality of opportunity would argue that the rich should be forbidden to set up schools of their own, which might turn out to be superior to those supported by the State." This is advocacy of a limited equality, an equality qualified by a good deal of inequality. If the schools established by the rich for the rich turn out to be better schools (though I do not believe this is altogether true) then what becomes of equality of opportunity? And how can we limit our equality to an equal opportunity to get a good education? If one child has better opportunities in life than another, merely because his parents are richer, will not many people regard this situation as unjust? It would seem that inequality in education is merely a special instance of inequality in general, and if we affirm a principle in one area are we not driven to accept it in all? Certainly, some English advocates of equality in education would go much further than, as I am told, American advocates do: they would abolish the private school and the privately endowed institution, or bring them all into the state system.

The usefulness of the phrase "equality of opportunity" is confused by the various meanings which we attach to the word "opportunity"—it means different things to different people, and different things to the same people at different moments, often without our knowing it. That everyone should, as far as we can make it possible, be able to pursue the activity for which he is best fitted, is an aim which we can all applaud. One has sometimes observed the son of people in well-to-do circumstances, admirably qualified by talent and temperament to be a first-rate garage mechanic, yet never having the opportunity to become one. Pressure of family and environment, the acquirement of tastes incompatible with the occupation for which he is best fitted, and perhaps also a defective education, usually stand in his way. I am afraid that to most people at most times "opportunity" means a good many other things than the opportunity to develop the latent powers and capacities: it means opportunity to make money, to acquire a higher social status, to have power over others. For some young women, opportunity means opportunity to get a screen test; and only a small number of those who crave this opportunity deserve it. In short, opportunity is an empty term unless we can answer the question "opportunity for what?"

It would seem, then, that most of the time, when we talk of "equality of opportunity," we either do not know what we mean, or do not mean what we say, or else are driven to conclusions from which most people would shrink. It is avoiding the issue if we assume vaguely that "inequality" means only the injustice of overprivileged and underprivileged social classes. It may happen that is child at a state school finds a teacher who will elicit his aptitude for a particular subject, and that a child at an expensive private school has just the wrong teacher. But what about overprivileged and underprivileged areas in the same country? A poor state or country may not be able to provide such good equipment or teachers, such good libraries or laboratories, as a richer one. Should not that inequality be redressed also? Thus, the claim of equality of opportunity, if pressed to its logical conclusion, seems to me to lead inescapably to a universal and exclusive state system of education, to the cost of which the richer parts of the country, like the richer individuals, will contribute proportionately, but from which they will derive only the same educational returns as their poorer neighbours. And next, is it just that the citizens of a wealthy or advanced nation should have greater opportunity for education than those of a backward one? Unless we maintain that some races or peoples are superior to others we seem to be forced toward the goal of a world system of education. And finally, if we are to have complete equality of opportunity in education, it seems to follow that we must have a uniform system for grading the intelligence of pupils, so that each shall receive just the kind and amount of education to which his gifts entitle him.

If, as I have suggested, the thoroughgoing application of the principle of equality of opportunity (reinforced by the other pressures of which I have spoken) tends towards increased control by the State, then the State will have something to say about opportunity. It will find itself limiting opportunity to those vocations which serve the ends of the State as conceived by those who happen to control the State. I am not suggesting that it would, in a Western democracy, reach the point of direction of labour; but by offering greater inducements and advantages and facilities in one direction rather than another, it might tend to limit education to the kinds of training which served the immediate purposes of the State.

The idea of equal opportunity, it would seem, has to be considered in relation to each of the three aims of education from which we started; and it might be that in this connection, also, one aim would be pursued in such a way as to interfere with another. The difficulty arises from the fact that we cannot, in practice, wholly separate one from another. There have been, no doubt, men who were animated by curiosity and the thirst for knowledge, to such a degree as to be able to pursue their studies quite apart from their actual calling in life. There have been Spinozas who, in order to be free to exercise a wholly unremunerative activity and one not regarded by the world as particularly useful, have been content to earn a modest livelihood by grinding lenses. There have been other men, in humble positions, in whom the speculative or contemplative motive has been so strong that they found happiness in this double life. On the other hand, there have been men so completely limited in interest to the duties of their occupation that they have seemed to be hardly more than machines. Most men escape from this only by way of recreations and hobbies, ordinarily of a rather trivial nature. The ideal is a life in which one's livelihood, one's function as a citizen, and one's self-development all fit into and enhance each other. For most of us, the full pursuit of any of these aims must interfere with another; and we are obliged, at best, to make almost day-to-day calculations and decisions between the several claims. We are all limited, by circumstances if not by capacities. To get anything you want you find you have to sacrifice something else that you want; and in getting it, you find that you have to accept other things that you do not want. Yet we must maintain that a man is not educated if he is merely trained to a trade or profession; that he has to play his part as a citizen; and that, as a citizen, to be something more than a voting machine, and, as a worker, to be something more than a working machine, he must be trained and developed to something more than citizenship and work. And we find that the principle of "equal opportunity" is meaningless—that is, susceptible of being interpreted by everybody in terms of what he *desires,* instead of what he ought to desire—unless we answer the question "opportunity for what?"

There are obviously some "opportunities" which ought to be available to everyone. Every man should have the opportunity of earning a livelihood in reasonable and decent conditions; of marrying and rearing a family who will also have the same opportunity; of rest and recreation, and so forth. You will observe that this sentence is made up of terms which will have different meanings in different social contexts: it is necessarily vague. But when we proceed beyond material necessities we get into a region of values. And so the assertion of "equal opportunity" leads us gradually to the point at which we must know what we mean by "the good life". The question "What is education?" or the question "What is the aim of education?" leads us to this point. Now it is unlikely that we shall all agree on an answer to the final question, "What is Man?" Therefore, what we mean in practice by "education" will be the highest common factor of what enough educated people mean by it. So you may say that "education" is likely to mean, in practice, a compromise between what different people mean by it.

I hope that it is by now clear that I do not complain of other writers that "they seek to use the schools to achieve social purposes which they have at heart." When we talk about education, we cannot stop at education as if it were a field which we could close off; an area in which we could come to agreement whatever our differences of philosophy. We must have a social purpose in education, and therefore, if we talk about education, we must be prepared to make clear to ourselves and to our hearers what our social purpose is. But the social purpose itself should not spring from a prejudice, and emotional bias in favour of equality or hierarchy, a bias in favour of freedom or of order. Nor is the social purpose in itself enough, for it does not take account of the whole nature of man.

We have seen that, just as we are led, the moment we begin to think seriously about education, to think about citizenship, so thinking about citizenship leads us to something beyond citizenship; for the good citizen in the end turns out to be the good man; and that leads wherever the whole problem of ethics is going to take us. Now a view of education such as Dr. Joad's, which suggests that training for citizenship and training for the development of one's latent powers and faculties can be carried on in separate departments, may seem clear enough about the discipline for citizenship, but offers no general prescription for the development, or we may say "the improvement" of man as man. As citizens, men must hold certain principles in common, and must agree on certain social habits; the fact of having to get on with other people imposes some discipline. But in the question of the development of latent powers, this view does not proceed to maintain that there are certain latent powers for good, and certain latent powers for evil, in man as man; it suggests rather, that each man has latent powers and faculties peculiar to himself, illustrated by the various ways in which men spend their leisure time. It is perfectly true that some men have an aptitude for and take enjoyment in doing their own repairs about the house; whereas others are much better advised to send for a plumber, a carpenter, or an electrician. I have no doubt that when Dr. Joad talks of latent powers and faculties, he is thinking of higher powers and faculties than those of the handy man. Nevertheless, he is leaving the area of latent powers and faculties uncontrolled. The danger of separation between the social and the private life—which has the corollary that the only criterion of morals is whether one's conduct is harmful to one's neighbours, and that every man should be free to do as he likes with *himself*—is that the social code, the code of citizenship, will become more and more constrictive, more and more exercising a pressure towards *conformity;* and that this public servitude to society will be compensated by extreme license in whatever conduct is supposed to be none of society's business.

It is true that in a society organised on this principle the social may prove in the end to encroach more and more upon the private. In a society organised to carry out this principle, the rules of matrimony and sexual relations may be, at first, much relaxed. But then it may be found that this relaxation has undesirable social consequences—that it affects the birth rate unfavourably, in a nation which finds that it needs more workmen and soldiers; or that it has an unfortunate effect upon the children, who may begin to show psychological aberrations, or may grow up to be less desirable citizens than the government wants them to be: and then private life will be interfered with in the name of society. People may be ordered to have larger families, or to have no families at all, according to whether they are judged to be suitable breeders of future citizens. Thus, the individual may find his privacy, his opportunity for exercising his moral freedom and responsibility gradually taken away from him in the name of society.

The restoration of a kind of order in people's private lives, however, when it is made in the name of a social purpose only, furthers the reduction of men to machines, and is the opposite from the development of their humanity. The assumption that you can have areas of control, and areas of complete freedom, must lead either to a suffocating uniformity of order, or to chaos. The actual degree of freedom or control may differ between one area and another. We are all more willing to submit to regulation of our public than of our private behaviour, and gradually, with the increasing complexity of modern civilisation, we are prepared to submit to more and more regulations in the public interest. There are still people who object to being vaccinated, but few people now resent being isolated when they have typhoid fever. Most people recognise that the state of their drains is a matter in which they have a duty to their neghbours; though not everybody recognises that he has the same duty in respect to the noise of his radio set. In a flat, one expects to have less freedom in many petty details of life than in a solitary cottage in the country. On the other hand, people in England since the war have objected, and they have my sympathy, to being forbidden to set up a tool shed in a country garden without a license from the government, or being forced to employ a workman to do what they are capable of doing themselves. Fortunately, we do not yet submit to universal regulation in the public interest; and fortunately, we are still capable of being shocked by private behaviour, even when it does not appear to injure anyone but the culprit himself. And so long as we are capable of resenting control, and of being shocked by other people's private lives, we are still human. We are, at least, recognising that man is something more than merely a social animal: that there should be limitations to social control. And by being shocked (when it is something more than a prejudice that is shocked) we are recognising, however dimly, that there is some law of behaviour which is something more than a duty to the State.

What, then, should we mean by the development of the individuals latent powers and faculties, if we go further than Dr. Joad, and consider the individual, not as if he were a seed out of a packet with no name on it, which we plant and tend out of curiosity to see what it will become, and what sort of flower or fruit it will bear; but as a seed of a known plant which has been cultivated for many generations—a plant about which we know what its flower or fruit ought to be, if it receives the right nurture and grows to perfection? How are we to try to educate good men, seeing that the idea of the good citizen implies the good man? Are we to be content with a rough-and-ready description of the good citizen, leaving everybody to define goodness according to his own taste and fancy? As you may have feared, this question raises for me the final question, that of the relation of education to religion.

Unless we can get complete agreement about religious truth—that is, the ultimate truth about Man—we must not expect to be able to agree upon an ideal system of education which can be put into practice. Many situations in life have to be dealt with by compromise, and we must not repine over this misforture of the human condition. But I think that it is very important, when we are forced by circumstances to stop short of the proper terminus of our speculations, to be aware of what we are doing; in respect to the present subject-matter, not to pretend that a theory of education can be complete which excludes the ultimate religious problems—and I have said that "What is Man?" is one of these—and which attempts to delimit for the theory of education an area within which religion can be ignored.

I am now, I hope, in a position to remark that the inquiry into "the place of religious teaching in education" with which I have been occupying myself for some minutes is really unimportant for the purposes which I set myself in these discourses. Only, it is a problem which has to be inquired into first, before we can see how and why it is unimportant in this context. In my "aims of education" it is not the place of religion in education, but the place of education in religion, that is the vital issue.

So far, our aims have been for the individual: to train him to become the best that he is capable of becoming. We have been concerned only with the present not with the past or the future. Now I suggest that one aim of education should be concerned with another obligation besides that towards the persons to be taught. If we consider only the latter, our curriculum may vary with every wind of doctrine; our notions of what is a good way of earning a living, of what is good citizenship, and of what is good individual development, may be at the mercy of the prevailing mood of one generation, or the caprice of individual educators. It should be an aim of education to maintain the continuity of our culture—and neither continuity, nor a respect for the past, implies standing still. More than ever, we should look to education today to preserve us from the error of pure contemporaneity. We look to institutions of education to maintain a knowledge and understanding of the past. And the past has to be reinterpreted for each generation, for each generation brings its own prejudices and fresh misunderstandings. All this may be comprehended in the term history; but history includes the study of the great dead languages and of the past of modern languages, including our own. Particularly, indeed, our own; for we need to understand the way in which our words have been used in the past, how they have developed and altered their meanings, in order to understand how we are using them ourselves. And to preserve the wisdom of the past, we need to value it for its own sake, not simply to defend it on the ground of its usefulness. To support religion on the ground of its usefulness is obvious error; for the question, of what use is man to God, is more important than the question, of what use is God to man; and there is an analogy—

though I admit the danger of drawing such an analogy with temporal affairs—in our relation to our culture. For if we estimate the wisdom and experience and art of the past only in terms of its usefulness to us, we are in danger of limiting the meaning of "usefulness," and of limiting the meaning of "us" to those who are now alive. What I wish to maintain is a point of view from which it appears more important—if we have to choose, and perhaps we do have to choose—that a small number of people should be educated well, and others left with only a rudimentary education, than that everybody should receive a share of an inferior quality of education, whereby we delude ourselves into thinking that whatever there can be the most of, must be the best. And what I plead for is what Matthew Arnold spoke of as "the knowledge of the best that has been thought and said in the world" (and, I might add, the best that has been done in the world, and that has been created in the arts in the world); that this knowledge of history, in the widest sense, should not be reserved to a small body of experts—reserved to them and parcelled out among them—but that it should be the common possession of those who have passed through the higher grades of non-specialised education; that it might well form, for most of them, the foundation for many of the more modern studies which now tend to be substituted for it.....

# 15

# Special Reading

## Several Thousand Books

....It has been frequently said that the mode of modern poetry is the mode of prophecy, a vision of the end of all things. This is obvious the moment we evoke the names of Rilke, Valery, Montale, Yeats, Eliot. If the mode of modern poetry is prophecy, the rhetorical mode of prophecy itself is hyperbole. We foresee a future dominated and perhaps eventually destroyed by the evils, with no redemptive power of any good, of our own time.

I am, therefore, about to preach a sermon; and because I am not properly ordained for this office. I shall adopt not a holy but a secular text, which is as follows:

> The price the man of today has paid for his increase in power is, it should seem, an appalling superficiality in dealing with the law of his own nature.

This sentence was written by the late Irving Babbitt in 1919. I shall not refer to it again but rather offer you three characters modelled after Theophrastus, one living, the two others dead.

Every September, almost a century ago, Charles Eliot Norton greeted the first meeting of his classes at Harvard with a snobbish irony that we today might have to take literally. He is reported to have said: "I suppose that nobody in this room has ever seen a gentleman." The New England scholar, if rumour be reliable, has not been famous for humility. I surmise that Norton was inviting the students to look at one gentleman, perhaps the last, before the species became extinct. I intend no irony whatever when I say that nobody in this auditorium, either you out there or we up here, has ever seen an educated person. I may not be the oldest member of the faculty on this platform. Allow me the rhetorical privilege of believing that I am. So it is possible that I may have seen, some fifty to sixty years ago, one or two educated men. (At that time it was not necessary to consider whether there were educated women.) I have not seen an educated man since, and I fear that you will never see one.

As a small boy I knew a man who lived on a farm a few miles from a Kentucky country-seat, the population of which was about five hundred. I suppose he had been born about 1840; he had fought in the Confederate army and it was said that after 1865 he refused to recognise one of his brothers who had fought on the other side. He was a lawyer whose office was up a dingy flight of stairs above the feed store on the courthouse square. He had "read" law after the war in the office of an older lawyer; but before the war he had been graduated from a small sectarian college, a day's buggy-ride from the family farm; and while he was reading law for the state bar examinations be taught mathematics at his *alma mater.* (I once had his books on Conic Sections and the Integral Calculus.) I think I must have seen him last when I was about twelve or thirteen. It was summertime. He wore a shapeless, sweat-stained panama, black alpaca coat, unpressed broadcloth trousers, and string tie; he was very tall and very fat, with a smooth round face and unkempt white hair. I could not then have understood that he saw no difference between his vocation and his avocation, or that he did not know which was which. From early spring to early fall he spent most of his time on his farm. He sat under a tree in a far corner of the yard—which in England would have been called a park—reading Mommsen's *History of Rome,* or perhaps Lord Clarendon's *History of the Rebellion;* for he fancied himself a Jacobite. Back of his house stood an abandoned ice-house, down in the depths of which, on the sawdust floor, he had his laboratory apparatus with which he performed his chemical experiments—for what purpose and to what conclusions I do not know; and I doubt that he knew: he was only increasing his knowledge. He might have answered questions with obvious appeal to authority—"As Plato *says* in the *Phaidros*"—putting the verb in the present tense because Plato had lived only recently; or he might quote the *Georgics* and look hurt if the company kept an uncomprehending silence. He sat in a split-bottom rocking chair next to a big field of tobacco, a palmleaf fan in one hand, in the other his book, perhaps Cicero's *Letters to Atticus.* If the field-hands suckering the tobacco needed an order, he rose, placed the fan on the seat of the chair, his index finger between the pages of the book to mark the place; walked over to the fence, shouted his orders; and came back to his chair to resume his reading.

He was not a scholar; that is to say, he was not a professional scholar. He knew a little about many things—mathematics, science, the ancient classics, agronomy, the law; yet all of the little that he knew was alive in his daily life and was constantly brought to bear upon the human condition as he could know it in his place and time. Without being conscious of representing anything at all, he was an exemplar of the classical apothegm: Nothing too much. One would know that he would be as considerate of the plain people of his community as of Senator James or Justice McReynolds. He was, in short, an educated man.

The second figure that I evoke for this occasion was a generation younger than our lawyer-planter. He was not only a scholar; he was a great classical scholar. Our lawyer was a private person; our classicist was a public character, a professor of Greek; so I shall name him; Herbert Cushing Tolman. He was born in Massachusetts, educated in the classics by William Dwight Whitney at Yale; went to the German universities, as was the irresistible imperative of that era; came back to this country to teach, for more than thirty years, at a small Southern university. It was there that I became his student. I knew him nine months a year for four years. In bearing and in temper he was remarkably like his rural, non-academic counterpart in Kentucky. Yet he was a specialist. Besides his Latin and Greek, which he could speak better than our American professor of French could speak French, his Indo-European philology included Sanskrit and Ancient Persian; and he had mastered Babylonian cuneiform.

In his Greek classes he usually gave towards the end of the period, a "prelection" of the assignment for the next day. On one occasion he recited a free translation of a Pindaric ode. When he had finished I raised my hand and asked; "Dr. Tolman, could we have read that translation somewhere?" "No, sir," he replied, "my reading is the way John Dryden might have rendered it into English prose." How he ever had time for English poetry we never knew. He had published a small book entitled *The Art of Translating.* He had time for everything that interested him because he was never in a hurry. One spring afternoon as I was passing his house I saw him lying in his hammock in the side yard. Some boyish impulse moved me to approach and speak to him. In my self-consciousness, and in a clumsy effort to impress him, I made up a Greek sentence to surprise him with. After he had risen and we had passed the time of day—which on my part included taking off my hat—I said: καιρε η *ἀταραξla ré* φιλὸσοφον εXει. He smiled. "No," he said, "not has me—*had* me from the beginning; I was born taking my ease. So your verb should be in the second aorist—not ἔχει, but ἔσχεν. He laughed and asked me to sit down in a garden chair, while he lay back in the hammock.

This man, a great scholar on the Renaissance model, no more than the Kentucky farmer-lawyer, knew the difference between vocation and avocation, between labour and leisure. These man were both in the strict sense amateurs; for what each did in his own way was done in the love of excellence. The competitive "advancement of knowledge"—produce or perish—the ostensible purpose of our university scholar, was incidental to the love of excellence. But love of anything is notoriously inept at getting one ahead in our world. When I try to revive the image of Tolman—the noble brow, the serene eyes, the benign mouth, all composed in an imponderable effect of innocence—think of the great lines by W. B. Yeats:

> ... all his Greek and Latin learning seemed
> A long blast upon the horn that brought
> A little nearer to his thought
> A measureless consummation that he dreamed.

Getting ahead in the world is now the purpose of education; and the university must therefore provide education for our time, not for all time; it must discover and then give to society what society thinks it wants and needs; and Government is now paying, perhaps bribing, the university to give the people what it, representing society, thinks that society ought to have. Society ought to have more and more technology, more and more specialisation, more and more occultation of knowledge. I must linger a moment over the word occultation. I use it in the sense understood by the philosopher Scott Buchanan in a brilliant, forgotten book *The Doctrine of Signatures*. Occultation means turning the sciences into Black Arts, hidden arts, the purpose of which no single mind can comprehend. These are the applied sciences over which the true scientist, after the applications have been made, no longer has control. When the late Robert Oppenheimer tried to control the making of the hydrogen bomb, be was disqualified on pseudo-political grounds. Who—or what—disqualified him? The slowest member of the class could answer the question: Government disqualified him. Oppenheimer was satisfied with scientific knowledge; Government was bent upon power, upon the use of scientific knowledge as a Black Art for the control—and destruction is the ultimate control—of man and nature. For once the bomb is made, it has as its final cause, its end, which it may achieve through the agency of man, an explosion; but the agent being dehumanised is neutral, and has no responsibility for the consequences.

We have recently heard another version of the doctrine of means-as-end, this time from a humanist, our third character, who declares that the printed book is obsolete. The audio-visual *media* have replaced it. In a series of dizzy non-sequiture, which remind one of Ralph Waldo Emerson, if Emerson were vulgarised and brought up to date, Mr. Marshall McLuhan assures us that the electronics *media* are their own subject-matter, or will eventually become so, when the rational, systematic thought, which developed after Gutenberg had invented movable type, has disappeared, as he promises it will speedily do. There will be less and less "content-analysis" and more and more identification of the auditor-spectator with the audio-visual medium. We shall give the television screen a catatonic state. In this prelapsarian, illiterate Elysium it will no longer be necessary to learn how to read. All is sound and sight; the medium is its own message. This attractive chimera, which if universally followed would relieve us, as it has evidently relieved Mr. McLuhan, of the burden of thought, would, I make bold to conjecture, have pleased the late George Orwell. Yet I doubt that Orwell could be convinced that Marshall McLuhan exists; he would recognise him as one of his own fictional characters who had just stepped out of the pages of 1984 and changed his name to McLuhan. Satire is frequently a mode of prophecy. When "content-analysis" is forbidden or—what is the same thing—no longer "necessary," and the medium is its own "message," we may safely infer that the message will have been prepared by invisible Big Brother. Another name for Big Brother is Government; another, Society; still another may possibly be the University itself. The University, still proud, may try to disguise itself as Big Brother, with an even Bigger Brother, named Brother State, back of him. Will the University then agree to give Society what it thinks it wants, not what it is the responsibility of the University to tell Society that it needs?

As I approach the conclusion of these meditations I must remind you that the rhetorical mode of satire is hyperbole. I have been assuming that the abstraction Society never knows what it needs, but only what it wants, or what it is told that it wants by distant persons whose interest lies in the frustration of the human being. In those departments of the American University which self-interest has led me to observe, we are told—and we tell others—that what we need is more scholarly research; a more and more rapid advancement of knowledge (by which is meant inert information); more and more "research" for more and more dissertations which nobody will read but the authors of previous dissertations who will be as bored as the persons who wrote them. This reciprocal boredom is enthusiastically perpetuated because it leads to power; power in an *occulted* world of Black Art. What is occulted is the true purpose of literary studies. That true purpose is not to produce more studies of Coleridge and Hawthorne, but more Hawthornes and more Coleridges. The name of this Black Art is Research, a term and a procedure borrowed from the natural sciences at a low level; that is, at the level of the applied sciences, which are, of course, the genuine and efficient Black Arts. One wonders where the laboratory for literary research is located. It is located, invisibly, in the heads of scholars who use the study of literature to maintain an academic power *elite.* I suggest that it would be better to try to *be* Coleridge than to *use* him, even if as pusillanimous Coleridges we fell flat on our noses and made fools of ourselves. Coleridge never did any research; he never even had a course in English literature. He had merely read, in six languages, by the time he died at the age of sixty-two, several thousand books.

Thus, far a secular gospel, or a vision of the end of all things.

# Bibliography

*A Laboratory School Evaluates Its Contributions to Teacher Education.* (Columbus University School, College of Education, The Ohio State University, 1943).

Alberty, Harold, *Reorganising the High School Curriculum* (New York, Macmillan, 1948).

Allport, Gordon, "The Psychology of Participation," *Psychological Review,* Vol. 52 (1945), pp. 117–132.

Anderson, Harold, *et. al, Studies of Teachers' Classroom Personalities,* Psychology Monographs, Stanford (Stanford University Press, 1946).

Angell, Robert C., *The Integration of American Society* (New York, McGraw-Hill, 1941).

Ash, F., *Effect of Teacher Adjustment upon Personality Adjustment,* University of Iowa Study, Sims Progressive Research, 1944, No. 76. Study Series No. 408.

Baruch, Dorothy, *Parents and Children Go to School* (Chicago, Scott, 1939).

Baxter, Bernice and Cassidy, Rosalind, *Group Experience, the Democratic Way* (New York, Harper, 1943). I. Group Leadership; II. Face-to-Face Group: Its Emergence and Guidance; III. Individuals in Groups; IV. Preparation for Tomorrow's Leadership.

Bode, Boyd H., *How We Learn* (Boston, Heath, 1940).

Brown, Francis J., *Educational Sociology* (New York, Prentice-Hall, 1947).

Brown, Francis J., *Sociology of Childhood* (New York, Prentice-Hall, 1939).

Brubacher, John S., *A History of the Problems of Education* (New York, McGraw-Hill, 1947).

Burr, James B. Harding, Lowry W., and Jacobs, Leland B., *Student*

*Teaching in the Elementary School* (New York, Appleton-Century-Crofts, 1950).

Butts, R. Freeman. *A Cultural History of Education: Reassessing Our Educational Traditions* (New York, McGraw-Hill, 1947).

Chambers, M.M., *The Community and Its Young People* (Washington, American Council on Education, 1940).

Cheskie, Sophie V., "A Flexible Pattern for Adult Education." *The Nations Schools,* Vol. 43, No. 4 (April 1950).

Christian, Johnie, "Curriculum Planning on a Community Basis," *Educational Administration and Supervision,* Vol. IV (January 1947), pp. 43–48; "Community Participates in Curriculum Building," *Texas Outlook,* Vol. XXXXI (February 1947, pp. 12–13.

Clapp, Elsie, *Community Schools in Action* (New York, Viking, 1939).

Collaborators in Child Growth and Development, *Child Growth and Development Emphases in Teacher Education* (Oneonta, N.Y., American Association of Teachers Colleges, 1944).

Cook, Lloyd A., and Elaine Forsythe Cook, *A Sociological Approach to Education* (New York, McGraw-Hill, 1950).

Cook, Lloyd A., *Community Action and the School* (Columbus, The Ohio State University, 1941).

Cook, Lloyd A., *Community Backgrounds of Education* (New York, McGraw-Hill, 1938).

Cook, Lloyd Allen and Elaine Forsythe, *A Sociological Approach to Education* (New York, McGraw-Hill, 1950).

Cook, Lloyd Allen, and Cook, Elaine Forsyth, *A Sociological Approach to Education* (New York, McGraw-Hill, 1950).

Coons, P.W., "School-Community Relations: A Report on a Poll of 67 Educators," *Social Education,* Vol. 14 (May 1950), pp. 223–225.

Counsellbaum, Stella, "Building Democracy Through Extra Curricular Clubs," *Education,* Vol. 68 (November 1947), pp. 62–68.

Crawford, Nelson Antrim, "The Little Professor of Piney Woods," *The Rotarian* (October 1945).

Criffin, Alan, *Freedom American Style* (New York, Holt, 1940).

Cubberly, E.P., *Public Education in the United States* (Boston, Houghton, 1934).

Cuber, J.F., "Changing Courtship and Marriage Customs," *Annals of the American Academy of Political and Social Science,* Vol. 229 (1943), pp. 33–38.

Cummings, Howard H. (ed.), "Improving Human Relation," *National Council for the Social Studies* (Washington, National Education Association, November 1949).

Cupps, R.D., "Dating at the University of Washington," *Marriage and Family Living,* Vol. 9 (May 1947), pp. 30-31.

Davis, R.G., "Group Therapy and Social Acceptance in a First-Second Grade," Bibliography F. Education School Vol. 49 (December 1948), pp. 219–223).

Department of National Elementary School Principals, "Building Community Understanding of the School," a cooperative set of materials in *Elementary School Principal's Bulletin,* 24th Yearbook, Vol. 25 (Washington, National Education Association, 1945-1946).

DuVall, Everett. *Personality and Social Group Work, an Individual Approach* (New York, Association Press, 1943). I. The Individual and the Group; VIII. Leadership as Relationship.

Edwards, Newton and Richey, Herman, *The School in the American Social Order* (Boston, Houghton, 1947).

Englehart, Fred, *Planning the Community School* (New York, American Book, 1940).

Everett, Samuel, *School and Community Meet* (New York, Hinds, Hayden and Eldredge, 1948).

Everett, Samuel, *The Community School* (New York, Appleton-Century, 1938).

*General Education in a Free Society,* Report of the Harvard Committee (Cambridge, Harvard University Press, 1945).

Good, Harry G., *The Development of Education in the Twentieth Century* (New York, Prentice-Hall, 1950).

Goslin, Willard E., "The Characteristics of a Community School," *Forthcoming Developments in American Education,* William C. Reavis, ed., (Chicago, University of Chicago Press, 1946).

Greenhoe, Florence, *Community Contracts and Participation of Teachers,* (Washington, American Council on Public Affairs, 1941).

Hambly, W.D., *Origins of Education Among Primitive Peoples* (New York, Macmillan, 1926).

Harnly, Paul W., and others, *Improving Intergroup Relations in School and Community Life* (Lincoln, Neb., The North Central Association of Secondary Schools and Colleges, 1946).

Havighurst, Robert J., Developmental Tasks in Education (Chicago, University of Chicago Press, 1951).

Heintz, Emil, "A Community College in Action," *The School Executive*, Vol. 66, No.7 (March 1947).

Hopkins, Thomas, "Techniques in Human Relations," *Teachers College Record*, Vol. XLVII (November 1945), pp. 89–97.

Hulburd, D., *This Happened in Pasadena* (New York, Macmillan, 1951).

Hullfish, G.H., "What Kind of Education?" *Educational Research Bulletin*, Vol. 26 (May 1947), p. 118.

Hullfish, G.H., *Education in Philosophy and Interaction* (Columbus, Ohio, Educational Collections, 1944).

Jeffers, Ruth Arnold, "An Orientation Conference for Parents, It Pays," *West Virginia Educational Bulletin*, Vol. XV, No. 5 (January 1948).

Kilpatrick, W.H., *Source Book in the Philosophy by Education* (New York, Macmillan, 1948).

Kirkendall, Lester A., *Factors Related to the Changes in School Adjustment of High School Pupils*, Contributions to Education, No. 705 (New York, Bureau of Publications, Teachers College, Columbia University, 1937).

Kirkpatrick, C., and Coplow, T., "Courtship in a Group of Minnesota Students" *American Journal of Sociology*, Vol. 51 (1945), pp. 114–125.

Lee, Doris and Lee, J. Murray, *The Child and His Curriculum* (New York, Appleton-Century-Crofts, 1950).

Leonard, Paul, "The School Cooperates," *The School Executive* (December 1946), p. 40.

Lewin, Kurt, "Experiments on Autocratic and Democratic Atmosphers," *Social Frontier*, Vol. 4 (July 1938), pp. 316–319.

Mangus, A.R. "Four Marks of a Mature Teacher," *Portfolio of Teaching Techniques*, Staff of Educator's Washington Dispatch.

Mangus, A.R. and R.H. Woodward, *An Analysis of the Mental Health of Elementary School Children* (Columbus, Division of Mental Hygiene of the Ohio State Department of Public Welfare, 1948).

Mangus, A.R. and R.H. Woodward, *An Analysis of the Mental Health of High School Students* (Columbus, Division of Mental Hygiene of the Ohio State Department of Public Welfare, July 1949).

McCandless, Boyd R., "Changing Relationships between Dominance and Social Acceptability during Group Democratisation" *American Journal Orthopsychiatry*, Vol. 12, (1942), pp. 529–535.

Mead, Margaret, *The School in American Culture* (Cambridge, Harvard University Press, 1950).

Melby, E.O., *American Education Under Fire* (New York, Anti-Defamation League, 1951).

Mitchell, Lucy Sprague, *Our Children and Our Schools* (New York, Simon and Schuster, 1951).

Moehlman, A.B., "Why a Community School?" *The Nations Schools,* (March, 1944).

New Jersey State Teachers College at Trenton, *Student Leadership in Community Clubs,* Studies in Education, No. 5 (Trenton, 1940).

Northway, Mary L., Frankel, Esther, and Potashin, Reva, "Personality and Sociometric Status," *Sociometry Monograph* (New York, Beacon House, 1947).

Olsen, E.G., *School and Community* (New York, Prentice-Hall, 1946).

Presey, Sidney and Robinson, F.P., *Psychology and the New Education* (New York, Harper, 1944).

Project in Applied Economics, *School-Community Cooperation for Better Living* (Gainsville, University of Florida, 1947).

Pumala, Edwin, "The San Diego, California, Community School Camp," *The Bulletin of the National Association of Secondary School Principals* (May 1947), pp. 100–105.

Reavis, W.C., ed., *Forthcoming Developments in American Education* (Chicago, University of Chicago Press, 1946).

Rice, Theodore, "Leadership Through Group Dynamics," *Nations Schools,* Vol. 43, No. 5 (May 1949), pp. 31–32.

Roper Study. "What the U.S. Thinks about Its Schools." *Life,* Vol. XXIX, No. 16 (Oct. 16, 1950), pp. 11-18.

Roucek, Joseph D., *Sociological Foundations of Education* (New York, Crowell, 1942).

Sharp, R.L., "School Public Relations Via A Community Council," *American School Board Journal* (August 1947).

Smucker, Orden, "The Campus Clique as an Agency of Socialisation," *Journal of Education Sociology,* Vol. 21 (November 1947), pp. 163-168.

Stolen, A.T., "Duluth Schools Provide Experiences in Community Life," *Nations Schools,* Vol. 45, No. 4 (April 1950), pp. 44–46.

Stone, Sybil A., *et. al., Children in the Community* (Washington, Government Printing Office, 1946).

Strang, Ruth, *Group Activities in College and Secondary School* (New York, Harper, 1946).

Waller, Willard, *The Sociology of Teaching* (New York, Wiley, 1932).

Whitcomb, Mildred E., "Play—the word that makes Milwaukee famous today," *Nations Schools*, Vol. 43, No. 6 (June 1949), pp. 24–27.

Wofford, K.V., *Teaching in Small Schools* (New York, Macmillan, 1947).

Young Essie, "The School Lunchroom," *Educational Leadership*, Vol. IV (February 1947), pp. 314–320.